Family and the Female Life Course

Life Course Studies

David L. Featherman
David I. Kertzer
Series Editors

Nancy W. Denney
Thomas J. Espenshade
Dennis P. Hogan
Jennie Keith
Maris A. Vinovskis
Associate Series Editors

Life Course Studies represents a broad disciplinary spectrum of inquiry into the formation, elaboration, and change in life timetables and biographies. All societies and cultures attach meaning and give structure to time and, in doing so, produce a periodization of the life course into phases. The series focuses on the life course as a biocultural phenomenon to be explained in biological, cultural, and social terms, and to be appreciated for its plasticity in history and its variability across sociocultural groups and societies.

The raison d'être of *Life Course Studies* is the need to integrate a sophisticated understanding of the biological life course with an equally well articulated appreciation of socially structured life timetables and culturally constructed norms regarding age and transitions. It is this biocultural life course that provides the context for studies of childhood, adolescence, adulthood, and old age as historically discrete life periods. The series encompasses works on life periods as well as on the life course as a whole, on life-span human development and aging. The special emphasis remains on the collective level by viewing individual-level processes as part of a larger set of systemic processes that express the workings of cultures, institutions, and social systems.

FAMILY
AND THE
FEMALE
LIFE COURSE

The Women of Verviers, Belgium, 1849-1880

George Alter

THE UNIVERSITY OF WISCONSIN PRESS

Published 1988

The University of Wisconsin Press
114 North Murray Street
Madison, Wisconsin 53715

The University of Wisconsin Press, Ltd.
1 Gower Street
London WC1E 6HA, England

First printing

Printed in the United States of America

Library of Congress Cataloging-in-Publication Data
Alter, George.
Family and the female life course.
(Life course studies)
Bibliography: pp. 209–221.
Includes index.
1. Women—Belgium—Verviers—History—19th century.
2. Working class women—Belgium—Verviers—History—
19th century.   3. Family—Belgium—Verviers—History
—19th century.   I. Title.   II. Series.
HQ1655.V47A47 1988   305.4'09493'4   87-40360
ISBN 0-299-11200-4
ISBN 0-299-11204-7 (pbk.)

To my parents, Pauline and Hyman Alter

Contents

Figures

Tables

Acknowledgments

One of the pleasures of completing a long project is the opportunity to thank the many people who contributed to its success. Funds for this project have come from a grant from the National Institute of Child Health and Human Development (PHS R01 HD 14965), an Indiana University Biomedical Research Support Grant (PHS S07 RR 7031G), and a fellowship at the Newberry Library from the National Endowment for the Humanities.

The communal administration of Verviers was very kind to give me liberal access to documents from the nineteenth century. I am especially grateful for the assistance of Mmes Douffet and Rutten of the Bureau de programmes, documentation, et archives. I am happy to have Mme Rutten as a friend as well as an archivist.

Historians at the Université de Liège have generously supported and encouraged my work. Etienne Hélin has been a valued advisor and an inspiration. René Leboutte has been a good friend as well as a valued colleague. Claude Desama and Pierre Lebrun have also offered their help. I am also grateful for the assistance of George Hansotte of the Archives de l'état à Liège.

This project is a continuation of work which I began as a dissertation at the University of Pennsylvania, and I am grateful for the encouragement of my advisors, Richard A. Easterlin, Lynn Hollens Lees, and Etienne van de Walle. My friends and colleagues Myron P. Gutmann and Susan Cotts Watkins are responsible for teaching me the promise and pitfalls of using historical population registers, and my work could not have been accomplished without our regular meetings and frequent telephone conversations. Many others have been kind enough to read early drafts of chapters and to offer technical advice. I would like to thank Gerhard Arminger, Caroline Brettell, Goran Brostrom, John Caldwell, Pat Caldwell, Barbara Hanawalt, David Kertzer, John Knodel, Leslie Page Moch, James C. Riley, Roger Schofield, Daniel Scott Smith, Harvey Smith, James Trussell, Maris Vinovskis. Robin Whitaker provided valuable editorial assistance.

The arduous task of preparing data was supervised with the utmost efficiency and dedication by Ann R. Higginbotham, to whom I am very grateful. I would like to thank the many student assistants who helped transcribe the data from microfilms to computers, especially Lisa Rappoport Thomas, Steven Abney, Georg'ann Catelona, Laura Gordon, Bradley Schaffner, Maureen Wolfenden, Katherine Workman.

My friend and companion Elyce Rotella has been a continual source of strength and confidence, and I am grateful for the sunshine she brings with her when we visit Belgium together.

Family and the Female Life Course

1

Introduction

WOMEN, FAMILY, AND THE LIFE COURSE

In 1873 an article appeared under the title "Section des femmes" in *Le Mirabeau*, the organ of the first International Workingmen's Association in Verviers, Belgium. The author, Hubertine Ruwette, exhorted her sisters to support the International, and she closed by proclaiming that they would march together under the banner "L'homme à l'atelier, la femme au ménage" ("The man in the workshop, the woman in the home") (*Le Mirabeau*, 24 October 1873, BV). Readers a century later cannot help being struck by the apparent traditionalism of this slogan. It betrays a backward-looking, patriarchal ideology, which Belgian socialists would soon discard. But at the time it was written, it was meant to be a revolutionary demand, and it marks a turning point in the history of the family. While Ruwette described an apparently traditional domestic role for women, in its context this was a radical demand, for she was addressing industrial workers in one of the foremost factory towns of Europe. Domesticity was still an aspiration for the women of mid-nineteenth-century Verviers, who spent only a small part of their lives as housewives. They married late, were widowed early, and more than one woman in four never married at all. This book describes the life histories of these women, their transitions from children to adults, and the families and households in which they lived. Its theme is the relationship of women to the family.

Until recently, discussion of family life in nineteenth-century cities was dominated by the sociological tradition which associated industrialization with social decay and family breakdown. Conservative social observers of the nineteenth century, influenced by Frédéric Le Play in France and Wilhelm Heinrich Riehl in Germany, emphasized the role of industry in weakening paternal authority (Mitterauer and Sieder, 1983, pp. 25–26). The spread of child labor created economic independence at an early age, and the pernicious environment of the factory undermined social and sexual morality. Signs of this development could be seen in the high illegitimacy rates in cities, the apparent disappearance of the large, extended family, and the declining birth rate. The small family, it was argued, did not develop the strong sense of moral obligation toward elderly and needy kin that had been essential to the survival of traditional society. Instead, industrialism lead to selfishness, vanity, and egoism—common charges against women who practiced family limitation.

Historians of the family have overturned most of this sociological tradition. Peter Laslett led the onslaught against accepted wisdom by attacking the very notion that preindustrial households had always been large and included many kin. From the work of Laslett and his many associates, we now know that the independent nuclear family was the dominant form of household organization in northwestern Europe well before modern industry appeared (Laslett, 1972). Research on nineteenth-century cities has failed to reveal the disorganization of the family feared by contemporaries. Michael Anderson's (1971) work on Lancashire shows that factory employment did not lead children to leave their parents earlier than their rural counterparts. Indeed, there is growing evidence that leaving home at an early age was a traditional, preindustrial pattern, which was reversed by the employment opportunities in cities and factory towns. Louise Tilly and Joan Scott (1978) have been influential in emphasizing the continued importance of female and child labor in the family economy of the early factory age.

There has been increasing recognition of the importance of the timing of marriage and the "European marriage pattern" described by John Hajnal (1965). Hajnal points out the relatively late age at marriage and high rate of celibacy in northwestern Europe in comparison with other culture areas. He attributes this pattern to a cultural and social system which demanded economic self-sufficiency as a prerequisite for marriage. Europeans appear to have behaved largely as Malthus recommended: restraining the rate of population growth by practicing the "preventive check." Malthus himself gathered numerous examples of late marriage among his contemporaries. While historians have not adopted Malthus's view that late marriage was specifically intended to reduce family size, the timing of marriage is once again central to explanatory models in historical demography and family history.

This Malthusian perspective still has a weak hold on the nineteenth century, however, and the writings of nineteenth-century Malthusians highlight the problem. It was widely expected and feared that marriage age would decline as the population moved from agriculture to industry, but this development failed to occur. Age at marriage dropped only slightly in the nineteenth century, and urban age at marriage was often later than that of rural areas. A more pronounced decline in age at marriage developed in the late nineteenth century, but western Europeans never married as early as eastern Europeans, much less Asians or Africans.

The expectation that factory workers would marry early was based on the assumption that the economic independence offered by wage labor would free them from family control, and the weakening of the nineteenth-century family has usually been tied to the emergence of individualism and the emancipation of individuals from family and social control. The rise of modern industry has long been associated with the spread of individualism. Modern industry requires the mobility of factors of production, including labor, and in Max Weber's classic formulation individualism is an intrinsic part of the spirit of capitalism. Those who see family breakdown in this period, like Le Play, tend to associate parental authority with economic power and the potential economic independence of children with a weakening of parental control. Even Anderson (1971), whose work discredits the family breakdown theory, sees the changing economic bargain between parents and children as a source of increasing independence among young people and a greater sense of individualism.

There is thus an inherent tension in descriptions of the nineteenth-century family between the persistence of an earlier logic of household formation and the presumed effects of industrialization and urbanization. On one hand, the signs of social disorganization, like high illegitimacy rates, show the weakening of social controls over demographic behavior. On the other hand, marriage continued to be late, even though wage labor had freed most of the population from the economic and social links that are supposed to have supported late marriage. A new family and demographic pattern based upon family limitation did emerge, but this behavior is not apparent until a half century after industrialism was well established.

Some historians have begun to suggest that a different kind of transition occurred in the nineteenth-century family. While the continued importance of the family as an economic unit was apparent, the moral cohesion of the family was no less important. The late age at marriage characteristic of this period seems to be a sign of the strength of this cohesion. As the economic basis of parental authority declined, parents' moral authority continued to be central to family life. Rather than leading to disintegration, economic development may have increased the salience of the emotional functions of the family, which were previously subordinated to pressing economic concerns. Earlier generations always lived in the shadow of impending economic or demographic disaster. Marriage for material advantage was the rule rather than the exception, and conflict and tension over land and property were commonplace. Despite the close

5

and vital cooperation of its members, sentiment was not always strong in the preindustrial family. The reduced economic functions of the family seem to have increased its emotional importance.

John Caldwell (1982) sees the late nineteenth century as a period in which the "intergenerational transfer" of wealth changed direction. Where parents in earlier times had seen children as a form of capital, working for them, late nineteenth-century society began to emphasize the obligations of parents to children. Tamara Hareven (1977) has written:

> The emergence of the private, child-centered family consciously separating itself from the outside world brought about major redefinitions of traditional family roles and functions. This new family type placed emphasis on the family as a center for nurture and affection rather than as a corporate unit. Their wages no longer needed, women and children in the middle class were exempted from the labor force. Wives were expected instead to be the custodians of the family and to protect the home as a refuge from the world of work, and children, although expected to help with household tasks, were freed from serious work responsibilities until their late teens. (p. 67)

This study investigates this period of changing and perhaps contradictory developments in the history of the family. The women studied here were at an important historical crossroads. The old system of social controls had indeed been removed, but the economic prosperity and social institutions that would become the framework of family life in the twentieth century had not yet emerged. Our problem is to find elements in their behavior that show continuity with the family system of earlier generations or anticipate the logic of generations to follow. These are not simple issues, and the explanations offered here are often tentative and complex. There were many reasons why women entered the labor force, married late or not at all, gave birth to illegitimate or premaritally conceived children. Nevertheless, the central importance of the family and the logic of the European family system is fundamental to this history. As Paul Spagnoli (1983) has suggested, the specific explanations are probably less important than the overall framework, and this framework is best represented by the independent nuclear family identified by Laslett and Hajnal.

The women of Verviers demonstrated a commitment to the family that was not diminished by the economic system of early industrialism. Often it was a commitment that resulted in sacrifices without the expectation of benefits. Despite the patriarchal bias in the movement from which it derived, the motto "L'homme à l'atelier, la femme au ménage" was a demand that the benefits of the new industrial system be turned to the advantage of women. Indeed, the next generation of women realized this demand, because their involvement in the wage economy declined (Alter, 1984a). It is hardly surprising that they would wish to avoid the lives

6

of toil suffered by their mothers or to demand the material advantages that their domestic labor could bring to their children and themselves. Furthermore, as bourgeois women were beginning to learn, the domestic ideal could be the moral basis of a new challenge to patriarchy (Moses, 1984).

TEXTILE CITIES AND FAMILY HISTORY

As the first industry to be mechanized on a large scale, the textile industry was the prototype of the new machine manufacture. In the nineteenth century the textile city became the symbol of the new industrial system, and the history of the industrial revolution has often been written as the history of textile machinery. The textile industry also became notorious for its effects on the family. The large-scale employment of women and children in a nondomestic environment became a cause of concern, and government inquiries revealed poor working conditions, long hours worked by children, mixing of sexes at work, and a catalogue of horrors. The tales of children slaved to machines which mangled their limbs and destroyed their youth were exceeded only by the horrors of children working underground in mines. Radicals, like Friedrich Engels, repeated the lurid tales of social breakdown, illegitimacy, and exploitation of children. Frédéric Le Play (1878), a conservative, proposed returning textiles to rural domestic industry as the only way to restore authority of fathers in textile families.

The study of life in textile cities has also played an important role in the development of family history. Earlier generations of historians often accepted the claims of middle-class contemporaries that the factory system had undermined the strength of the family. In *Social Change in the Industrial Revolution*, however, Neil Smelser (1959) reinterprets the evidence presented to British factory commissions. Smelser has found that families often moved into early factories as work groups, so that the family continued to operate as a unit of production. Factory operatives used their own children as assistants, just as they had on the farm or in the workshop. Resistance to legislation restricting the hours of labor for children came not only from employers, but also from parents who supervised their own children at work and needed the wages they earned. The elaborate theoretical superstructure within which Smelser presents the history of family life in the early cotton mills has been largely abandoned, but his work marks a turning point in the reinterpretation of the history of the family.

Michael Anderson's (1971) work on Preston provides a comparison of families in a nineteenth-century industrial city with those in rural areas of

7

Lancashire. Anderson found little evidence that factory labor had caused children to abandon the family. On the contrary, children tended to reside with their parents longer in Preston, where factory jobs were available, than in villages, where the lack of employment required them to leave their homes. Anderson concludes that individual wages tended to create a "calculative" orientation in the relationship between parents and children, but this new orientation had surprisingly few consequences for their behavior with respect to household formation.

Other textile cities have been studied by Louise Tilly (Roubaix, France) and Tamara Hareven (Manchester, New Hampshire), with particular emphasis on the occupational and demographic patterns of women. Tilly (1979) has shown how the employment opportunities in Roubaix affected the economic and demographic strategies of the women and families living there. Hareven (1982) has shown how kin ties were carried into the factory, and how the family mediated the demands of the industrial system.

The work of Louise Tilly and Joan Scott (1978) has been most successful in describing an alternative model for the evolution of the family in the nineteenth century. In *Women, Work, and Family* they describe a "family wage economy," which they associate with the urban and industrial system of the nineteenth century. This stage intervened between the preindustrial family economy of the peasant farm and the "family consumer economy" of advanced industrial society, and shared characteristics with both earlier and later family forms. Tilly and Scott emphasize that work was expected of all family members in the nineteenth century, just as it had been in the peasant family. The difference in the nineteenth century was that the development of wage labor in factories removed production from the household. While the peasant farm and the protoindustrial workshop had always been both a unit of production and a unit of consumption, modern industry removed production from the household. In the early stages of industrialization women and children continued to make economic contributions to the family, as they always had, but their money earnings now replaced their participation in a family enterprise. At the end of the nineteenth century married women increasingly directed their labor toward work in the home and became central to the emerging consumer economy.

If family behavior did not undergo a radical change in early textile cities, it is partly because they were slow to develop many of the characteristics that we associate with modern industry and modern cities. The important social consequences attributed to the factory have tended to obscure the full range of experiences of women and families even in these textile cities. While most women worked both before and after marriage, only a minority ever worked in the factories. Since married women tended to work part-time, few of them could work in the mills, although some factories provided domestic work for these women. Even unmarried women were by no means employed strictly in the factories. Many single women were employed in domestic service (including laundering and charring) and the needle trades, even in textile areas. It is important not to lose sight of the variety of their experiences.

Large manufacturing firms did not develop complete managerial control over the process of production until late in the century. Relationships with workers often resembled subcontracting more than wage employment, with foremen and senior workmen frequently controlling hiring and even purchasing. Factory production and domestic out-work usually went hand in hand, creating opportunities for married women to work part-time in their homes. The incomplete development of industrial organization created opportunities for abuse, like the foremen's alleged coercion of workers to buy from certain stores, but it also created opportunities for the family. Married women could find work that was more compatible with their domestic duties, and the needs of the family could be insinuated into the discipline of production.

It is also easy to overestimate the modernity of mid-nineteenth-century urban life. The development of modern retailing and services awaited the higher incomes of the consumer society emerging in the last quarter of the century. Earlier generations still depended on the myriad of peddlers and hawkers described so vividly by Henry Mayhew (1861–62) in London. This system imposed greater burdens on the domestic labor of women, creating the necessity of servants in the bourgeoisie, but it also offered many ways for women to supplement the family's income by selling and trading. Petty commerce had always been an area of female employment. A small city, like Verviers, did not have the variety and color of the London street scene, but it depended on street sellers for fruits and vegetables and on secondhand dealers for clothes and furniture. These part-time vendors were often married women and widows. Thus, we must evaluate the significance of the new industrial system in terms of the life experiences of the women and men who encountered it.

THE LIFE COURSE AND THE FAMILY

The women and families of nineteenth-century Verviers are examined here from a "life course" perspective, which emphasizes the transitions in individual lives. This approach differs in important respects from the emphasis on family life cycle and structure found in the seminal works in family history by Laslett, Anderson, and Berkner. These writers are primarily interested in determining the composition of domestic groups.

9

In contrast, the life course perspective focuses on transitions in individual lives and the decisions associated with them: the decisions to work, leave the parental household, marry, bear children, and so on. Each of these decisions was affected by a woman's personal and family resources, and her life history can be viewed as a sequence of transitions, each one affecting her choices in the next phase of her life. This is a framework which lends itself to both economic and social analysis, because it describes economic constraints as well as social interactions at the moment each choice is faced.

The life course approach, as used here, is part of a movement away from the concept of a family life cycle as the organizing principle in family studies. While the family life cycle was once hailed as a way to study family dynamics, it has recently drawn increasing criticism. David Featherman (1983) has written:

> Because of the life-span orientations, family researchers now recognize that the concept of the family cycle has been ahistorical, static, culture bound, and unduly focused on the impact of children on the parental relationship. To be sure, the concept has aided the analysis of longitudinal change in behavior, but it was based on typological thinking and on assumptions about the prevalence of marriage and the nuclear family and of the durability of marriages throughout a lifetime. (p. 37)

Glenn Elder (1978) points out that the typologies inherent in family cycle models are designed for static "snap-shots" but pose numerous problems with longitudinal data. As Kertzer and Schiaffino (1983) argue, family life cycle schemata are particularly weak when it comes to describing the processes of household formation and dissolution. Families do not have simple beginnings and ends, as the cycle models suggest. Over time households divide and combine, and we face a series of basic accounting problems: When has a new family been created? When did the original family die? If a family splits into two households, do we have one new family or two? This problem is largely hidden in cross-sectional studies of household or family structure, because each individual can always be assigned to a family or household. But difficulties arise in longitudinal studies when people move among households.

The problem is not simply that family life cycle approaches are based on typologies. In essence the family life cycle focuses on the career of a marital dyad, and it assumes a normatively prescribed sequence of events. Since these models are about couples, not individuals, they have little to say about how individuals sort themselves into couples or when individuals choose to leave one family to form another. Individuals are assigned to categories because of their relationships to married couples, and those

10

who never marry play a significant role only when they are children. The "normal" pattern of a couple's married life underlying the family life cycle model has the effect of omitting from consideration individuals who follow some other course. Women and men who do not marry, those who are widowed or divorced, and unwed mothers and their children are largely ignored. By turning to the individual life course we can study these different paths.

As a concept, the life course still lacks the intellectual tradition and resonance of the term *life cycle*. Life cycle conveys the ideas of process and continuity. In contrast life course is without direction or shape. This is a necessary and beneficial ambiguity. Life cycle analysis has often assumed too much regularity and left out too many who followed divergent paths. In place of the abstract continuity of the family cycle, we substitute the strivings of individuals in the act of creating families. We avoid the insoluble question of when families begin or end, and instead we look for alliance, negotiation, and the shift of resources and allegiances from one group to another. In the end rejecting the family cycle as an organizing principle for research actually increases our awareness of the importance of the family in individuals' lives.

The life course approach also restores to individuals the responsibility for their own actions. If the family is used as the unit of analysis, it is difficult to separate the interlocking and conflicting interests of different family members. Since the actions of each family member affect the choices of others, it is important to identify the actor responsible for each change. Did the child leave his parents, or the parents leave the child? In some analytical models, particularly those motivated by the "New Home Economics" (Becker, 1981), we are asked to assume that a family makes a single decision, as if it were governed by a benevolent dictator. This approach has useful applications, but there are situations, such as the decision to move out of a household, in which individual and group interests may be in conflict. Our analysis must leave room for conflict, compromise, and even for sacrifice. There are good reasons to believe that wives and children often deferred to the decisions of male heads of households. But the existence of patriarchy cannot be tested when it has already been assumed. It is the decisions made for the benefit of others that show the importance of the family as an organizing principle in individual lives.

This does not mean that the family is to be ignored. On the contrary, the life course approach enriches our understanding of the family, but it inherently views the family from the perspective of one family member. The family remains the context in which individuals make their decisions, and important insights such as the life cycle balance of income and consumption must be retained. The family can be viewed as a social contract

11

which specifies the rights and obligations of each family member, and our purpose is to identify the terms of this contract for each individual. The shift of focus from the group to the individual, however, solves some inherent problems with family life cycle analysis and opens the analysis to new questions.

The life course perspective also allows for the incorporation of historical development into our discussions of the family. As Hareven (1977, 1978b) puts it, we can examine the interaction of "historical time" and "individual time." The life course approach is particularly well suited for data organized by cohorts, and it is possible to examine the impact of events experienced by different cohorts at different ages. Glenn Elder's (1974) study of the cohorts who experienced the Great Depression is the classic example of this type of investigation.

Since few historical studies have been based on a life course perspective and fewer still have had longitudinal data about individuals, there is no simple definition of a life course analysis. In some respects this study will take a more individual-oriented approach than that found in the programmatic statements of Elder and Hareven. They have tended to emphasize the synchronization of individual transitions with the family cycle, in Hareven's words the relationship between "individual time" and "family time." Susan Watkins (1980), however, argues that the individual life course and the family cycle are two incompatible ways of looking at the same data. In her view, we can aggregate our information by individuals or by families, but both perspectives cannot be taken at the same time. This study adopts the individual's perspective, and we see the role of the family through the decisions of individual family members. Thus, the focus here is on how family characteristics affected the life course transitions of individuals, and family patterns are considered the outcome of these individual decisions.

This focus on individual decision-making leads to another difference from earlier work. While most previous historical studies have described distribution of statuses by age, this study attempts to focus on the determinants of transitions between statuses. Elder (1978), in particular, has tended to emphasize the importance of patterns of sequence and timing and the consequences of age-grading in society. His approach is partly grounded in a theoretical perspective which assumes the existence of strong norms regarding the appropriate ages for transitions. In contrast, the focus here will be on how individual and family characteristics affected the likelihood of transitions. This is not to deny the existence of age norms, but it is likely that age norms were more often subordinated to other economic and family considerations in the nineteenth century. Modell, Furstenberg, and Hershberg (1976) have shown that the variance in ages

12

at life course transitions, like marriage, narrowed significantly from the nineteenth to the twentieth century in the United States. The apparent compression of ages at marriage around the modal age appears to have resulted both from the lessened importance of economic and demographic crises and the increased influence of formal institutions like schooling (see also Uhlenberg, 1978).

It is possible to give greater attention to the determinants of transitions here because of the longitudinal data available from the Belgian population registers used in this research. Most historical research on the family has been based on censuses and other cross-sectional data sources. These sources can describe the patterns of status by age, like distribution of household types by age. Without longitudinal data, however, we cannot study the factors affecting transitions. Cross-sectional data do not help us examine questions like: Were women living with parents less likely to conceive children outside of marriage? Or did women with older sisters tend to marry later? The population registers and other longitudinal data sources allow us to raise new questions, but they also require new methodological tools.

METHODS AND THE LIFE COURSE

Most readers will find the methods used in some parts of this study unfamiliar. Some of these methods, like hazard models, have only recently become common in the social sciences, and there have been few previous applications in family history. The development of a new methodology, which is presented below in Chapter 2, was dictated by the characteristics of the Belgian population registers, from which data on nineteenth-century Verviers have been drawn. These sources are inherently longitudinal records, showing not a static cross-section but a span of time. Each population register records all of the demographic events that occurred in Verviers between a pair of censuses. Longitudinal records are ideal for life course analysis, but the dimension of time in these data poses a series of methodological problems. The work of van de Walle, Gutmann, and Watkins points to a new approach to these data (van de Walle, 1976; Watkins and McCarthy, 1980; Watkins and Gutmann, 1983).

The first step in using the population registers is to move away from the counting of individuals to the counting of "person years." Each of the women selected from the Verviers population registers was observed for a different amount of time. Those who lived all their lives in the city may have been observed for more than 30 years. Others migrated into and out of Verviers in as little as a few months. Still others left and returned several times. It would be inappropriate to equate the experience of 30 years as equivalent to that of a few months. The concept of the "person year" is used to weight the observations drawn from the population registers by the amounts of time that they represent. Thus, we do not ask what proportion of women lived with their parents, but rather what proportion of their time was spent living with parents at each age.

In addition to describing the amounts of time women spent in different statuses, population registers also tell us about transitions between statuses. The longitudinal dimension in the population registers describes sequences of events occurring over time. The population registers are limited in a fundamental way, however, because they do not yield complete life histories. The spans of time covered by population registers are arbitrarily divided, and the sequences reconstructed from them rarely include the complete life histories of the subjects of our study. The Verviers registers vary in length from 3 to 16 years. While each register reflects the events that occurred while it was open, the lives of our subjects continued after the register was closed. A woman who was single at the end of a register may have married after the register closed. Even while the register was open, some women migrated out of the reporting area. It is possible to link the population registers together to construct complete life histories, but this process is so costly that it is usually impractical.

The termination of observation at the end of each register creates a potential bias in some of the most familiar calculations, like the average age at marriage. The average age at marriage of women who married in a certain register is almost always lower than the average age at marriage of all the women in that register who eventually married. In the simplest terms, the women who married the latest are the most likely to have married after the register ended. The technical term *censoring* is used to describe the arbitrary end of observation in records like population registers. Fortunately, methods are available to overcome this problem, and recently developed statistical techniques allow us to fully exploit the information from the population registers.

Chapter 2 examines the nature of data from population registers and offers a methodology for overcoming the problem of censoring. The centerpiece of this methodology is the life table. The life table is an accounting device which follows a real or hypothetical cohort of people over time. It offers a way of relating the status an individual reached at each moment in time to the probability of a transition between statuses over periods of time. We can derive an estimate of the probability of a certain transition by a particular age from the population registers, and use the life table to translate this probability into an average age for each transition. This is analogous to using the death rates computed from censuses and vital registration to estimate life expectancy, which is the expected average age at death.

The final statistical step in the analysis is the construction of models showing relationships between transitions and individual and family characteristics. These models will be used to examine the effects of age, occupation, and family composition on the chances that a woman would marry. The results speak directly to the question: Did women adapt the timing of their marriages to the needs and resources of their families? In statistical terms these models are known as hazard models, because the likelihood of a transition, the "hazard," is the dependent variable in the models. This hazard is closely related to the probabilities of transitions depicted in the life table, and it is possible to think of hazard models as multivariate models of life table processes. The estimates produced by these models are similar to those resulting from the more familiar technique of multiple regression. We obtain estimates of coefficients which show the expected relationship between changes in explanatory variables and changes in our dependent variable. Although the statistics behind hazard models differ from common techniques like least squares regression, the results can be presented in a way that many readers will find familiar.

While these methods are new and in some respects radical departures from the ways in which other family historians have used their sources, they represent not a rejection of those methods but a return to basic principles. Thirty years ago the manual of Fleury and Henry (1956) revolutionized demographic and family history by showing how parish registers could be exploited despite their limitations. The methodology developed here uses the same logic and insights that underlie family reconstitution, but applies them to the possibilities and limitations of the population registers.

THE SETTING: VERVIERS IN THE MID-NINETEENTH CENTURY

Verviers is situated in eastern Belgium, 20 kilometers east of the provincial capital of Liège and 25 kilometers west of the present border with Germany. The heart of the city lies in a narrow, steep valley beside the Vesdre River. The river was essential to the city's woolen textile industry, and during the nineteenth century canals drew water from the river to be used in washing the dirt and oils from unprocessed wool. The Vesdre is too shallow at Verviers to be navigable, however, and the steep ridges and valleys which surround the city made transportation costly and difficult before the arrival of the railroad.

The history of nineteenth-century Verviers is inseparable from the history of its woolen textile industry. This one industry employed 40 percent of the city's work force, and the rhythm of its expansion was the rhythm of the city itself. Although the textile industry was not of ancient origin, by the beginning of the nineteenth century it was firmly established and vigorous. Its evolution into a modern form can be traced back at least to the seventeenth century, when it began to depend upon foreign trade. Exports went first to Germany and the Netherlands, and in 1672 manufacturers started to import fine wool from Spain and Portugal (Lebrun, 1948; Lebrun et al., 1979; Dechesne, 1932, p. 307; Mathieu, 1946, p. 33). Imported wool soon became indispensable, because the wool of local sheep was too coarse to produce the high quality product needed for an export trade (Dechesne, 1932, p. 217). In the nineteenth century Verviers imported its wool from South America and sold its products throughout the world. Their interests in foreign trade led Verviétois to consular posts as far away as New York and Singapore (*L'Industriel*, 11 October 44, AV; *Nouvelliste*, 6 April 45, AV).

Throughout the nineteenth century the textile industry in Verviers showed signs of its protoindustrial origins (Lebrun, 1948). In the seventeenth and eighteenth centuries merchant-manufacturers had learned to utilize the large supply of rural domestic labor surrounding the city. The land around Verviers, especially the plateau of Herve, was better suited to grazing than to farming. This type of agriculture left a large part-time labor force that could be used in the textile industry (Dechesne, 1932, pp. 218–9). The early merchant-manufacturers of Verviers "put-out" wool to domestic workers for spinning and weaving. Operations of preparation and finishing were kept in the city where water and water power were available (Dechesne, 1908, p. 31). By 1800 the woolen industry in the area around Verviers was employing 30,000 people found in 52 villages and 580 small hamlets (St. Lewinski, 1911, p. 28).

Verviers is best known for its leadership in the introduction of mechanized manufacturing (Lebrun, 1948). In 1798 two leading manufacturers brought John Cockerill to Verviers to build for them the textile machinery that he had learned in England. Cockerill set up the first spinning machinery on the continent in Verviers in 1802 and the first steam engine in Belgium in 1816 (Renier, 1881, pp. 80–90). In 1846 Verviers still had the largest concentration of steam engines in all of Belgium (Belgium, Ministère de l'intérieur, 1851). Cockerill and his sons went on to build an industrial empire in machinery and metallurgy, and other inventors were attracted to Verviers. James Hodson came from England in 1802 to build textile machinery, and in 1821 A. Houget established a firm to build shearing machines and steam engines (Renier, 1881, pp. 82, 91). The leadership of the woolen industry in Verviers was recognized by foreign governments, who tried to acquire the latest techniques by attracting artisans from Verviers (Dechesne, 1932, p. 308).

During the course of the nineteenth century the domestic form of textile production was replaced by centralized and mechanized production.

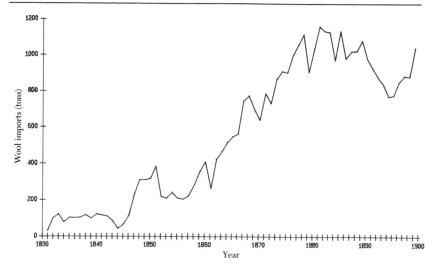

Figure 1.1. Imports of wool, by year, 1831–99

Operations which had once been "put-out" were drawn into factories, and hand labor was eventually replaced by steam-powered machines. This transformation took a long time, however, especially in weaving, and for most of the nineteenth century domestic industry around Verviers was very important. In 1846, of the 20,000 persons employed in the textile industry in the province of Liège 8,000 were in domestic industry (Thonnar, 1904, p. 62). Even in 1896 there were still 1,000 rural persons weaving on handlooms in the arrondissement of Verviers, although young people were no longer learning the trade (Thonnar, 1904, p. 13).

The 1840s were a period of both promise and crisis. The railroad reached the city in 1843 and finally provided good transportation to the port of Antwerp. A technological foundation was laid which would later lead to great expansion of industry in Verviers. This can be seen in the number of steam engines in the city, which increased from 68 in 1837 to 99 in 1845 and 122 in 1849, more than tripling the available horsepower from 513 to 1,468 (Dechesne, 1908, p. 37). But the prosperity promised by the new railroad was cut short in 1845 by the economic crisis that accompanied the potato famine. The price of potatoes, the mainstay of the workers' diet, rose by 300–400 percent, bread prices rose by 38 percent, and the price of rice doubled (Fohal, 1927–28, p. 30). The famine and its economic consequences had hardly passed when the city was struck by the cholera epidemic of 1849.

After 1850, expanding foreign trade and rapid technical innovation made Verviers a wealthy and proud city. The course of this expansion can be

17

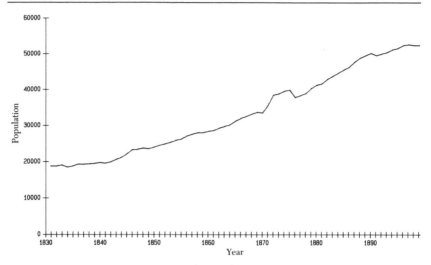

Figure 1.2. Population of Verviers, 1831–99

traced in Van Houtte's (1949) collected statistics for exports and imports (see Figure 1.1 for imports). Wool consumption increased 10-fold between the 1840s and the 1870s, exports of woven goods quadrupled, and exports of spun wool rose from just 34 tons in 1845 to 7,606 tons in 1873 (F.-X. Van Houtte, 1949, pp. 256–58, 265–67).

The depression of 1873 marked another turning point in the industrial history of Verviers and the beginning of its decline. Protectionism and the diffusion of textile technology abroad reduced the advantages that Verviers had enjoyed. Exports of woven goods never returned to the levels of the early 1870s, and exports of spun wool did not recover until the mid-1880s (F.-X. Van Houtte, 1949, pp. 256–58, 265–67). Changes in fashion reduced demand for the products in which the city specialized, and the transition to new products did not restore prosperity until the end of the century (Dechesne, 1932, pp. 435–36).

The demographic history of Verviers is traced in Figures 1.2, 1.3, and 1.4. The city experienced continued growth from 23,339 in 1846 to 41,256 in 1880, but much of this growth was due to migration into the city. The death rate was high and volatile, averaging 31.1 per 1,000 people between 1846 and 1880, with peaks at 63.7 and 59.4 in the cholera years of 1849 and 1866, respectively. The birth rate was similarly high and variable (34.1 per 1,000 between 1846 and 1880), although its swings were never as wide as those in the death rate. There is a suggestion in Figure 1.3 that fertility had been higher in the 1830s than it was in the 1840s and 1850s,

18

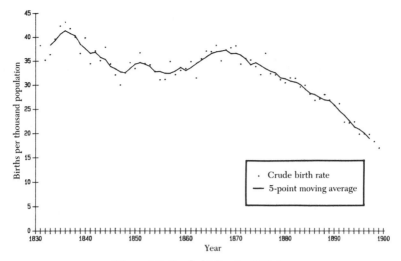

Figure 1.3. Crude birth rate, 1831–99

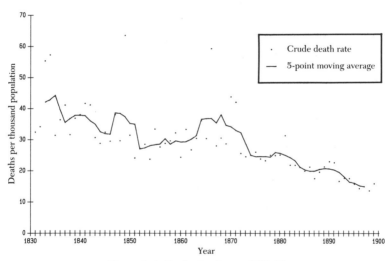

Figure 1.4. Crude death rate, 1831–99

and we shall see in Chapter 7 that the level of fertility increased in the 1860s and 1870s from the 1850s. The turning point in the demographic transition in Verviers occurred around 1870. Both birth and death rates began their long-run declines. In the classic pattern, death rates declined more rapidly, and 1871 was the last year in which deaths exceeded births.

THE WOMEN AND FAMILIES OF VERVIERS

Each of the following chapters addresses a life course choice encountered by the women of Verviers. Chapters 3 and 4 describe household and occupational patterns, which are choices faced throughout the life course. These chapters also describe how these patterns developed and their relationship to the family. Chapters 5, 6, and 7 focus on turning points in the life course: initiation of sexual activity, marriage, and childbearing. These chapters direct attention to the personal and family logic behind these life course choices.

Chapter 3 examines the household patterns of the female population of Verviers from the perspective of the demographic formation of the city. In particular, residential patterns were related to two important transitions, migration and marriage. Both of these transitions affected household patterns by changing the types of kin available for coresidence. In Verviers marriage and migration were deeply intertwined, and Chapter 3 attempts to unravel these processes. Like most rapidly growing industrial cities, Verviers experienced rapid in-migration from surrounding rural areas, and we will attempt to sort out different types of migrants as they varied by age.

In Verviers women left their families of origin when they married, as was typical of the European marriage pattern. Also typical was the high percentage of women who never married. While it is tempting to attribute these marriage patterns to the in-migration of unmarried from outside the city, we find that migrants were actually more likely to be married than urban natives. Migration did increase female celibacy in Verviers, but it did so by depressing the marriage market for natives, rather than by bringing unmarried women into the city.

There is no evidence in Chapter 3 that the unmarried women of Verviers abandoned the family; rather, residential patterns show the opposite. Most unmarried women lived in their households of origin as long as possible. The transition to a different type of household was more often caused by the death of parents than by unmarried women attempting to assert their independence. There is a suggestion in these data that unmarried women were relatively immobile, and that their households of origin often dissolved around them.

While we see strong attachment of unmarried women to the family of origin, we also see the exclusive nature of the nuclear family. The boundary around the nuclear family was such that other kin were rarely admitted. Few married women had other types of kin living in their families, and even widowed women tended to maintain independent households when they had older children. Consequently unmarried women tended to

20

form households with other unmarried and widowed women, and seldom lived with married kin.

Chapter 4 examines the structure imposed on these life histories by their positions in the economic life of the city. Women in nineteenth-century Verviers were limited to a small number of occupations, but the social hierarchy of female occupations was as clear as the hierarchy of male occupations. At the top were the women whose families could afford to hire servants. These women emphasized the privilege of their idleness by reporting no occupations, while women who said they were *ménagères* (housekeepers) did the backbreaking work of a nineteenth-century household. At the bottom were the casual laborers, who did unskilled work in the factories or other odd jobs. In between these extremes were the female artisans, like seamstresses, and the workers who did the factory and domestic labor of the textile industry.

Each female occupation had a social position analogous to that of the male occupation to which it corresponded. Moreover, occupational status was passed from father to daughter, just as it was passed from father to son. The daughter of a shopkeeping artisan, like a butcher or baker, often became an artisan herself by learning one of the needle trades, while the daughters of textile workers followed their fathers into the female jobs associated with spinning and weaving. The domestic ideal is apparent in the behavior of women from the city's economic elite, who rarely had occupations. In the generation of women forming households at midcentury, however, few achieved that ideal.

Marriage and the childbearing, which quickly followed, decisively changed the working lives of these women. They continued to work, but their domestic responsibilities prevented most of them from earning wages full time. Nevertheless, many continued to make economic contributions to their families. There are signs in Verviers of a world of part-time female work, which has been hidden because married women usually told the census taker their most important occupation, housewife. Factory wage books show that many women worked part-time, and tax records show a myriad of small shops and cabarets which were often run by women.

Chapter 5 addresses one of the key arguments in the indictment of working-class morality: the high levels of illegitimacy and bridal pregnancy in the nineteenth century. This problem is particularly relevant to nineteenth-century Verviers, where illegitimacy was moderately high and more than one bride in three was pregnant. The historical issue was posed in its clearest form in an exchange between Edward Shorter (1973, 1977) and Louise Tilly, Joan Scott, and Miriam Cohen (1976). Shorter argues that their newfound economic independence created a wave of sexual liberation among the young women of the nineteenth century. They were freed from the constraints of family and community supervision, and found an expression of their freedom in sexual activity. Tilly, Scott, and Cohen, on the other hand, see no sexual revolution, but rather the continuation of peasant courtship customs, in which sexual activity often preceded the marriage ceremony. Women were behaving no differently from the way they had before, but the urban community could not reproduce the social control used by the peasant village to force marriage on young men whose partners had become pregnant.

Were the women of Verviers emancipated and pleasure-seeking, as Edward Shorter would have us believe, or were they isolated and exploited, as Louise Tilly, Joan Scott, and Miriam Cohen suggest? The answer offered here comes closer to the position of the latter three researchers, but it proceeds from different principles. Following the lead of Tilly, Scott, and Cohen, I view the sexual activity of unmarried women from the perspective that their culture was one in which premarital sex was often tolerated. The transition to marriage had many stages, only one of which was the marriage ceremony itself. This pattern is not simply a legacy of peasant society, however. Working-class cultures in the twentieth century also exhibit a striking ambivalence about premarital sexual activity; this ambivalence can be traced to the "double standard" applied to male and female sexual behavior. Chapter 5 proceeds by describing courtship as a three-way negotiation involving a woman, her partner, and her family. Each of these parties had different goals and different understandings of the courtship process. For males, nonmarital sexual activity was part of the process of self-identification. Women faced greater risks and were more motivated to use sexual activity to strengthen commitments leading to marriage.

The data on illegitimacy and bridal pregnancy in nineteenth-century Verviers fit this model of negotiation surrounding marriage in several key respects. We can identify four different outcomes: spinsterhood without children, illegitimacy, bridal pregnancy, and marriage without pregnancy. These outcomes form a continuum, in the sense that women made a series of decisions in the face of demands from potential husbands and their changing positions in the marriage market. Unwed motherhood was not the fate of the young and inexperienced. Mothers of illegitimate children were on average older than brides, and they were also more likely to be migrants or orphans. These women were not isolated from the urban community, but their ages and weaker social supports made them more vulnerable in the marriage market.

Bridal pregnancy shows how sexual activity fitted within the social system, and these cases may even have been viewed favorably by those involved. When pregnant and nonpregnant brides are compared, we find that coresidence with parents did not have the effect of preventing premarital sexual intimacy. Indeed, since parents had an economic interest in delaying the marriages of their daughters, premarital pregnancies may have been used to pressure reluctant parents to consent to these marriages. Pregnant brides were somewhat younger than other brides, but their postmarital household patterns do not indicate that they were unprepared for marriage.

Chapter 6 views the marriage process in a different way, and asks what individual and family characteristics affected the tendency to marry. The central problem addressed here is: Why did marriage occur so late? The economic demands of establishing an independent household have always been stressed by historians, but little research has examined the demands placed upon women by their families of origin. An important element in Verviers appears to have been the duties that daughters performed for their households of origin. In particular, we see a strong binding force holding women to their families. This force was partly economic, and women with working-age siblings found it easier to leave. But economic factors do not explain why women living with parents were less likely to marry than those living by themselves. Surprisingly, women who lived with both parents were the least likely to marry, holding the availability of family labor constant. This suggests that the family of origin had a special hold on children, which was broken when one parent died. Late marriage, then, was a response to the demands of both family of origin and family of procreation. Marriage was delayed, because the economic demands of parents and siblings often conflicted with the need to accumulate savings needed to form a new family.

In 1870 the birth rate in Verviers began its long decline to present low levels of fertility. It is highly likely that the cohort of women sampled here was the first in which a significant minority practiced family limitation. The records of working-class leaders of the time exhibit an ambivalence toward child labor, which we can associate with the transition in social values taking place. Chapter 7 examines the family-building process in late nineteenth-century Verviers and the characteristics of couples most likely to have practiced family limitation. Although most earlier research has emphasized differences among social strata in the practice of birth control, these differences were less pronounced in Verviers than might have been expected. The very wealthy families in the city's economic elite did indeed practice more extensive and effective family limitation than the rest of the population, but evidence of birth control is found throughout the population. There is no sign that this practice "trickled down" from the bourgeoisie to the petty bourgeoisie to the skilled workers and so on. It seems more likely that the advantages of small families and the means for achieving them were perceived by and spread quickly through all social classes. The variable most clearly associated with family limitation is early residence in the city, and it would seem that the urban environment had a formative influence on the values and expectations of native Verv)étoises that adult migrants from rural and semi-industrial areas did not experience.

2

Methods and Data: Time, Events, and the Study of the Life Course

Chapter 2 describes the methods that are used elsewhere in this monograph.[1] Although some of the topics discussed here involve sophisticated statistical techniques, I have attempted to keep the explanation of these methods as simple and intuitive as possible. The discussion is illustrated with schematic diagrams and examples based upon simplifying assumptions. It is hoped that this chapter will make the substantive chapters accessible to a wide, quantitatively literate audience, without demanding specialized knowledge in demographic and statistical methods.

Underlying the methods used here is a new and powerful way of thinking about the life course. Much of the analysis presented here will be unfamiliar even to readers well versed in quantitative analysis. The continuous observation of time in the population registers requires methods that are fundamentally different from those applied to other data sources. This time dimension is missing in cross-sectional data, like censuses and surveys, and even time series and panel methods observe time in a different way. The methodology used here does more than make a virtue of necessity, however. Rather these methods are both more powerful and more relevant to the theoretical issues that I want to address. In fact, more familiar methods are really special cases of the general approach used here (see Tuma, Hannan, and Groeneveld, 1979).

We can appreciate how these methods differ by considering a motion picture film. Motion picture film is actually composed of a series of still photographs separated by very brief intervals of time. A census is like a single frame of film. In a census the population is frozen at an instant in time. Census data can show composition and relations within a population, but it cannot show change over time. We can see those changes

1. The methodology described here is derived from the pioneering work of Etienne van de Walle and his associates Myron Gutmann and Susan Cotts Watkins on the Belgian village of La Hulpe. In addition to the articles cited, van de Walle, Gutmann, and Watkins offered me the benefit of their experiences in numerous personal conversations and meetings.

by comparing successive frames in the film, and most time series analysis operates in this way. The data are composed of a series of snapshots, which can be compared and contrasted. The interval between observations may vary (one year, one month, one day, etc.), and the data may be averaged or summed over an entire interval rather than referring to its beginning or end. Nevertheless, the observations are evenly spaced in time, like the frames in a film.

Although the time series approach captures the information on the film, there are some aspects of the film that are difficult to describe in this way, and an alternative approach is also used on motion picture film. Consider the sound track of a motion picture. The sound track on the film is continuously recorded and not divided into a succession of snapshots like the picture. When we stop the film, a picture is frozen on the screen, but the sound disappears entirely. Sound, by its nature and representation on the film, exists only in time. When we stop the film we hear an instant of sound, which is so small that it vanishes. Of course, we could describe the sound track in the same way that the picture has been represented. At each moment there is a certain combination of sounds with different intensities and wavelengths, and the sound track can be divided into a sequence of intervals of equal length. The information on the film can be described in this way, but something important about the continuity of sound is lost. Any series of arbitrary intervals will not conform to the underlying rhythms of music and speech of which the sound track is really composed. These patterns are the processes that we really want to describe.

If we turn to musical notation, we find a very different way of describing sound. Each note in a musical score represents a tone of a certain pitch and also a certain duration. The sounds are not divided into arbitrary intervals, rather the natural continuities are preserved by a notation explicitly showing how long each tone should be played. This time dimension is as much a characteristic of each note in the score as its pitch. When we listen to music, however, we do not simply hear tones of different lengths. We also hear sequences and movements. We hear the melody rise an octave or fall two tones lower. The transitions between notes are instantaneous events, and yet we hear transitions as well as long and short continuous tones.

These two characteristics of music, duration and transition, are also important ways of looking at individual life histories. A life course can be thought of as a sequence of stays in different statuses and transitions between statuses. For example, a marital history describes time spent single, married, and perhaps also widowed and remarried. By analogy, each of these statuses is a different tone, and the time spent single can be thought of as a "note" with a duration in time. We are interested in describing both the durations of time spent in each status and the timing of transitions between statuses. The methods presented here are designed to capture these aspects of the life course.

The methodological implications of recognizing the time dimension in population registers are far-reaching. This is not a matter of using more or less elaborate statistical techniques; it amounts to redefining what and how we count. When observation is in continuous time, the samples consist of lengths of time in individual life histories, and the amount of data is measured in durations of time not numbers of individuals. Indeed, there is no simple correspondence between the number of individuals and the amount of data that they contribute to the data set. A woman who is observed for 10 years contributes 10 times more data than a woman observed for only 1 year.

This means that we can use the population registers to ask new questions and that we will often approach old questions in new ways. Earlier historians of the family asked how many persons lived in simple nuclear households as opposed to households including other kin and nonkin. Population registers tell us not just "how many" but "how long." What is the average proportion of life that women spent living with their parents? their siblings? other kin and nonkin? their husbands and children? Moreover, we can ask whether the composition of their households affected the timing of other events in their lives. Did women who lived with parents marry sooner or later than women who lived alone? How did the family's economic and demographic resources affect the decision to marry? Did women with unmarried older sisters delay their own marriages in deference to their sisters, as tradition required?

There are also new problems associated with this type of data analysis. Some familiar quantitative measures, for example, the average age at marriage, are more difficult to calculate from the population registers than one might expect. These problems are due to the incompleteness of life histories included in the population registers. Fortunately, methods are available that allow us to reconstruct the measures which cannot be computed directly.

An Illustration of Time in the Population Registers

Table 2.1 and Figure 2.1 illustrate some of the important features of the representation of time in the population. Table 2.1 is an example of the reporting of a household in the population register for the period 1856–65. The household consists of a woman in the sample (Barbe), her husband (Arnold), their four children (Constance, David, Edouard, Françoise), and

27

Table 2.1. Sample Household in Verviers, as Reported in the Population Register for 1856–65

Name	Marital Status	Relationship	Year of Birth	Place of Birth	Year of Entry	Year of Exit	Year of Death	Changes in Marital Status
Arnold	Married	Husband	1821	Hodimont	1835		1862	
Barbe	Married	Woman in sample	1823	Verviers				
Constance	Single	Child	1849	Verviers				
David	Single	Child	1851	Verviers				
Edouard	Single	Child	1857	Verviers			1858	
Françoise	Single	Child	1859	Verviers				
Gertrude	Single	Servant	1832	Herve	1855	1858		
Harriet	Single	Servant	1834	Soiron	1859			1858 (marr.)

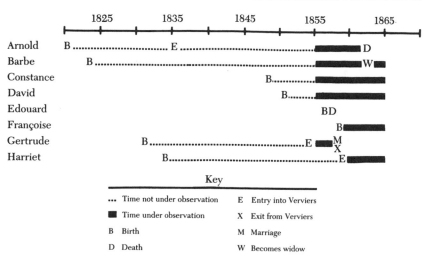

Figure 2.1. "Time lines," by year, for each individual in the sample household of Table 2.1

two servants (Gertrude, Harriet). The population register reports the date of birth for each person, and dates are reported for other demographic events in other columns. Three persons migrated to Verviers from other communes (Arnold, Gertrude, Harriet), and the dates that they entered Verviers are recorded. One servant out-migrated (Gertrude), two family members died (Arnold, Edouard), and one servant married (Gertrude).

Figure 2.1 presents "time lines" for each individual constructed from the information in Table 2.1. Events are marked on each time line with letters, such as "B" for birth. The figure also shows two implicit events of great importance for our analysis. The population register was opened 1 January 1856, and closed 31 December 1865. Although we have information about some events that occurred before 1856, a person who was not in the household between 1856 and 1865 was not recorded. The family may have had children who were born and died or servants who entered and exited before 1856, but these individuals would not have been observed while the 1856–65 population register was open. Similarly, events that occurred after 1865 were recorded in the register opened in 1866. Persons in the household were under observation, or "at risk," only from 1856 to 1865. The time at risk is indicated in the diagram by using a bold line (▬▬) while the register was open. A dashed line (- - - -) is used for periods before or after this register.

The diagram also shows that some people were not under observation during all 10 years the register was open. Two children (Edouard, Françoise) were born after the register began, and one servant (Harriet)

29

Figure 2.2. "Time lines," by age, for each individual in the sample household of Table 2.2

entered in 1858. Similarly, three persons left the household before the register closed. Two family members (Arnold, Edouard) died, and one servant (Gertrude) exited. These individuals were under observation only while they were alive, living in the household, and the register was open.

We can see changes in the composition of the household over time by noting that a vertical line marks a specific date. Although there are eight people listed in the register, the household never had more than six persons at any time. When the register opened in 1856, there were two children (Constance, David) and one servant (Gertrude). The household size grew to six when Edouard was born. But Edouard died as an infant and Gertrude married and exited shortly afterward. The household again grew to six persons with the birth of another child and the entry of another servant. This configuration lasted only three years before the male head of the household (Arnold) died. When the register was closed at the end of 1865, there were still five people in the household; however, only three of them had been present for all 10 years (Barbe, Constance, David). The diagram shows clearly that several combinations of persons listed in the household were never actually present at the same time (e.g., the two servants Gertrude and Harriet).

Many of the questions of interest in life course analysis deal with processes that are in some way related to age, like marriage and mortality. Figure 2.2 shows how the information in the population register can be organized by age. The time lines in this figure are the same as those in

30

Figure 2.1, but they are now compared by a scale showing age rather than date. Figure 2.2 shows dramatically that the arbitrary opening and closing of the register captured very different periods in the lives of each person in the household.

In Figures 2.1 and 2.2 an artificial event ("becomes widow") has been added to the time line of the woman in the sample (Barbe) to illustrate a very useful device for the analysis of population registers. In this example, when Arnold died, his wife's marital status changed from "married" to "widowed." The usefulness of this device becomes apparent when we move from Figure 2.1 to Figure 2.2. When the life histories are arranged by age, the temporal sequence of events occurring in different individuals' lives is lost. By creating artificial events or "pseudo-events," like "becomes widow," we can easily show when and how the woman in the sample was affected by changes occurring in the lives of those around her.

The term *event* is used here to refer to any kind of demographic change that affects some analytically interesting characteristic of a person in the sample. In the example, "becomes widow" is an event that marks a change in marital status. For the purposes of analysis the beginning of her widowhood was an event in her life history of equal standing with the beginning of her marriage. Just as it is useful to consider "becomes widow" as an event comparable to marriage, it is also useful to consider the birth of a child as an event in the mother's life history. We may refer to this as "becomes mother" or "motherhood" to distinguish it from the event of "birth," which will be treated as an event in the life history of the child that was born. This device makes every important transition in the household a part of the life history of the woman in the sample. The "pseudo-events" were first developed to simplify the computer programs needed to process the population registers, but they are also a useful way to think about the data.

In the analysis that follows, a variety of household characteristics will also be treated as attributes of the women in the sample. For example, when we are interested in examining the correlates of household size, household size will be treated as a variable describing an individual woman. This involves counting the number of other persons living in the household of each woman in the sample at each point in time. As Table 2.1 indicates this is a straightforward process of listing the consequences of events recorded in the population register in chronological order. In earlier studies I have referred to the computer program that performs this task as a "household simulation" program, because it simulates the dynamics of movements into and out of the household. Among the different variables that have been generated from the population registers are

31

variables describing coresidence with parents, siblings, and the age and sex composition of the household. Each of these variables refers to a point or period of time in the history of a specific woman.

COUNTING PROCEDURES:
PERSON-YEARS OF OBSERVATION AND EVENTS

The Belgian population registers are a hybrid of two demographic instruments, censuses and vital registration, and they contain two kinds of data corresponding to each of these instruments. Like censuses, the population registers show the characteristics of the population. Like vital registers, the population registers recorded the number of transitions from alive to dead, unmarried to married, etc. However, the time frame of the population registers is different from those of other sources, and this has important consequences for the ways in which they can be used.

It is possible to use the population registers to reconstruct the censuses and vital registers from which they were derived. We could identify which persons were present at the censuses marking the beginning and end of each register. We could also count the number of births, deaths, and marriages in each calendar year to reproduce the vital registers. If this were done, then standard techniques for using these data sources could be applied. Unfortunately, this approach would ignore the most exciting research possibilities in the population registers. There is much more information in the population registers than in the censuses and vital registers considered separately. The additional information comes from the linkage of information from the census to the demographic events and the linkage of events occurring in the life of each individual in the population registers. The life histories that we can construct from the population registers show variations in household characteristics over time and sequence of events. A host of questions beyond the scope of conventional techniques can be addressed with this type of data. For example, how does the marriage of a woman depend upon the current composition of her household? Or, how does the likelihood of another birth depend upon the mortality of the previous child?

The basic nature of the methods used here can be explained by comparing them with more familiar techniques for analyzing censuses and vital registers. Censuses are used to count the number of people with each type of characteristic or in each status. Thus, censuses give us counts or proportions by occupation, marital status, age category, etc. Population registers also record these same characteristics. But censuses refer to moments in time, whereas population registers refer to periods of time. For this reason it is not appropriate to count each time a characteristic occurs in a

32

population register without also counting how long it was observed. As Figure 2.2 shows, different individuals are observed for different amounts of time, and it is even possible to observe the same person more than once. A person who stayed in the same household for all 10 years of the register would have been recorded only once. But a person who moved to a different household every year, like some domestic servants, would have been recorded 10 times in 10 different households. Clearly, the latter should not be counted 10 times more than the former. The solution to this problem is to weight our counting by time spent in each status. A person who was observed for 10 years should contribute 10 "person-years" of experience to the sample, whether she was observed once for 10 years or 10 times for 1 year.

The inclusion of vital registration in the population registers makes it possible to calculate vital rates: birth rates, death rates, marriage rates. In addition, the population registers record migration, which is usually not directly observed in vital registration systems. The difference between population registers and other vital registers lies in the calculation of the denominator in these rates. The counts of births, deaths, and marriages in vital registers are converted to rates by dividing the number of events in a given period of time, usually a year, by the average size of the population during this period of time. The size of the population is not derived from the vital registers but from a census.

The population registers can be used to derive both the numerator and denominator of these vital rates, and again, it is appropriate to count "person-years at risk." This is actually no different from the procedure used in conventional calculations. The duration of time in the denominator in calculations from vital registers and censuses is usually disguised, because these calculations are computed on an annual basis. Implicitly, the usual calculation is births per person-year at risk, but the average number of person-years contributed by each person in the denominator is one year. The population registers, however, allow us to observe time at risk directly and to make a number of distinctions not otherwise possible.

Figure 2.2 suggests how these calculations can be made. The total amount of observation of the woman in the sample (Barbe) is the length of the bold line indicating the time she was under observation, 10 person-years in this example. Most of the variables of interest to us are best broken down by age. In Figure 2.2 we can see that the woman in the sample was under observation during the five-year age groups 30–34, 35–39, and 40–44. A full 5 person-years of exposure were observed in the category 35–39, and about 2.5 person-years were observed in both the 30–34 and 40–44 age groups. The "W" symbol, indicating the beginning of her widowhood, shows how her time spent in different marital statuses can be broken into age groups. She was married for about 2.5 and 3.5 person-years at ages 30–34 and 35–39, respectively, and she was a widow for about 1.5 and 2.5 person-years at ages 35–39 and 40–44, respectively.

The calculation of vital rates from the population registers is best illustrated by considering the age-specific death rates of all members of the household shown in Figure 2.2. The numerators for the age-specific death rates are constructed by allocating the two observed deaths (Arnold and Edouard) to their respective age groups (40–44 and 0–1). The denominators for death rates are calculated by summing the amount of observation of all persons in each age group. Figure 2.2 shows that every age group from birth to 40–44 is represented by at least one member of the household; thus, there was some exposure to the risk of death in each age group. Some age groups were observed for only short periods (e.g., Constance in the age group 15–19), while the overlap of more than one life history in other age groups generates more data at those ages (e.g., Constance and David in the age groups 5–9 and 10–14 and Arnold and Barbe in the age group 35–39). These numerators and denominators can be tabulated across all women in the sample or all persons in the data to obtain estimates of age-specific death rates.

Readers familiar with demographic history will notice that the methods used here are very different from those used in the family reconstitution method developed by Louis Henry (Fleury and Henry, 1956; Henry, 1980). Family reconstitution is based upon family histories derived from vital registers by linking all of the births, marriages, and deaths associated with a marital union. Periods at risk of demographic events are reconstructed from recorded events showing that members of the family were alive and present in the commune under study. René Leboutte (1984) has shown that population registers as well can be used for family reconstitution. The population registers facilitate the necessary linkages of births, marriages, and deaths, and all of the techniques used by classic family reconstitution can be applied to data constructed with the assistance of the population registers.

There are several reasons for my taking a new approach here. First, the methods I have used produce a number of important new measures—in particular, measures involving household composition and dynamics—that are beyond the scope of family reconstitution.

Second, the family reconstitution approach is costly in terms of both the labor required to prepare the data set and the amount of useable data that it produces. Family reconstitution requires the linkage of events to produce individual and life histories, ideally from birth to death. Since each population register is too short to cover an average life span, successive population registers would have to be linked together to generate these data. Under the best conditions this linkage process is a time-consuming and expensive undertaking. Two of the samples used here are linked across successive registers from 1849 to 1880. This linkage was a laborious process, and even with indices and frequent cross-references in the registers themselves these samples were an order of magnitude more expensive than unlinked samples of the same size. Furthermore, most of the information in these linked samples would be discarded under standard family reconstitution rules. For example, many measures of fertility used in family reconstitution studies are computed only for couples that are observed from marriage until the wife passed age 45. Data from incomplete unions, the majority of all unions, is discarded. The techniques used here allow us to compute comparable measures using all the available data.

Finally, family reconstitution is subject to biases that can be avoided in population register research. Family reconstitution can be accomplished only on couples that were geographically stable. Couples who migrated across the boundaries of communes left records in the registers of each commune, which are impractical to link. The behavior of the "reconstitutable minority" may have differed in undetectable ways from the more mobile part of the population. As we shall see, migrants in Verviers were often very different from natives of the city. These differences could not have been examined with family reconstitution techniques.

Despite the apparent differences in approach, the techniques used here are an attempt to remain true to the underlying logic of family reconstitution. Part of Louis Henry's insight is the recognition that the way in which a partial life history ended affects the purposes for which it can be used. If fertility rates are calculated from partial histories that ended in a birth, the estimates will be biased toward showing higher fertility. Every history ending in a birth contributes an event to the numerator of the fertility rate, but observation ends at that birth without contributing an appropriate amount of exposure to risk to the denominator of the rate. The rules by which Henry decides when a partial history can be used for a particular kind of calculation are designed to prevent this kind of bias. However, the underlying problem in family reconstitution is that migration is not observed directly, and exposure to risk must be inferred from other events. Couples who migrated out of the commune after a birth were at risk of another birth for an unmeasurable amount of time after their last observed birth.

In contrast to the sources used by family reconstitution, the population registers did record migration explicitly, and they can be used to produce unbiased estimates of exposure to risk, the denominator in all vital rates. The problem in the population registers is that they refer to relatively

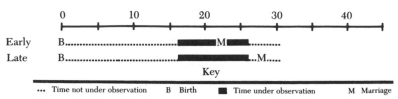

Figure 2.3. The effect of censoring on observations of age at marriage

short periods of time and provide only partial life histories. Certain types of calculations result in biased estimates when performed on these data. In general, the average of observed ages for some transitions, like marriage, is biased toward underestimating the average age of the transition in the population. The average age in the observed marriages does not include information about the age at marriage of persons who married after the register closed, and these marriages tended to be at higher ages than the marriages that are observed. A more complete explanation of this problem and its solution are presented in the next section.

THE LIFE TABLE APPROACH TO CENSORED LIFE HISTORIES

The life histories examined here are characterized by an important limitation, known in the statistical literature as censoring. As Figures 2.1 and 2.2 show, the histories derived from the population registers are "censored" on both the "left" and the "right," because most of them begin after birth and end before death. Censoring has important effects on the calculation of average ages for transitions like marriage, migration, first birth, last birth, and so on.[2] This section explains why censoring creates biases in these calculations and how alternative measures can be constructed.

Figure 2.3 has been constructed to provide a simplified illustration of the censoring problem. Suppose that we are interested in the average age at marriage in a cohort of women observed in a population register. For the sake of simplicity, let us assume that all women were born at the same time and all were observed for all 10 years of a population register which opened when they were age 17 and closed when they were age 26. Finally, suppose there were only two ages at marriage in this hypothetical cohort: Assume that half of the cohort married at the "early" age of 22, and half married at the "late" age of 28. These assumptions yield a true average age at marriage for this cohort of 25 [= .5 (22) + .5 (28)].

Figure 2.3 shows that it would not be possible to derive the true aver-

2. The standard discussion of this problem is Ryder, 1975. Watkins and Gutmann (1983) explore this problem in the context of population registers.

36

age age at marriage from the data found in our hypothetical population register. Some of the events of interest occurred in the period after the population register closed, thus censoring the observation. Since the register closed before the cohort reached age 28, only the "early" marriages were recorded. The average age at marriage *observed* in the population register is 22. By construction, only the marriages of the "early" subpopulation are observed, whereas none of the marriages of the equally numerous "late"-marriage subpopulation are. The average of observed ages at marriage ignores the latter part of the population entirely.

The problem illustrated in Figure 2.3 can be generalized by moving to a more realistic model in two steps. First, consider an alternative distribution of ages at marriage. In the diagram this would be represented by adding many more life history lines with different ages at marriage. No matter what distribution of ages at marriage we use, only marriages under age 26 will be observed in the register. The exclusion of marriages above age 26, whatever proportion they may be, means that the average of the observed ages at marriage will always be too low. Second, consider a distribution of birth cohorts, that is, women who were different ages when the register began and ended. We could draw a diagram like Figure 2.3 for each of these birth cohorts. The end of the register will truncate the observation of each birth cohort at a different age, but it will always exclude later rather than earlier marriages. Thus, the end of the register will always create a downward bias in the average age at marriage for each observed birth cohort.[3] The overall estimate for the whole population is a weighted average of the averages for the different birth cohorts, and it too will be downwardly biased.

The implication of this illustration is that averaging observed ages at marriage in a censored data set yields downwardly biased estimates. This is a general conclusion, and it does not depend upon the simplifying assumptions introduced in the illustration in Figure 2.3. Furthermore, the bias due to censoring is not related to the composition of the population or its rate of growth. Bias is also introduced by censoring of other kinds, such as migration out of the commune covered by the population register. In contemporary sociology and economics, event histories collected by retrospective or longitudinal surveys are censored by the date of the last survey (Ryder, 1975).

3. The beginning of the population register will exclude marriages at younger ages for earlier birth cohorts. For example, if the women in the sample were all 25 when the register began, no marriages under age 25 will be observed. Thus, truncated observation at younger ages, "left" censoring, will lead to estimates that are upwardly biased. Although the averages of observed ages at marriage are biased in opposite directions with "left" and "right" censoring, they will not necessarily compensate each other in any particular sample.

In population registers, censoring affects not only the calculation of average age at marriage but other average age estimates, including age at first birth, last birth, migration, widowhood, death. A number of other variables of interest, like the length of the average birth interval, are affected by the same problem. In general, any variable that can be thought of as a "waiting time to an event" must be called into question. The average age at marriage is the average waiting time from birth to marriage. Although it refers to a different starting point, the average birth interval is also an average waiting time: the waiting time from one birth to the next.[4] Average waiting times can be estimated from the population registers, but to do so we must draw upon other methods, in particular the life table.

Figure 2.3 helps us see the problem with averaging observed ages at marriage. One of the two types of data provided by the population register is handled incorrectly. The population register provides very good information about time (person-years) spent in each marital status. Age at marriage is equivalent to time spent unmarried. When we use only the observed marriages, we systematically exclude the experience of the "late"-marriage subpopulation. The time that the "late"-marriage group spent unmarried is excluded from the calculation, because it cannot be associated with an observed marriage. An unbiased estimator of age at marriage will have to include data from women in the sample without respect to the eventual age at marriage.

One type of measure that is not subject to bias from censoring is the age-specific rate described above. The marriage rate at ages 20–24 for the data in Figure 2.3 is the number of observed marriages divided by the number of observed person-years in which women were unmarried at ages 20–24. Each member of the "early"-marriage subpopulation contributes one marriage to the numerator of this rate and two person-years of exposure to the denominator. The "late"-marriage half of the population is not observed marrying, and they each contribute five person-years to the denominator of the marriage rate. The age-specific marriage rate for 20–24 is 0.14 $[= 1/7 = .5(1)/.5(2+5)]$. All of the available data are used in the calculation of this marriage rate. A decrease in the age at marriage would increase the marriage rate at ages 20–24 in this example. We can assume a lower age at marriage by increasing the proportion of the population following the "early"-marriage pattern. An increase in the number of "early" marriages increases the numerator of the marriage rate and decreases the number of unmarried person-years in the denominator.

---

4. Life table methods applied to birth interval data are used not only to estimate the average birth interval but to estimate proportions closing the interval at each parity, a measure similar to a parity progression ratio. See Trussell, 1984, and Alter, 1984b.

Although the age-specific marriage rates are directly related to the average age at marriage, the relationship is not obvious and can vary from age to age. Demographers use the life table to estimate an expected (or average) age at marriage from this kind of data. The first step in construction of a life table involves converting the age-specific rates to probabilities of transition between specific ages. These age-specific rates are called central rates and are analogous to the rates that are computed by dividing the number of events in a year by the midyear population. The central marriage rate for ages 20–24 can be converted to the probability that someone who is unmarried at age 20 will marry before reaching age 25. In our example this probability is .5, that is, one-half of the persons unmarried at age 20 marry before reaching age 25.[5] The relationship between this probability and the construction of the hypothetical population is apparent. Only the half of the population with the "early" age at marriage marries between ages 20 and 25. Since half of the population is still unmarried at age 25, the average age at marriage could not possibly be 22.

In practice the computation of an expected age at marriage will differ from the illustration presented in Figure 2.3 in two ways. First, we will have estimates of marriage rates for all relevant age groups. There is no way to derive an expected age at marriage from the data given in our example, because there is no information on marriages after age 26. The samples drawn from the population registers of Verviers cover a wide enough range of ages (15–55) to provide data on all of the relevant age groups. Second, in a real population some women never marry. The expected age at marriage refers to the part of the population that does marry, and it is necessary to convert the observed probabilities of marriage to probabilities that apply to the "ever marrying" population. This can be accomplished by assuming that no marriages will take place after age 50.

The life table is an analytical device for presenting the steps involved in calculating an average waiting time in a life history. The life table presents the experience of a hypothetical cohort of people subject to a set of probabilities of transitions between different statuses. Mortality tables, the most familiar life tables, display two statuses, alive and dead, and show the age-

---

5. The population registers provide the information needed for an exact conversion from central rates ($_nm_x$) to the conditional probabilities of the life table ($_nq_x$). The conversion formula requires the average age at transition within the interval, which is denoted by $_na_x$ in life table notation. The conversion formula is

$$q_x = \frac{n_n m_x}{[1 + (n - {}_na_x)_n m_x]},$$

in which n is the length of the interval.

Table 2.2. Life Table Estimates of the Proportion Married, by Age, and Expected Age at Marriage, Linked Random Sample, 1849–80

| | Observed | | | Life Table Estimates | | |
| | | | | | Number Unmarried: | |
Age	Person-Years	Marriages	Marriage Rate	Probability of Marriage (q_x)	of all Women (l_x)	of Ever Married (l_x)
15–19	615.46	8	0.0129	.0640	100,000	100,000
20–24	1,235.08	91	0.0736	.3078	93,600	90,902
25–29	947.44	72	0.0759	.3149	64,789	49,950
30–34	542.05	32	0.0590	.2521	44,387	20,949
35–39	343.15	3	0.0087	.0425	33,197	5,043
40–44	286.91	2	0.0069	.0342	31,786	3,037
45–49	142.18	1	0.0070	.0342	30,699	1,492
50–54	29.85	0	0.0000	.0000	29,649	0
55–59					29,649	0

Expected age at marriage: 26.06

specific probabilities of transitions for one type of transition, from alive to dead. More elaborate "increment-decrement" life tables can be constructed for processes involving more than two statuses. A marital status life table can be constructed with four statuses (unmarried, married, widowed, and dead) and six types of transitions (single to married, married to widowed, widowed to married, single to dead, married to dead, widowed to dead). Readers may consult one of the standard demographic references for a complete explanation of the mathematics of life tables. My purpose here is to point out the general usefulness of life tables for analyzing population registers.

Table 2.2 presents a life table analysis of marriage in one of the Verviers samples.[6] The second and third columns of the table show the number of person-years of unmarried women and the number of marriages observed in the sample during each age group shown in the first column. The fourth column presents marriage rates calculated from this information. The last three columns of the table present life table parameters. The "q_x" column of the life table is the probability of marriage in the next five years for women at a given age x.[7] Thus, .064 is the estimated probability that a

6. Examples of life table analyses of population register data can be found in Watkins and McCarthy, 1980, for marriage and Kertzer and Hogan, 1985, for migration.

7. The probabilities presented in Table 2.1 are probabilities of marriage without regard to mortality. If we assume the independence of the probabilities of marriage and death, the table can be interpreted as the experience of survivors to each age.

15-year-old woman will marry before reaching age 20. These probabilities are calculated from the observed marriage rates, as discussed above.

The sixth column shows the experience of a hypothetical cohort of 100,000 women from age 15 to age 50, subject to the probabilities of marriage in the preceding column. This column indicates that the number remaining unmarried would decrease from 93,600 at age 20 to 29,649 at age 55. The last column of the table shows a hypothetical cohort of women, all of whom eventually marry at the observed rate. This column is obtained from the previous column by subtracting the women who never marry (29,649) from those remaining unmarried at each age and rescaling the numbers to obtain 100,000 at age 15. For age 20 this computation is

$$l_{20} = \frac{100,000\,(120 - 155)}{(100,000 - l_{55})} = \frac{100,000\,(93,600 - 29,649)}{(100,000 - 29,649)} = 90,902.$$

The expected age at marriage calculated from this table is 26.06 years.

We can describe any kind of event or "pseudo-event" recorded in the population registers as a life table process. The important first step is to express the event as a transition between two statuses. Marriage is the event marking the transition between the statuses of single and married. In the analysis of birth intervals the "motherhood" pseudo-event marks the transition between the statuses of "x children ever born" and "$x + 1$ children ever born." The birth interval analysis can be conducted for all married women regardless of the value of x or separately by number of children ever born. In addition to the expected age of transition, the life table shows the proportion of the population in each status by age.

HAZARD ANALYSIS

The life table model offers considerable advantages for analyzing the life histories in population registers, but it is severely limited as a tool for examining the determinants and covariates of life course transitions. The only way to analyze the effects of variables other than age on transition rates in life tables is to divide the population into groups and compute separate life tables for each group. For example, if we would like to know whether working women married earlier or later than nonworking women, we need to produce separate marriage life tables for each subgroup. This procedure is possible for a simple dichotomous variable like working/nonworking, but it becomes unwieldy when the number of subgroups grows large. Multivariate models with several explanatory variables are almost impossible to handle with the life table method. If we are

41

interested in separating the effects of occupation and household size upon the timing of marriage, we must produce life tables for each combination of categories of these two variables. Even with two categories of occupations and five categories of household size, this requires the calculation of 10 life tables. The resulting tables would be too voluminous to summarize easily, and few data sets are so large that we would have reliable results for so many small subpopulations.

Recent developments in applied statistics have made it possible to employ a multivariate technique referred to as hazard analysis, which can be considered an extension of the life table model. The hazard model describes life course transitions in terms of underlying "hazard rates," which are defined as instantaneous probabilities of the event in question. The hazard rate is closely related to the probabilities of transition (q_x) in the life table. The probabilities in the life table refer to intervals of time, such as the probability of marriage in the interval from age 20 to age 25. If we could shrink the length of the intervals in the life table, these probabilities would approach the hazard rates as the length of the intervals approaches zero. Mathematically, the hazard rate is the derivative with respect to time of the probability in the life table.

Explanatory variables are added to the hazard model by assuming a simple relationship between the hazard rate, h_t, and the independent variables $(x_1, x_2, x_3, \ldots, x_k)$. This relationship is given by these two equivalent formulae:

$$h_t = \exp(b_0 + b_1 x_1 + b_2 x_2 + b_3 x_3 + \cdots + b_k x_k) \qquad (1)$$
$$\ln(h_t) = b_0 + b_1 x_1 + b_2 x_2 + b_3 x_3 + \cdots + b_k x_k \qquad (2)$$

in which exp and ln refer to exponentiation and natural logarithms. Many readers will notice the similarity between Equation 2 and the more familiar multiple regression formula. As in multiple regression, a dependent variable, here the natural logarithm of the hazard rate, is expressed as a function of a constant (b_0) and the sum of a set of independent variables $(x_1, x_2, x_3, \ldots, x_k)$ multiplied by coefficients $(b_1, b_2, b_3, \ldots, b_k)$. The interpretation of coefficients estimated from observed data is also similar to regression coefficients. A positive coefficient implies that an increase in the corresponding independent variable is associated with an increase in the hazard rate.

The model in Equation 1 is often described as the proportional hazards model. The exponential form of Equation 1 implies that a change in one independent variable results in proportional changes in the hazard rates associated with the values of every other independent variable. This rela-

Table 2.3. Estimates of Two Hazard Models of Marriage,
Linked Random Sample, 1849–80

Variable	Estimated Coefficient	S.E.	t-Ratio
MODEL WITH AGE EFFECTS			
Constant	−4.3450	0.3374	−12.87
Age (15–19 omitted)			
20–24	1.7200	0.3536	4.86
25–29	1.7570	0.3576	4.91
30–34	1.5160	0.3809	3.98
35+	−0.3793	0.6586	−0.57
MODEL WITH AGE EFFECTS AND EFFECT OF TEXTILE EMPLOYMENT			
Constant	−4.4010	0.3390	−12.98
Age (15–19 omitted)			
20–24	1.6890	0.3541	4.76
25–29	1.7290	0.3581	4.82
30–34	1.5040	0.3810	3.94
35–39	−0.3777	0.6589	−0.57
Textile worker	0.2946	0.1525	1.93

tionship comes from the underlying multiplicative form of Equation 1. We can rewrite Equation 1 in the following way:

$$
\begin{aligned}
h_t &= \exp(b_0 + b_1 x_1 + b_2 x_2 + b_3 x_3 + \cdots + b_k x_k) \\
&= \exp(b_1 x_1) \exp(b_0 + b_2 x_2 + b_3 x_3 + \cdots + b_k x_k)
\end{aligned}
\tag{1a}
$$

Equation 1a shows that the estimated hazard rate can be viewed as the product of the effect of variable x_1 and the total effect of the other independent variables. For example, suppose that we estimate a model of the marriage rate including variables for age, household size, and occupation. The model implies that each occupation has the same proportional effect on the hazard rate for every combination of age and household size.

Tables 2.3 and 2.4 present examples of two simple hazard models of the type used here.[8] The first model includes only the effects of age mea-

8. A number of examples of hazard analysis have appeared recently. Hogan and Kertzer (1985a, b) use hazard models in the study of migration using Italian population registers from 1865–1921. Menken, Trussell, Stempel, and Babakol (1981) present hazard models of marriage dissolution. Pickens (1978), Rodriguez et al. (1984), and Trussell et al. (1985) apply hazard analysis to the study of fertility. A recent application to the study of household dynamics is found in Richards, White, and Tsui, 1985.

Table 2.4. Age-Specific Estimated Hazard Rates for
Marriage, Linked Random Sample,
1849–80

Age	All Women	Nontextile Worker	Textile Worker
15–19	0.0130	0.0123	0.0165
20–24	0.0724	0.0664	0.0892
25–29	0.0752	0.0691	0.0928
30–34	0.0591	0.0552	0.0741
35+	0.0089	0.0084	0.0113

sured in the same five-year age groups used in the life table. Age effects are introduced by constructing "dummy" variables, which are assigned a value of one when the woman in the sample was in the indicated age group and zero otherwise. As is done in multiple regression with dummy variables, one category is omitted. The estimated coefficients for the included dummy variables compare the effects of that category with the effects of the omitted category—in this case, ages 15–19. In the second model, an additional dummy variable is introduced to identify women within occupations in the textile industry. The estimation procedure does not restrict the model to dummy variables, and continuous variables will be used in some models.

The statistical procedure used to estimate the hazard model produces estimates of the constant (b_0) in Equation 1 and the coefficients (b_1, b_2, b_3, ..., b_k). It also yields standard errors for each coefficient, also shown in the Table 2.3. This information is used for tests of hypotheses involving individual variables. A test statistic following the chi-squared distribution can also be derived for hypothesis tests on all variables or groups of variables in the hazard model. The ratios of estimated coefficients and standard errors shown in Table 2.3 can be compared with the standard normal distribution to show that we can reject the null hypothesis that the true coefficients are equal to zero for all of the estimated coefficients, except for the coefficients for ages 35 and over, at conventional levels of statistical significance.

The interpretation of these models is straightforward. The estimated coefficients of the age effects implicitly compare the probabilities of marriage at ages 20–24, 25–29, 30–34, and 35 and over with the probability of marriage at ages 15–19. The estimates indicate that the probability of marriage was higher between ages 20 and 34 and lower after age 35 than at ages 15–19. The estimated hazard rates are fairly constant between 20 and 34, with the rate for ages 25–29 slightly higher than the preceding and following age groups.

The model with a variable identifying women working in the textile industry suggests that those women married earlier than other women. The positive coefficient for the textile-worker dummy variable has the effect of raising the estimated hazard rate for each age group. A higher hazard rate results in a lower average age at marriage and a higher proportion eventually marrying.

Table 2.4 shows the estimated hazard rates implied by the coefficients in Table 2.3. The estimates in Table 2.4 are reached by inserting the information in Table 2.3 into Equation 1 to solve for values of h_t. The second column, "All Women," shows the hazard rates derived from the first model in Table 2.3. The second model is converted into the two columns showing women without and with occupations in the textile industry. The hazard rates in Table 2.4 are close to the probabilities of marriage (q_x) in a life table estimated for single-year intervals of age.[9] It is possible to derive all of the features of a life table from a corresponding hazard model.

The columns for textile workers and other occupations in Table 2.4 show how independent variables have proportional effects on the estimated hazard rates. The ratio between the estimated rate for a textile worker and a woman with any other occupation is the same for every age group (1.34). This ratio is obtained by exponentiating the coefficient for the textile-worker variable (0.2946) in Table 2.3.

A number of more elaborate hazard models have been introduced recently.[10] At this early stage of research on the population registers, however, the practical advantages of the proportional hazards model were judged more important than the gains from a more sophisticated statistical procedure. The proportional hazards model is both easier to understand and easier to compute with readily available statistical software. Refinements, like coefficients dependent on duration measured in continuous

---

9. The hazard rates shown in Table 2.4 are not exactly comparable to the life table probabilities in Table 2.2, because they employ different assumptions about the occurrence of events over time. The hazard rate is an instantaneous probability, while the life table uses probabilities computed over intervals. This difference is analogous to the difference between using continuous and discrete compounding in calculations of present values for financial purposes. The hazard model used here can be converted to estimates of the $_nq_x$ values in a life table by the formula

$$_nq_x = 1 - e^{-nh_t},$$

in which h_t is the estimated hazard rate for ages x to $x + n$ (see Tuma, Hannan, and Groeneveld, 1979). The estimates in Table 2.4 for ages 15–19 and 20–24, 0.0130 and 0.0724, imply five-year probabilities of .0628 and .3039, respectively. The corresponding probabilities in Table 2.2 are .0640 and .3078.

10. Discussions of different models used in the analysis of event histories can be found in Allison, 1982, Arminger, 1984a, and Trussell, 1984.

time, are not likely to change any of the conclusions that can be drawn from simpler hazard models. Furthermore, some nonproportional effects can be approximated by the construction of additional independent variables. For example, interactions between age and other variables can be introduced to detect effects that vary by age.

There are some important differences between the hazard model and the multiple regression model. The hazard model lacks the "error term" included on the right side of the regression equation to introduce random effects. Instead, the hazard models used here assume that the events from which the hazard rate is estimated can be described by a Poisson process. This assumes that these events are distributed randomly over time with a low probability that two events will occur in any given small interval of time. Hazard models have also been shown to produce biased estimates of coefficients when certain characteristics of the underlying population are unobserved. This is a problem receiving a great deal of attention from statisticians, and it is too technical to be discussed here (see also Arminger, 1984b).

The Verviers Data Set

Four population registers were open in Verviers during the years 1846 through 1880 covering these periods: 1846–48, 1849–55, 1856–65, and 1866–80.[11] The Verviers data base consists of four separate samples. Three samples were drawn from women in the birth cohort 1826–35: (1) a random sample which is linked from 1849 to 1880, (2) an elite sample which is also linked from 1849 to 1880, and (3) an unlinked random sample from the 1866–80 register. The fourth sample is an unlinked random sample of an earlier cohort (1805–19) drawn from the 1849–55 register.

The cohort of women born between 1826 and 1835 was selected, because they were at the end of their childbearing years in the decade of the 1870s, when the city's birth rate began to fall. Other studies of fertility transitions have shown that couples tended to limit fertility by avoiding later births rather than by postponing earlier births. Most of the decline in fertility in Verviers during the 1870s must have been due to the behavior of the women in this target cohort. The sample from the 1805–19 cohort provides a comparison with a period before the fertility transition had begun. It shows the amount of change that took place in the first generation of the fertility decline, and it is helpful in evaluating methods of examining that change.

11. Descriptions of the origins and contents of Belgian population registers with consideration of their uses in historical demography can be found in van de Walle and Blanc, 1975, and Leboutte, 1984.

The elite sample provides a contrast of a different sort. Higher economic and social strata have lower fertility in most populations, and there are reasons to suspect that they limited their fertility earlier than other parts of the population. The elite sample was selected by identifying women who lived in the wealthiest households listed in an 1849 tax register. These households were assessed by the tax commission of that year for incomes of 2,000 francs or more. This group was less than 10 percent of the total population of Verviers, and they had to be sampled separately to achieve a sample large enough for comparison with other social strata.

The linked samples were constructed to give complete fertility histories. The samples were drawn from women in the target cohort found in the 1849–55 population register. These women were followed forward in time until they disappeared or until the end of the 1866–80 population register. Women who were reported as married in the 1849–55 register were also linked backward in time to the 1846–48 population register.

The unlinked samples were drawn from the population register of 1866–80 for the target cohort and from the 1849–55 register for the 1805–19 cohort. The 1866–80 sample includes only women from the birth cohort of 1826–35, but it also includes women who migrated into the city after 1856. The women in this sample were not linked, so they are under observation at most from 1866 to 1880.

CHARACTERISTICS OF THE SAMPLES

The linked and unlinked samples provide very different perspectives on the life course. Table 2.5 shows the amount of information in each sample, by age. In both types of sample, observation of a woman ended when she migrated out of Verviers, died, was widowed, or when the last register ended in 1880 (1855 for the 1805–19 cohort). The linked samples include some histories that span the entire 31 years from 1849 to 1880, but in fact most histories are censored by death or migration before 1880. Since women do not enter the linked samples after 1856, these samples have more observation of younger than older ages. The unlinked samples, on the other hand, were constructed to include information on older ages. A woman in the target cohort could enter the unlinked sample by migration at any time while the 1866–80 register was open.

LINKED RANDOM SAMPLE FROM 1849 TO 1880

The linked random sample follows 651 women selected from the 1849–55 register.[12] Each time a woman was written in a population register,

---

12. The linked random sample was collected in three waves. Each wave is a random sample of 1 in 10 women from the 1826–35 birth cohort in the 1849–55 population register.

Table 2.5. Percentage Distribution of Person-Years Observed in Sample, by Age

| | | Cohort of 1826–35 | | |
Age	Cohort of 1805–19	Linked Random	Unlinked Random	Elite
15–19	0.0	7.6	0.0	8.4
20–24	0.0	18.3	0.0	16.7
25–29	0.1	19.6	0.0	18.8
30–34	18.3	18.5	7.3	18.9
35–39	32.1	14.0	26.2	14.1
40–44	34.1	12.8	37.9	12.9
45–49	15.4	7.6	22.9	8.1
50–54	0.0	1.7	5.7	2.1
	100.0	100.0	100.0	100.0
Number of person-years	1,889	8,382	6,161	2,554

Note: In this and subsequent tables, some columns and rows may not add to the exact total of 100.0 because of rounding.

information on her household was collected. Women were rewritten at the beginning of each register, when they changed households after marriage, or when they returned to Verviers after living in some other commune. Women who moved among households are recorded more than once in the same population register. The data for a woman in the sample consist of all the information about her and the people in the households in which she lived from 1849 to 1880, and they are organized as a succession of households.

Table 2.6 shows the amount of information drawn from each of the four population registers used in the linked samples. The top panel of Table 2.6 shows the number of household entries taken from each register. The largest number of entries, 697, is from the 1849–55 register. A small number of women (29 households) were traced backward to the 1846–48 register, because they were married when located in the 1849–55 register. Migration and death reduce the number of household entries drawn from the 1866–80 register to 258. The bottom panel of Table 2.6 shows that the amount of information in the sample, measured in person-years, is

---

Since each wave sampled the entire register, some women were selected in the sample more than once. There is also some overlap between the elite sample and the random sample. This overlap does not affect the statistical characteristics of the sample. Each wave is a random sample, and each woman in the population register had an equal probability of being drawn once or more than once. The sample design and its implementation are described in a research note available from the author.

Table 2.6. Number of Households and Person-Years
Observed, by Register, Linked Random
and Elite Samples

	Linked Random		Elite	
	Number	Percent	Number	Percent
HOUSEHOLDS				
1846–48	29	1.9	14	3.3
1849–55	697	46.0	183	43.0
1856–65	531	35.0	145	34.0
1866–80	258	17.0	84	19.7
Total	1,515	100.0	426	100.0
PERSON-YEARS				
1846–48	48	0.6	23	0.9
1849–55	2,101	25.1	629	24.6
1856–65	3,323	39.6	1,015	39.7
1866–80	2,909	34.7	888	34.7
Total	8,381	100.0	2,555	100.0

not proportional to the number of household entries shown in the top half of the table. Although the number of households drawn from the 1849–55 register is large, the register was open for only six years. In contrast, the 1866–80 register covers 15 years, and a smaller number of household entries produces a larger number of person-years of observation. Table 2.7 shows the distribution of data in each five-year age group across the four registers. Since we are following a birth cohort over time, older ages are observed in later registers. Table 2.8 shows the number of person-years and women by year. The gaps in certain years, represented by zeroes in the table, reflect problems in transitions between registers, which are discussed below.

The purpose of this sample is to provide a set of complete fertility histories in which both duration of marriage and parity are known. Some sort of linkage among population registers covering different periods is necessary to construct these variables, and linkage forward in time is more desirable methodologically than backward linkage. Forward linkage assures that only women with complete fertility histories are in the sample at any point in time. Since records in the study are limited to the city of Verviers, migration and mortality effect changes in the membership of the sample. A backward linked sample would have included in-migrants for whom parity and age at marriage would not be ascertainable.

This sample also provides unbiased information about age at marriage and circumstances of first birth. Since Verviers had a high level of pre-

Table 2.7. Percentage of Person-Years, by Age, in Each Register, Linked Random
and Elite Samples

Age	1846–48	1849–55	1856–65	1866–80	Total	Number
Linked Random Sample						
15–19	2.5	96.8	0.7	0.0	100.0	638
20–24	2.1	73.1	24.8	0.0	100.0	1,530
25–29	0.0	22.1	77.4	0.5	100.0	1,645
30–34	0.0	0.0	82.6	17.4	100.0	1,547
35–39	0.0	0.0	31.8	68.2	100.0	1,174
40–44	0.0	0.0	1.4	98.6	100.0	1,071
45–49	0.0	0.0	0.1	99.9	100.0	636
50–54	0.0	0.0	0.0	100.0	100.0	141
Entire sample	0.6	25.1	39.6	34.7	100.0	8,382
Number	48	2,101	3,323	2,909	8,382	
Elite Sample						
15–19	6.5	93.0	0.5	0.0	100.0	214
20–24	2.0	77.1	20.9	0.0	100.0	427
25–29	0.0	20.1	79.5	0.5	100.0	481
30–34	0.0	0.7	87.0	12.3	100.0	482
35–39	0.0	0.1	34.2	65.7	100.0	361
40–44	0.0	0.0	0.2	99.8	100.0	329
45–49	0.0	0.0	0.0	100.0	100.0	208
50–54	0.0	0.0	0.0	100.0	100.0	53
Entire sample	0.9	24.6	39.7	34.7	100.0	2,555
Number	23	629	1,015	888	2,555	

nuptial conceptions and a moderate illegitimacy rate, the timing of the
first birth is an important issue. A backward linked sample would not
have provided equivalent information because of the unknown correla-
tions between mortality and migration, on one hand, and age at marriage
and circumstances of first birth, on the other.

The Verviers population registers provide a good environment for linkage, but complete linkage is difficult if not impossible to achieve. The
registers include cross-references and indices, which facilitated linkage
in a great majority of cases, but they do have limitations. The numerous
cross-references in the Verviers population registers are more likely to
refer to earlier than to later registers. Officials in Verviers were mostly
interested in completing the information found in the register currently in
use. This sometimes required information from earlier registers, but there
was less often a need to make additional notations in registers that had
been closed. Since the samples used here were linked forward in time,
the cross-references were often incomplete.

Similarly, the indices to the population registers are very helpful, but
not all that we would desire. These indices were only partly alphabetized.

Table 2.8. Number of Person-Years and Number of Cases,
by Year, Linked and Unlinked Samples

Year	Linked Sample		Unlinked Sample	
	Person-Years	Number of Cases	Person-Years	Number of Cases
1846	0.0	0		
1847	26.6	28		
1848	21.5	24		
1849	0.0	0		
1850	520.3	542		
1851	530.1	555		
1852	530.2	570		
1853	515.6	549		
1854	0.0	0		
1855	0.0	0		
1856	0.0	0		
1857	395.3	372		
1858	394.5	387		
1859	392.8	379		
1860	377.1	364		
1861	369.5	368		
1862	363.1	349		
1863	351.2	346		
1864	342.5	333		
1865	333.6	333		
1866	0.0	0	0.0	0
1867	255.0	254	486.3	507
1868	248.2	256	495.2	520
1869	241.6	245	499.6	518
1870	237.5	242	493.2	521
1871	231.2	233	489.9	510
1872	228.0	229	486.9	507
1873	223.3	226	473.0	492
1874	218.6	221	461.2	476
1875	210.9	215	456.7	474
1876	207.9	208	453.7	463
1877	204.9	206	452.4	464
1878	200.9	203	453.5	461
1879	197.5	200	451.4	460
1880	0.0	0	0.0	0

Note: Years of transition (1846, 1849, 1854–56, 1866, 1880) between population registers have been omitted to avoid poor recording while registers were being revised.

51

Names were arranged by first letter of the last name and then by location. The compilers apparently went through each volume of a register, copying names to the index by first letter of the last name as they went. Omissions are also common. These indices are very useful, but finding a particular individual is still a very labor-intensive process. Use of the indices is also limited by variations in the orthography of names, a common problem in historical populations with low levels of literacy.

The information provided by the population registers is so extensive that a highly varied and opportunistic linkage strategy was used. The search for successive occurrences of a woman in the sample began with the cross-references and then moved to indices. If these steps were unsuccessful, a variety of other types of information were exploited. Often, it was possible to locate a woman's father or husband more easily than the woman herself. The vital registers were also searched to locate unreported deaths and marriages. The 1849–55 and 1856–65 registers were found to have particularly incomplete information about new marriages, a problem discussed below. A number of links were made by searching the locations in these registers where new marriages were recorded.

The level of certainty that we can attach to any particular linkage is usually very high. Since the population registers provide several types of information about each individual, we can verify linkages by comparing dates of birth, places of birth, and often dates of in-migration and places of origin. Furthermore, we have similar information on every person in the household, and we can verify the linkage of the woman in the sample by examining her parents, siblings, spouse, or children. The linkage of women is also considerably improved by the official practice of continuing to record married women under their maiden names. Widows were listed with their maiden names and the names of their deceased husbands, for example, "Marie Lecomte veuve Rahier." This creates an unusual situation in which married women are easier to link than either men or unmarried women. A common problem hindering the study of the female life course is that married women are listed with their husband's names, making them difficult to follow in official records.

UNLINKED RANDOM SAMPLE FROM THE POPULATION REGISTER
OF 1866–1880

This sample consists of 709 women, a random sample of one in three women in the target cohort found in the 1866–80 population register. It supplements the forward-linked random sample in two ways. First, it increases the number of women observed at older ages, and second, it provides information on migrants to Verviers. Unfortunately, this sample does not cover the entire population of Verviers between 1866 and 1880. Only the first 30 of the 41 volumes of this register have been microfilmed, and it was not practical to sample the remaining volumes. The omitted volumes include two kinds of information. First, certain streets and parts of streets are in these volumes. Second, the later volumes of the register include more migrants who arrived in the 1870s and households that were rewritten, because all of the blank space in the original location had been exhausted. Nevertheless, it is reasonable to treat the first 30 volumes as a representative sample of the city's population. The areas enumerated in the omitted volumes are scattered around the city, and the sample does include some information from every part of the city. The omission of later migrants is unfortunate, but these migrants would have contributed relatively small periods of exposure before being censored by the close of the register.

Both random samples have their weaknesses, but their strengths tend to complement each other. While the linked sample becomes progressively less representative of the total female population over time, the unlinked sample provides a new representative sample for the 1866–80 period. In later chapters several differences between samples will be noted, especially the exclusion of most migrants from the linked sample. Nevertheless, when well-defined subpopulations are examined, the two samples give very similar results.

LINKED ELITE SAMPLE FROM THE "TAXE SUR LA FORTUNE PRÉSUMÉE"

In 1849 the city of Verviers imposed an unusual income tax on its citizens. The records of this tax provide unique estimates of the incomes of the wealthiest 40 percent of the population. While all persons in the random samples were linked to the tax register, a special sample has been drawn from households assessed for 2,000 or more francs of income in 1849. The sample consists of 175 women who are principally the daughters of the persons taxed. This oversampling of the economic elite is important because most research has found that family limitation began first among the highest socioeconomic strata. The random samples provide too few women from this level of society for most purposes.

RANDOM SAMPLE FROM THE 1849–1855 POPULATION REGISTER, FOR THE 1805–1819 COHORT

The sample of the 1805–19 cohort includes 549 women, selected as a random sample from the 1849–55 register. A 15-year birth cohort was used to increase the ages covered in the sample during the 6 years that the register was open.

QUALITY OF THE VERVIERS POPULATION REGISTER

Population registers require a high level of administrative skill, and in this respect Verviers appears to have had two advantages over other nineteenth-century Belgian communes.[13] First, the intermediate size of the city worked in its favor. Verviers was large enough to have permanent, full-time bureaucracies for both police and vital registration. The population registers in small communes were often the responsibility of a part-time official. The quality of these population registers has been found to vary, depending upon each individual's ability and diligence, and periods of poor recording often occurred when a new official took responsibility. On the other hand, Verviers was still small enough to be manageable. In larger cities, like Liège and Brussels, the size of the transient population put disproportionate demands on the surveillance capabilities of the police.

Second, when the national population registers were instituted in 1846, officials in Verviers already had 40 years of experience with a similar document. From 1806 to 1846 a nominative list of the population of Verviers was compiled every year. The first list was required by the Napoleonic regime, but the system persisted on local initiative. These lists, called *Relevés des habitants*, were indexed periodically and cross-referenced to preceding and following years. Notations in the *Relevés des habitants* show most of the same information found in the later population registers. Births, deaths, and marriages were recorded in the margins, and in-migrants were added at the end of each register.

Another factor favoring the population registers in all of Belgium is that officials were also compiling a number of other lists of the population. Annual tax registers for the *contribution personelle* covered every household in the city, and many households were also listed in the *Registres des patentables* as well. The recording of the poorest part of the population is almost certainly incomplete, because the very poor escaped taxes and tended to move frequently. But disreputable and criminal elements in the population may be recorded unusually well. For example, the records of brothels show that they were under constant surveillance. Indeed, the police chief of Verviers refers to this surveillance in his correspondence with the mayor. The police chief favored at least two applications for licenses to open *"maisons de débauches,"* because the applicants would be easier to watch if their activities were brought into the open.

All indications are that the population registers of Verviers are quite

13. Discussions of the quality of reporting in Belgian population registers can be found in Gutmann and van de Walle, 1978, Leboutte and Obotela, 1982, and Leboutte, 1984.

high in overall quality. This is particularly important to this project, because this research has relied more heavily on the population registers than similar research has. Van de Walle and his associates, who are studying the Belgian village of La Hulpe, linked the population registers to the vital registers of births, deaths, and marriages to compensate for periodically poor reporting in the population registers. Such linkage would be prohibitively expensive in Verviers, which was more than 10 times as large as La Hulpe.

A test of the quality of the Verviers registers was conducted for one of the most sensitive variables in the study, infant mortality.[14] If registration in the population register had been slow or faulty, infants who died in the first week of life were likely to be underrepresented in the population register. Gutmann and van de Walle (1978) conclude that delays in the transfer of information from the vital registers were the most common cause of inaccuracies in the population registers. We compared the population register with the death register by constructing the pattern of infant deaths, by age, as recorded in each. Since the death register is considered highly accurate, this is a good test of the completeness of the population register. We were pleased to find an almost exact correspondence between the two different patterns of infant deaths. Although this does not prove that all infants were recorded in the population register, it does show that births and deaths were recorded promptly. There was no reason to record in the population register an infant who had already died, so this test suggests that entries in the population register were made at the same time as those in the birth register. The population register does not include those infants recorded in the death register as *"enfants sans vie,"* who had died in the first day of life before their births were registered. We found, however, that these infants can be located quickly in the indices of the death register, and they have been added to the data from the population register.

The Belgian population registers were officially records of the *de jure* rather than the *de facto* population.[15] This has important consequences for the recording of short-term migration patterns. The population registers undercount people who came to Verviers for short periods to work as servants or in the textile factories. It is likely that many servants and workers never reported their movements to the authorities in either Verviers or their communes of origin.

On the other hand, there are many indications that city officials took

14. This test is reported in a research note available from the author.
15. See Leboutte, 1984, on the legislation defining *résidence habituelle* and *population de fait* as they affected recording in Belgian population registers.

a broad view of the usefulness of the population registers, and that the distinction between *de jure* and *de facto* residents was often blurred in practice. Migrants who spent less than one year in Verviers and Verviétois who spent less than one year outside of the city were often recorded, even though their movements were not necessarily changes of legal domicile. Short-term movements are undoubtedly underreported, but they were not completely unrecorded. The population registers were also used to record much extraneous information for administrative or legal reasons. We often find notations referring to dates of death or migration many years after the close of the register. One unusual marginal note records a man's sworn statement that he did not marry while he was abroad working in Pennsylvania. We can surmise that this statement was demanded by his future in-laws before his marriage.

Several features of recording practices in Verviers have emerged from experience in working with the registers. The most important of these concern the 1849–55 and 1856–65 registers. All Belgian communes were required to open registers based upon the census of 1846 and later the census of 1866. The two intermediate registers in Verviers seem to have been based on local considerations, although other communes probably started new registers after the 1856 census. An official explanation for the timing of these registers has not survived. The new registers were probably introduced because there was too little blank space for making additions to each household in the old registers.

The 1849–55 and 1856–65 population registers highlight a particular problem in dating the beginning and end of population registers. Examination of the 1856–65 register shows clearly that some records date from 1854. There appears to be a period of about two years when both registers were open simultaneously. During this time information from the old register was being gradually copied into the new register. Households that had not been recopied were updated in the earlier register, but newly formed households were usually added to the new register only. Although the bound volumes of the second register now have "1856" embossed on their spines, internal evidence clearly indicates that some were started almost two years earlier.

It is very likely that the 1849–55 and 1856–65 registers were not the only ones that overlapped. Starting a new register was a major undertaking that must have taken months. The 1849–55 register, which has the least blank space on each page, fills 11 volumes, and the 1866–80 register has more than 40 volumes, some of which were started after 1866. This suggests that there are periods of questionable reporting at the beginning and end of every register. For this reason a cautious approach to the beginning of each register has been taken. Periods of questionable reporting near the start and end of each register, like 1854–56, have been excluded. This reduces the amount of data taken from the registers but does not affect the analysis.

The most serious problem associated with the population registers concerns the recording of mobility, both migration between communes and movements between households within a commune (cf. Watkins and Gutmann, 1983). Although it had been hoped that the population registers would eliminate the need for censuses after 1846, it soon became clear that this was not the case. The most troublesome to my study is the undercounting of out-migrants. Migrants were expected to report their movements to officials in both the communes of origin and of destination, but they more often neglected to report departures than arrivals (cf. Leboutte, 1984).

Movements within the city were also likely to be underreported. When a household changed address, it was not always recopied to a different location in the population register. Instead, the new address was indicated in an appropriate location. In the registers of 1846–48, 1849–55, and 1856–65 changes of address were recorded in the indices. In 1866 a column showing changes of address was introduced in the register itself. At this time a full analysis of the information on changes in address has not been attempted. When the change-of-address information has raised a question whether a woman in the sample was present in a particular household, it has been treated as a censoring event which ends observation.[16]

These uncertainties regarding mobility bias the data in a definite direction. Persons with unreported exits are erroneously counted as having been under observation until the end of a register. This leads to downward biases in observed rates by increasing the denominators of those rates. Since the risk of an unreported exit is continuous, the bias is greater with increasing time from the opening of a register.

There are some tests we can do to check on the extent of bias due to undercounting of exits from households. Many of the rates calculated from the sample can be compared with standards from other sources or

---

16. A special problem regarding movement between households was detected in the 1856–65 register. We noticed that the register often did not record when a newly wed woman formed a new household with her husband. Since this register covers the prime marriage ages of the target cohort, this is a serious problem. We also discovered, however, that new households were being recorded in a specific location in the registers: they were written in the blank spaces at the bottoms of pages in certain volumes. The data set was corrected by collecting the names of all women in these new households. This list was sorted alphabetically and compared with the list of women in the sample. Entries located in this manner were added to the data set.

other evidence in the population registers themselves. For example, mortality rates can be compared with life tables based on vital registration and censuses. The marriage life table produces estimates of the proportion remaining unmarried at each age, which can be compared with the observed proportions in the censuses and population registers themselves. So far, none of these comparisons have indicated that the rates calculated from the population registers are seriously biased.

The questionable reporting of movement within the city also has important implications for the descriptive measures of household composition used here. Again, comparisons with reasonable standards support the value of the population registers. Two standards have been used. First, a sample of marriages linked to the *Relevés des habitants* is available for the years 1844 and 1845. Since this earlier form of population register was compiled annually, it should be much more sensitive to short-term mobility. Second, the population register data can be used to reconstruct the populations enumerated in the censuses of 1856 and 1866. Since the population registers were either based upon or checked against these censuses, these reconstructed enumerations should be very accurate. Both of these tests also confirm the accuracy of the population registers.

There is one important exception to the dynamic nature of data in the population registers. Occupations are reported only once in each register, at the time that a person was recorded. In general, the occupations listed in the register will be attributed to each individual for the duration of the register. This obviously misses a great deal of occupational mobility. The linked samples allow another kind of analysis of this variable, however. Since we observe the same individuals several times, we can produce social mobility tables by cross-tabulating successive observations.

OTHER SOURCES OF DATA

THE MARRIAGE REGISTER SAMPLE, 1844–1845

Marriage registers contain extremely useful information on occupations of parents, literacy, and exact dates of birth. In earlier research a data set containing all of the marriages in the years 1844 and 1845 was constructed (Alter, 1978). These years were selected for their proximity to the 1846 census, but 1846 was omitted to avoid the distorting influence of the potato famine in that year. The marriages in these years were linked to the birth registers to locate the first birth in each marriage. They were also linked to the *Relevés des habitants* to gather information about household composition before and after marriage.

LITERACY

A simple measure of literacy is available from the vital registers in Verviers. When an event was recorded, the persons concerned were required by law to sign the register. Marriage registers contain the signatures of bride, groom, attending parents on both sides, and four witnesses. Birth registers contain the signatures of the person reporting the birth, usually the father, and four witnesses. Although the ability to sign is a poor indicator of level of education, it is a very useful measure for the population under study here. At the start of the period of interest only about half of the adult male population could sign their names.

Information on literacy has been added to the population register samples in two ways. Most of the women in the linked samples have also been linked to marriages listed in the marriage registers. The information on signatures of the woman in the sample, her husband, surviving parents, and witnesses has been added to these data sets. For women in the unlinked samples and those whose marriages were not located, we have turned to the birth registers. The birth registers usually provide evidence of the signature literacy for the husband of the woman in the sample. With the use of these two sources, literacy has been added for most of the married women in the sample or for their husbands.

TAXE SUR LA FORTUNE PRÉSUMÉE

The Taxe sur la fortune présumée, an unusual income tax mentioned briefly above, allows us to classify individuals by their current incomes. It distinguishes between employers and employees, which is not always possible from occupation titles, and it gives an indication of the importance of income from secondary sources. As a direct measure of income it is an unusual and important source. We have used the registers of the tax from its first and last years, 1849 and 1855. The 1849 tax register has been linked to the 1849–55 population register; the latter also provided ages, which are lacking in the tax register. The 1849 and 1855 tax registers have also been linked to each other.

CONCLUSION

The methodology presented here has a number of important and even surprising implications for the design and implementation of future research on population registers and other event histories. Although life course analysis has often been advocated by historians of the family, few studies have actually had the data necessary to explore this approach. Most research relies upon census data, which can show the distribution of statuses by age but cannot show either sequences of events or the effects of different characteristics on the timing of transitions. The population registers are the only available data source that shows both household characteristics and demographic transitions.

The most important practical implication of the methods described here is that research questions requiring event-history data can be explored with incomplete life histories. The linkage of consecutive population registers to create complete life histories is usually unnecessary and results in unrepresentative samples. The idea of reconstructing complete life histories is so appealing that many people will find this conclusion surprising. This chapter has shown how transition rates, which are the empirical data needed to study the life course, can be derived from censored histories. These transition rates already reflect existing conditions and the sequence of previous events, and the study of transition rates at any age does not require information about later ages. Events at later ages were still in the future from the point of view of our subjects, and could not be known with certainty. Presumably, they tried to anticipate the future in each of their decisions, but the only guide to the future was their own experience of the past.

Similarly, complete retrospective histories are also usually unnecessary. Of course, people do know the past with certainty, but most of the demographically important aspects of their past are carried with them in the population registers. Age, marital status, and place of birth are all results of past events that accompany people in their official records. Many earlier events are not recorded, but substitutes are often available. For example, when we observe a woman living on her own, we do not know if has she left her parents or if her parents have died. In many cases, however, the difference between an orphan and a woman alone for other reasons is less important than the simple observation that she has no coresident parents. The linked samples were constructed primarily to have complete information on children ever born and on marital duration for fertility analysis. In the final analysis these variables do not appear to be necessary. Fertility analysis using surviving children and age, which can be applied to the unlinked samples, provides the same information and results as the analysis using children ever born.

Furthermore, samples of linked records end up referring to unrepresentative portions of the population. A linked sample is representative of the population only during the period from which it was drawn. Unless linkage is carried out on a regional basis, a large part of the population will be lost through migration. The linked random sample used here diverges from the population more and more after 1856, as it comes to consist of

60

only the less mobile part of the population. By 1866 there are clear differences from the later random sample of the same cohort, which includes large numbers of migrants who arrived after 1856.

There are some questions that will still require linkage, such as the study of occupational mobility. But linkage, even with population registers, is very expensive, and the advantages of a linked sample must justify the costs. The implication of the methodology developed here is that the range of research problems requiring linkage is much smaller than we may have expected.

The population registers also suggest a new way of looking at family and demographic dynamics, a view that is much more in keeping with a life course analysis. Many important questions concern not the overall length of a life history but the sequence of events that it describes. An individual's experience through time is sequential, and a decision made at a moment in time reflects the results of events experienced earlier. Individuals are constantly making new decisions in the face of the conditions prevailing at each point in time. Rather than viewing the life course in terms of an overall strategy that can be decided early in life, we see it as a sequence of age-specific, contingent decisions.

In marriage analysis, this is the difference between a model in which an individual decides upon an ideal age at marriage early in her life and an alternative model in which the choice between marrying and not marrying is repeated at every age until a marriage finally occurs. The marriage life table shows this as a series of probabilities for persons who are still unmarried at each age. Those who have already married are not under consideration. In viewing each age separately we do not ignore the past history of each individual, rather we consider the consequences of this history. A sequential approach to the life course reflects the inescapable fact that the past cannot be changed.

There is a way to see this problem in terms of the mathematics of probabilities. Most researchers are accustomed to thinking of problems in terms of probability distributions. For the study of age at marriage, the relevant probability distribution is the distribution of marriages by age, in other words, the distribution of waiting times from birth to marriage. However, there is an alternative framework for studying these processes which is implicit in both the life table and hazard model. We can also view marriage as a sequence of conditional probabilities of marriage for those who are unmarried at any age, for example, the conditional probability that a woman who is still unmarried at age 24 will marry before age 25. These are mathematically equivalent ways of viewing the problem, and the conditional probabilities can be derived from the probability distribution and vice versa.

61

There is an important practical difference between these two approaches, however, especially when we are interested in the effects of other events on the timing of a transition. Consider, for example, the effect on marriage of a parent's death. This effect is easy to describe in terms of conditional probabilities: a parent's death will affect all conditional probabilities for every age after the woman's age when her parent died. It is not so easy to describe this problem in terms of the probability distribution of ages at marriage. This framework is not well suited for describing the effects of events occurring between the starting time (birth) and the event of interest (marriage), but it can be done. We can compute the probability distribution of ages at marriage from the age-specific conditional probabilities. The result is a two-dimensional probability distribution in which there is a probability for each combination of age at marriage and age at parent's death. Thus, instead of a distribution with one probability for each age at marriage, for each age at marriage we get a set of probabilities associated with all of the ages at which a parent could have died before the woman married.

In applied research there is always a dialectic between the questions we ask and the tools at our disposal for finding answers. This monograph is an attempt to ask new questions about old problems in family and demographic history. The sequential and contingent nature of the data available in the population registers has been a stimulus to formulate new theories and models, as well as an opportunity for new kinds of empirical research.

3

Marriage, Migration, and Household Composition

An important characteristic of family life in northwestern Europe in comparison with other societies has been the relatively late age at marriage. Hajnal (1965) has identified this as the "European marriage pattern" of late age at marriage and a high proportion never marrying. An important implication of this pattern for household composition is the existence of a large number of unmarried adults, both adults awaiting marriage and those who will never marry. Hajnal (1983) has more recently emphasized the circulation of adolescents and young adults that seems to have been common in preindustrial western European societies. Young people often left home to work as servants, farm laborers, and apprentices between age 10 and marriage. This redistributed labor to households where it could be used more effectively. Thus, preindustrial households had large numbers of servants and nonfamily workers in them, and many individuals spent time outside of their families of origin before they married.

The rise of industry and cities in the nineteenth century created a different set of opportunities for allocation of family labor. Many contemporary Malthusians expected and feared that the new proletariat would contract early and imprudent marriages.

> The ease that women have in earning their living in the cities is the determining factor in a crowd of marriages. . . . Each shuttle, each scissors, each wheel, each hammer constitutes a sort of small capital that is employed to feed a family. Any kind of instrument and a room is sufficient. Matters are different in the countryside. Capital is difficult to acquire there. It consists of a cottage surrounded by a certain amount of land. Everyone who wants it cannot obtain it. (Coomans, [1849])

These fears were usually misplaced. Age at marriage in urban areas was not consistently earlier than that of the surrounding rural areas, and even where the age at marriage did fall, it remained very late in comparison with other cultures.

Urban residence and industrial employment does appear to have changed life course patterns of household composition, however. The circulation of young adults described by Hajnal reflects the demand for labor in a society in which the household was still the unit of production. In the nineteenth century, however, work was no longer organized in the household. Although many observers feared that the factory would weaken the family, coresidence with parents may have actually increased in early industrial towns. The availability of wage labor in cities may even have facilitated the continued coresidence of unmarried adults with their families of origin. Michael Anderson (1971) has found a greater tendency for young people to have lived with parents in Preston, a textile center in Lancashire, than in the surrounding rural areas.

This chapter describes life course patterns of household composition for women in nineteenth-century Verviers. The employment opportunities in textile cities were particularly attractive to female migrants, and such cities characteristically had a large excess of women over men. Contemporaries were interested, as subsequent historians have been, in the impact of female employment opportunities on family life. It was often assumed that the urban experience weakened the family, and it has been suggested that the availability of employment for women decreased parental authority and fostered feelings of independence and emancipation (Anderson, 1971; Shorter, 1973, 1977). Empirical studies of the family during nineteenth-century industrialization and urbanization, however, have tended to emphasize the continued importance of the family (Tilly, 1979).

This chapter will differ from previous work in this area in two major respects. First, the sources used here allow a more explicit consideration of the effects of migration on household composition than most previous research. The Belgian population registers allow us to reconstruct patterns of migration by age and to compare the households of migrants with those of natives. There were several different types of migrants in the nineteenth century. Some young women were labor migrants of the type described by Hajnal, while others arrived with their families and were very similar to natives.

Second, the perspective of this analysis will also differ from the discussions of household composition that have become common in family history since the publication *Household and Family in Past Time* (Laslett, 1972) called the attention of historians to the study of household structure. Most historical research on household composition has focused attention on the family, and the residential patterns of the unmarried population have not always been examined. Households are usually classified according to a typology developed by Peter Laslett, which emphasizes the difference between nuclear family households and those containing stem families. Unfortunately, these categories are not well suited to the problems of life course analysis raised here. Laslett's categories were designed to identify types of households, and they fail to make the distinctions among individuals within households that are important for life course analysis.[1]

The fundamental problem with existing household typologies for the question examined here is that they do not show roles within households. Each woman in the household must be assigned the same household type regardless of her position in the household. For the present purposes, however, it is more important to know her standing in the household than the overall composition of the household. For example, even within a nuclear-family household, we may want to distinguish between the roles of mother and daughter, and we would classify a domestic servant according to her occupation regardless of the type of family in the household. Furthermore, household typologies do a poor job of describing the experiences of those who do not marry. They are based on a model of the family life cycle that assumes eventual marriage, and the unmarried are considered only if they become heads of households.

In contrast, this chapter uses a life course approach that views the household from the perspective of an individual, and classifies the household according to the individual's role in it. This perspective makes it possible to capture relationships and life course stages that do not involve the head of the household. For example, a woman living with her widowed mother as a boarder can be distinguished from a boarder without any coresiding kin. The life course approach also avoids the problem of defining when households begin and end, which tends to frustrate dynamic analysis of the family life cycle. Each life course has a single beginning, birth, and a single end, death. Households, on the other hand, can merge and divide repeatedly within the lifetime of one individual.

OVERVIEW

The picture of household composition that emerges in this chapter will emphasize three important and interrelated transitions: marriage, migration, and movement away from the family of origin. These three are so closely intertwined that it is almost impossible to examine one without simultaneously discussing the other three. Furthermore, these variables highlight differences between the samples drawn from Verviers. Each sample refers to a different part of the city's population, and most dif-

1. The focus on households and household heads has characterized Laslett's critics, as well as his supporters. Lutz Berkner (1972), the most widely quoted critic, has introduced an analysis in which household composition is linked to the family life cycle. David Kertzer (1985) has recently pointed out that Berkner's alternative approach is as oriented to household-level phenomena as Laslett's. In recent years the continuing debate between Laslett and Berkner and their associates has failed to extend the range of the discussion, despite the increasingly imaginative and sophisticated methods that have been applied.

ferences between samples turn out to be differences in composition with respect to marital status and migration. Since the discussion below is sometimes very complicated and specific, this section offers an overview and perspective.

The first step in understanding patterns of household composition is to recognize that migration was constantly changing the female population of Verviers. It is helpful to think of this population as a combination of several streams of natives and migrants that converged and diverged at different ages. At each age we see a different combination of natives and migrants, and there were important differences within each group.

Within the native population the main division was between the unmarried and married. Unmarried women tended to stay with their families of origin as long as possible. Even at age 45 two out of three unmarried natives lived with either a parent or a sibling. Indeed, unmarried natives appear to have been an immobile group who remained in their families of origin, which gradually dissolved around them. As they grew older, parents died and siblings married and formed new households, while native spinsters tended to stay with the remnants of the nuclear family. There was little tendency, at least by age 55, to move into households headed by married siblings; rather, unmarried women tended to combine with other unmarried and widowed women.

Marriage in Verviers was the occasion for establishing a new household. Verviétois obeyed the Walloon saying: "Mariage demande ménage" ("Marriage requires a household") (Dejardin, 1891–92). There is some evidence of coresidence with parents immediately after marriage, but this was a short-run solution for a minority of couples. Fewer than 10 percent of married women lived with either a parent or sibling, and fewer than 25 percent lived with anyone besides their husbands and children.

The widowed tended to follow a path between the unmarried and married. Young widows sometimes returned to their families of origin, but most women with children became heads of their own households. Many widows, however, accepted kin or nonkin into their households, presumably as boarders and lodgers who increased the economic viability of the household.

Considering the common argument that employment loosened the bonds of family on unmarried women, it is perhaps surprising to note that unmarried women in Verviers were not very mobile. In fact, they were less likely to leave the city than their married sisters. In part this reflects the opportunities for employment in Verviers. The textile industry in Verviers was the largest employer of women in the region. There were other processes at work, however. The migrant population observed in Verviers shows that there were several kinds of female migrants.

Three major types of migrants can be associated with stages in the life course. First, there were unmarried women who had entered Verviers with their parents in a migration that involved the entire family of origin. Almost all women who arrived as children came with parents, but this type of migration continued at older ages as well. In most respects these family migrants are very similar to unmarried natives of the city.[2]

Second, there were unmarried women who entered the city as adults to find work. Migrants were not confined to any particular female occupations, but they were especially common in domestic service. In fact, almost all of the servants in the city were migrants. The outstanding characteristic of these women was their instability. Most of them remained in the city only one or two years before moving on, and this created a rapid turnover of women in their 20s and early 30s.

Although most women who arrived in Verviers as unmarried adults departed in a short time, some did become permanent residents of Verviers, and the tendency to remain increased with age. Even a small proportion of young adult migrants remaining in Verviers more than a few years gradually accumulated. At older ages a majority of unmarried migrants had been in the city more than five years. These older unmarried migrants appear to have been very different from their native counterparts. Since they had arrived without their families, they could not choose the residential pattern preferred by natives. It is likely that most of these women stayed in the city precisely because they had no families to return to.

Third, we see a number of women at older ages who had migrated into Verviers with their husbands and children. These women were noticeably more stable than unmarried migrants. At older ages, an increasing proportion of migrants were married, and overall, migrants were more likely to be married than natives.

AGE, MARITAL STATUS, AND HOUSEHOLD COMPOSITION

Household composition is examined here with a view to women's roles within households. The categories in Table 3.1 and subsequent tables have been designed to show movements away from the family of origin. Women were assigned to the first category, "parent present," if they lived in a household with at least one parent, whether the household included other types of persons or not. If the household included no parents but at least one sibling, they were assigned to the category "sibling present." Similarly, "other kin" means "other kin present and no parents or siblings" and "nonkin" means "nonkin present and no kin of any kind." Women

2. Moch and Tilly (1985) have also found that most migration in the three French cities that they studied occurred in family groups.

Table 3.1. Household Composition of Women in the Sample, by Marital Status and Age

	15–19	20–24	25–29	30–34	35–39	40–44	45–49	50–54
Unmarried, Linked 1849–80								
Parent present	83.1	79.2	72.0	67.5	58.8	50.4	36.4	25.1
Sibling present	11.8	9.0	12.8	15.0	27.4	29.4	33.7	18.0
Other kin	0.0	0.7	0.4	1.6	1.4	0.0	0.0	0.0
Nonkin	3.3	4.6	5.1	5.8	3.9	13.0	22.2	48.4
Solitary	0.4	3.0	3.4	3.3	1.6	0.4	0.0	0.0
Servant	1.3	3.4	5.9	4.8	3.8	3.3	2.5	0.0
Spouse/own child	0.0	0.2	0.4	2.0	3.1	3.5	5.3	8.4
	100.0	100.0	100.0	100.0	100.0	100.0	100.0	100.0
Married, Linked 1849–80								
Parent present	4.4	4.9	3.0	1.6	5.0	6.8	10.0	6.1
Sibling present	3.1	0.8	0.7	1.2	2.0	3.0	2.8	0.0
Other kin	0.0	2.0	2.9	3.2	3.6	1.2	6.5	6.8
Nonkin	8.8	6.4	4.9	4.3	8.6	13.4	11.3	15.6
Solitary	0.0	3.4	0.3	0.6	0.0	0.0	0.8	0.0
Servant	0.0	0.0	0.0	0.0	0.5	0.8	1.1	0.0
Spouse/own child	83.7	82.5	88.2	89.2	80.2	71.8	67.5	71.5
	100.0	100.0	100.0	100.0	100.0	100.0	100.0	100.0
Widowed, Linked 1849–80								
Parent present	0.0	68.6	38.6	13.8	19.1	11.7	6.2	0.0
Sibling present	0.0	0.0	16.5	17.8	22.5	11.7	11.1	6.7
Other kin	0.0	0.0	12.8	5.1	5.6	19.3	16.5	16.3
Nonkin	0.0	0.0	9.9	13.9	21.8	29.9	34.3	46.9
Solitary	0.0	20.9	10.5	7.9	3.7	1.7	4.0	13.4
Servant	0.0	0.0	0.0	0.0	0.0	0.0	0.0	0.0
Spouse/own child	0.0	10.5	11.7	41.5	27.2	25.7	27.9	16.7
	0.0[a]	100.0	100.0	100.0	100.0	100.0	100.0	100.0
Unmarried, Unlinked 1866–80								
Parent present				35.0	29.3	23.9	16.0	10.8
Sibling present				6.6	14.8	23.3	33.8	32.8
Other kin				2.3	2.1	1.1	1.5	0.8
Nonkin				22.0	20.4	23.0	24.0	37.0
Solitary				4.4	7.4	8.4	7.4	6.2
Servant				23.2	20.2	15.3	13.3	11.7
Spouse/own child				6.4	5.8	5.0	4.0	0.8
				100.0	100.0	100.0	100.0	100.0

Table 3.1. Household Composition of Women in the Sample, by Marital Status and Age
(*continued*)

	15–19	20–24	25–29	30–34	35–39	40–44	45–49	50–54
Married, Unlinked 1866–80								
Parent present					3.7	6.0	4.0	3.8	1.8
Sibling present					2.1	2.5	3.2	2.3	3.0
Other kin					7.0	3.7	3.8	5.7	6.3
Nonkin					15.5	11.8	11.7	12.3	10.9
Solitary					1.3	2.6	2.7	2.8	4.6
Servant					0.0	0.1	0.0	0.0	0.0
Spouse/own child					70.5	73.4	74.5	73.0	73.4
					100.0	100.0	100.0	100.0	100.0
Widowed, Unlinked 1866–80								
Parent present					46.0	10.6	8.6	5.4	6.2
Sibling present					0.0	5.0	6.5	9.3	13.9
Other kin					0.0	4.5	5.0	7.6	6.2
Nonkin					6.4	15.7	22.6	26.0	39.2
Solitary					5.0	7.4	8.6	8.8	11.7
Servant					0.0	6.9	5.2	5.3	2.3
Spouse/own child					42.6	49.9	43.6	37.6	20.5
					100.0	100.0	100.0	100.0	100.0

[a] No observations in this category.

who lived with parents are all assigned to the "parent present" category whether their households included others or not. Women in the "nonkin" category, however, had no other coresiding kin. "Solitary" women lived by themselves, and "servants" are identified by their roles in the household. Thus, the categories are hierarchical: when a woman coresided with more than one other type of individual, the classification is based upon the other person most closely related to the woman's family of origin.

Implicitly, these categories assume a life course pattern in which women begin their lives in the household of their parents and move away to live with either their families of procreation or more distant kin and nonkin. Thus, the categories can be divided into three subgroups: (1) women living with their families of origin (parents or siblings), (2) women living with more distant kin or in nonfamily situations (other kin, nonkin, solitary, servant), and (3) women living with their families of procreation only (spouse/own children). Figures 3.1, 3.2, and 3.3 show this simplified form of the household categories for women in the linked sample.

Unmarried women in Verviers showed a very strong tendency to remain with their families of origin even at older ages. This is most apparent in the first panel of Table 3.1, which examines women in the linked sample (see also Figure 3.1). The proportion living with either parents or siblings

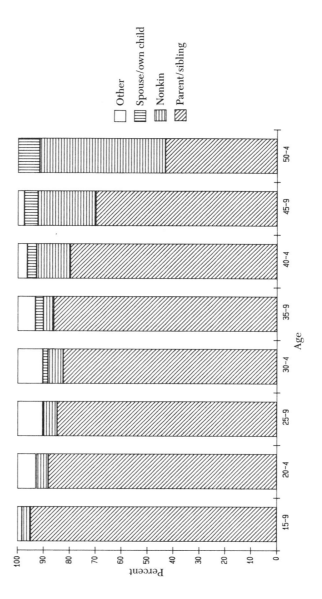

Figure 3.1. Household composition, by age, unmarried women, linked sample

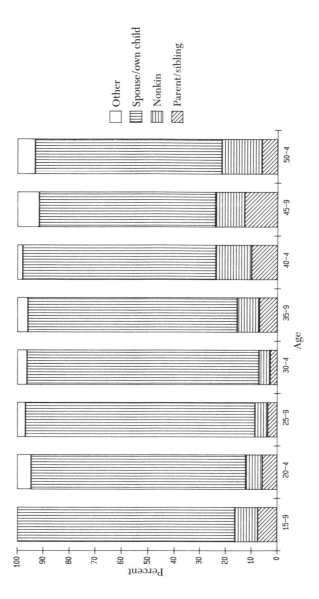

Figure 3.2. Household composition, by age, married women, linked sample

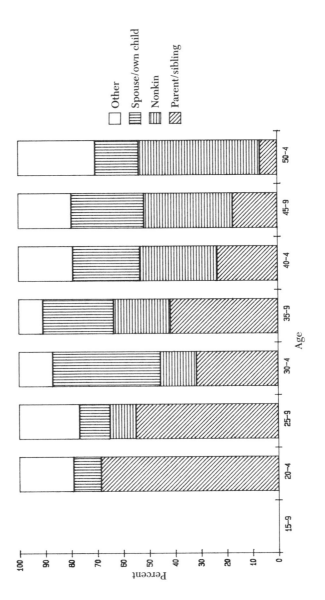

Figure 3.3. Household composition, by age, widowed women, linked sample

was about 95 percent at ages 15–19 and did not drop below 50 percent until after age 50. Mortality caused a gradual decline in the proportion of women living with parents, whereas an increase with age occurred in the category of living with other siblings.

Elite women, tabulations for which are not shown here, remained in their families of origin to an even greater degree. Even after age 40, two-thirds of unmarried women in the elite sample were living with parents, and nearly all of the remaining third were living with siblings. Since a very high proportion of elite women remained unmarried (nearly 40 percent of those in the sample), households consisting of two or more unmarried siblings were not uncommon.

The same pattern is present in the unlinked sample, but at a lower level. In that sample 40–45 percent of the women at all ages lived with representatives of their families of origin. The explanation of this difference is the much higher proportion of migrants in the unlinked sample. The unlinked sample captured many women who migrated in their 20s and early 30s to find work in the city. Often these women arrived in the city without their families and found work as domestic servants, an occupation that native women avoided.

When unmarried women were separated from their parents, they tended to remain with unmarried siblings but rarely joined the households of married siblings. Tabulations not presented here show that few women lived with sisters- or brothers-in-law. We also see in the second panel of Table 3.1 that fewer than 4 percent of married women had a sibling living with them.

While unmarried women maintained coresidence with their families of origin for a long time, marriage marked the transfer of obligations to a newly formed household. In the overwhelming majority of cases married women stopped living with their parents and siblings soon after marriage (see Table 3.1 and Figure 3.2). The proportion of married women living with a parent or sibling is below 15 percent at all ages. There is, however, a suggestion of a U-shaped pattern with age. The proportion of married women living with representatives of their families of origin was lowest at ages 30–34 and highest at younger and older ages. It is reasonable to suppose that young married couples were receiving assistance from their parents, while older married couples were giving assistance to elderly parents and unmarried siblings.

The widows examined in Table 3.1 and Figure 3.3 show a different pattern of household choices. The proportions of widows living with members of their families of origin were not as high as those of unmarried women, but they were much higher than those of married women. Like unmarried women, widows were less likely to live with parents and siblings as they

Table 3.2. Percentage Born in Verviers, by Age, in the Random Samples

	15–19	20–24	25–29	30–34	35–39	40–44	45–49	50–54
Linked	69.8	68.6	66.1	69.4	69.7	69.4	70.3	79.4
Unlinked				36.7	35.3	37.6	38.4	40.3

Table 3.3. Marital Status, by Age, for Natives in the Random Samples

	15–19	20–24	25–29	30–34	35–39	40–44	45–49	50–54
Linked 1849–80								
Unmarried	98.2	83.2	59.8	37.6	33.3	31.0	26.7	25.4
Married	1.8	16.0	38.2	56.5	60.3	58.7	55.0	47.8
Widowed	0.0	0.8	2.0	5.5	6.3	10.3	18.3	26.8
Divorced	0.0	0.0	0.0	0.3	0.1	0.0	0.0	0.0
	100.0	100.0	100.0	100.0	100.0	100.0	100.0	100.0
Unlinked 1866–80								
Unmarried				33.4	34.3	31.7	30.1	26.6
Married				63.0	58.2	55.7	52.4	48.7
Widowed				3.6	7.4	12.1	16.6	22.9
Divorced				0.0	0.1	0.6	0.9	1.8
				100.0	100.0	100.0	100.0	100.0

grew older. It seems that young widows often sought the assistance of parents and siblings. Older widows, however, were less likely to have surviving parents, and more likely to have children old enough to contribute to the family budget.

NATIVES

The sampling criteria for each sample resulted in different proportions of migrants and nonmigrants in each. Table 3.2 shows the proportion born in Verviers, by age.[3] At all ages, more than two-thirds of the linked sample was born in Verviers, but almost two-thirds of the unlinked sample was born elsewhere. Since the linked sample was selected from the 1849–55 register, it includes only women who were in the city by age 28. After 1855 the women selected were followed forward in time, but no new women

3. Age at migration is available in all samples, but it is not always reliable in the 1866–80 population register. Earlier registers give the date of entry into Verviers, even when it had occurred much earlier. The 1866–80 register, however, did not record dates of entry for persons who were long-term residents of the city.

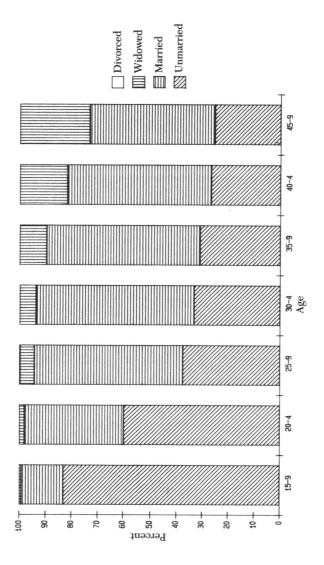

Figure 3.4. Marital status, by age, natives, linked sample

Table 3.4. Migration Rates, by Age, for Natives in the Random Samples (out-migrants per 1,000 person-years)

	15–19	20–24	25–29	30–34	35–39	40–44	44–49	50–54
Linked 1849–80								
Unmarried								
All	11.7	14.9	18.5	9.9	0.0	8.7	0.0	[a]
Without parents	0.0	13.8	12.3	4.9	0.0	4.3	0.0	[a]
Married	133.7	55.0	38.5	23.3	4.1	16.0	4.1	[a]
Widowed	0.0	0.0	0.0	0.0	0.0	13.1	0.0	[a]
Unlinked 1866–80								
Unmarried								
All				0.0	17.8	6.1	0.0	0.0
Without parents				0.0	17.8	6.1	0.0	0.0
Married				0.0	27.5	32.9	3.5	14.6
Widowed				0.0	0.0	9.4	0.0	31.0

Note: Migration at the time of marriage is not included here.

[a] Data have been omitted because the sample was too small to be meaningful.

were added to the sample. The unlinked sample, on the other hand, can include any woman present in the city after age 30. The difference between these two samples reflects changes in the nature of migration with age.

Table 3.3 and Figure 3.4 show the marital statuses by age for women born in Verviers in the two random samples. The striking aspects of the table are the high proportion of women who never married and the late age at marriage of those who did. The average age at marriage in this cohort was 26 years (see Table 2.1). Almost a third of each sample had not married by age 40, and at least one woman in four was still unmarried at age 50. High rates of permanent celibacy have been observed in European cities, but the proportions in Table 3.3 and Figure 3.4 are unusually high. Widowhood was also a common fate for women in nineteenth-century Verviers. By age 50 more than one woman in five had been widowed. Consequently, the proportion of married women never reached two-thirds of the native women at any age.

Both age and marital status were important in the decision of natives to migrate out of the city. Since the textile industry in Verviers itself was the most important source of employment for women, it is perhaps not surprising that unmarried and widowed women were not very likely to out-migrate. Migration often occurred at the time of marriage, but even when migration associated with marriage is excluded, unmarried natives migrated less than their married sisters. Widows were the least likely of all to migrate. Migration rates are shown in Table 3.4 for each age and marital

Table 3.5. Migration Life Table for Native Women in the Linked
Random Sample, Out-migration without Parents Only

	Observed		Migration Rate	Probability of Migration	Percent Remaining
Age	Person-Years	Exits	(m_x)	(q_x)	(l_x)
15	426.3	0	0.0000	.0000	100.0
20	870.9	12	0.0138	.0667	100.0
25	650.3	8	0.0123	.0590	93.3
30	404.4	2	0.0049	.0243	87.8
35	272.4	0	0.0000	.0000	85.7
40	230.0	1	0.0043	.0217	85.7
45	119.5	0	0.0000	.0000	83.8
50	28.0	1	0.0353	.1532	83.8
55					71.0

status (out-migrants per 1,000 person-years of observation). Migrations occurring simultaneously with marriage are excluded from Table 3.4.

The migration rates of unmarried women are shown in two ways in Table 3.4. The table presents rates in which all exits from Verviers are counted and also for exits without parents. The latter is intended to identify migration that involved an independent decision of the woman in the sample, as opposed to women who migrated with their families. This second migration rate is calculated by examining the event histories of parents living in the household of the woman in the sample. If the woman in the sample migrated out of Verviers on the same day as her parents, this exit is not counted in the numerator of the migration rate. This rate focuses attention on migration that involved a departure from the family of origin. The rates for migration without parents are necessarily the same or lower than the rates for all migration. This difference is most significant at ages 15–19. Although the migration rate for all unmarried women in this age group was 11.7 per 1,000, all of these moves occurred in the context of a move by the woman's family of origin. It is only after age 20 that unmarried women began to migrate away from their parents.

Table 3.5 provides another perspective on the migration patterns of unmarried women. In this table the migration rates for women in the linked sample moving without parents have been used to construct a life table showing the timing of migration from age 15 onward. The low rates of out-migration in the linked sample imply that fewer than 30 percent of unmarried women would leave Verviers before age 55. Even in the prime ages for migration, 20–35, less than 15 percent of women who remained unmarried would have set out on their own.

Table 3.6 shows the household patterns of unmarried natives, by age. When one looks at the first two categories, "parent present" and "sib-

Table 3.6. Household Composition of the Unmarried Natives, by Age

	15–19	20–24	25–29	30–34	35–39	40–44	45–49	50–54
Linked 1849–80								
Parent present	86.3	84.9	79.3	72.6	59.0	49.1	31.0	22.9
Sibling present	11.7	9.2	12.1	13.6	28.1	30.3	39.7	19.0
Other kin	0.0	1.0	0.6	2.1	1.7	0.0	0.0	0.0
Nonkin	1.9	3.2	5.0	5.5	2.0	11.7	20.1	49.2
Solitary	0.1	1.5	2.0	2.3	1.7	0.4	0.0	0.0
Servant	0.0	0.3	0.9	2.1	3.6	4.1	2.9	0.0
Spouse/own child	0.0	0.0	0.1	1.7	3.9	4.3	6.3	8.8
	100.0	100.0	100.0	100.0	100.0	100.0	100.0	100.0
Unlinked 1866–80								
Parent present				62.4	48.0	38.1	22.3	16.1
Sibling present				10.0	27.2	33.4	50.2	48.2
Other kin				6.4	5.1	2.5	3.1	1.3
Nonkin				7.0	10.5	20.8	23.7	34.4
Solitary				4.6	3.2	1.8	0.3	0.0
Servant				0.0	0.0	0.0	0.0	0.0
Spouse/own child				9.6	6.0	3.5	0.3	0.0
				100.0	100.0	100.0	100.0	100.0

ling present," it is difficult to avoid inferring that these women were strongly attached to their families of origin. Although the proportion living with parents declined steadily with age, most women continued to live with siblings. More than half of all unmarried women continued to live with part of their family of origin until at least age 50. In both samples fewer than 30 percent of the women aged 45–49 lived apart from parents or siblings.[4]

When native women lived apart from their families, most seem to have found places as boarders. Few women were living alone or in households with kin other than parents or siblings. These arrangements peaked at

4. We also see here a resolution of the apparent contradiction in Table 3.1 between the linked and unlinked samples. The differences in the households of unmarried women in the linked and unlinked samples are primarily due to the much higher proportion of migrants in the unlinked sample. Natives in the unlinked sample were very similar to natives in the linked sample. The linked sample still appears to overestimate the proportion of women who remained in their families of origin. A comparison of the two samples suggests that this overestimate is at most about 10 percent. This appears to be a maximum, because some migrant women in the unlinked sample are erroneously reported as having been born in Verviers. Research assistants linking women across registers sometimes noted that migrants were incorrectly recorded in later registers. This kind of mistake is common in censuses, where information is often given by one person for an entire household.

Table 3.7. Percentage of Unmarried Natives Living with Parents, by Age

	15–19	20–24	25–29	30–34	35–39	40–44	45–49	50–54
Linked 1849–80								
No parents	13.7	15.1	20.7	27.4	41.0	50.9	69.0	77.1
Mother only	26.7	27.4	26.1	33.7	29.9	24.2	17.3	17.6
Father only	7.3	9.5	15.6	14.8	17.6	19.7	10.8	5.3
Both parents	52.4	48.0	37.6	24.1	11.5	5.5	2.9	0.0
	100.0	100.0	100.0	100.0	100.0	100.0	100.0	100.0
Unlinked 1866–80								
No parents				37.6	52.0	61.9	77.7	83.9
Mother only				40.6	28.1	24.6	8.9	4.0
Father only				9.1	8.4	6.3	7.0	5.4
Both parents				12.8	11.5	7.2	6.4	6.7
				100.0	100.0	100.0	100.0	100.0

ages 30–34 with only 11 percent of the unlinked sample. Domestic service was even more unusual. None of the women in the unlinked sample were servants, and fewer than 5 percent of the linked sample were ever servants.

Table 3.7 examines the number of parents coresiding with unmarried natives. The effects of high mortality are very clear in this table. Even at ages 15–19 only about half of all women lived with both parents, and about a third lived with one parent. At younger ages there was a steady shift from living with both parents to living with only one parent. From age 20 onward fewer than half of all unmarried women lived in a household with both parents, but women living without parents were not in a majority until age 40. We will return to the question of the effects of mortality after the migrants have been examined.

MIGRANTS

Nineteenth-century cities often seem to have been magnets for unmarried women. Cities were the primary location for the most common of all female occupations, domestic service, which attracted many women from the countryside. Most cities had low ratios of males to females because of differences in migration patterns. Less is known about the details of this process of migration: the ages at which migration occurred, the marital statuses and occupations of migrants, and the process of remigration. Leslie Page Moch's (1983) work on the French city of Nîmes is one of

Table 3.8. Marital Status, by Age, for Migrants in the Random Samples

	15–19	20–24	25–29	30–34	35–39	40–44	45–49	50–54
Linked 1849–80								
Unmarried	98.1	74.4	52.7	29.0	18.5	16.6	12.0	5.2
Married	1.9	25.6	45.7	68.1	75.5	67.5	65.6	69.4
Widowed	0.0	0.3	1.6	2.9	6.1	15.9	22.5	25.4
Divorced	0.0	0.0	0.0	0.0	0.0	0.0	0.0	0.0
Separated	0.0	0.0	0.0	0.0	0.0	0.0	0.0	0.0
	100.0	100.0	100.0	100.0	100.0	100.0	100.0	100.0
Unlinked 1866–80								
Unmarried				34.2	26.1	22.2	18.6	10.9
Married				61.2	63.6	65.1	63.4	71.7
Widowed				2.9	9.7	12.6	17.3	15.6
Divorced				0.0	0.0	0.0	0.0	0.0
Separated				1.6	0.5	0.0	0.6	1.8
				100.0	100.0	100.0	100.0	100.0

the few historical studies that addresses these issues, and the results for Verviers are very similar to her findings.

Table 3.8 and Figure 3.5 show the marital status distribution by age of women born outside of Verviers. The surprising aspect of this table is that migrants were more likely to be married than natives (see Table 3.3).[5] While more than 25 percent of the natives were unmarried at ages 50–54, only 5 and 11 percent of the migrants in the two random samples were unmarried at these ages. Furthermore, the proportion of married among the migrants was 10–20 percent higher at the older ages. This pattern was due to the ebb and flow of married and unmarried migrants, which are examined more closely in Tables 3.9 and 3.10.

Table 3.9 shows out-migration rates for migrants, as compared with those for natives in Table 3.4. It is not surprising to find that migrants were more likely than natives to leave Verviers. These women had family and social networks in their places of origin to which they often returned. We see here that there was actually a constant circulation within the migrant population in which new arrivals replaced those who departed.

Simple migration rates, such as those in Table 3.9, do not show this circulation of migrants. Many accounts suggest that the young women who came to cities like Verviers were often short-term labor migrants. Women in domestic service, for example, were often saving money toward a dowry and not planning to remain servants. Table 3.10 shows that this

5. Moch (1983) found a similar pattern in the French city of Nîmes.

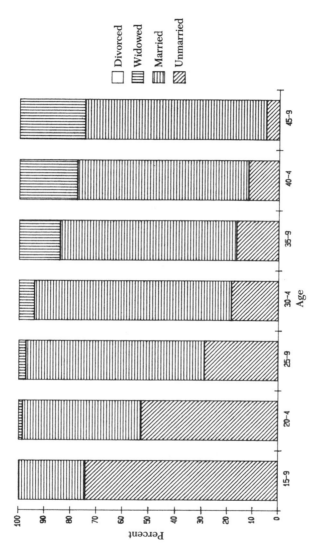

Figure 3.5. Marital status, by age, migrants, linked sample

81

Table 3.9. Migration Rates, by Age, for Migrants in the Random Samples (out-migrants per 1,000 person-years)

	15–19	20–24	25–29	30–34	35–39	40–44	45–49	50–54
Linked 1849–80								
Unmarried								
All	31.7	61.4	54.4	43.6	28.2	17.6	0.0	[a]
Without parents	5.3	58.6	40.8	29.0	28.2	0.0	0.0	[a]
Married	0.0	74.2	20.1	18.7	15.2	27.4	16.1	[a]
Widowed	0.0	0.0	0.0	0.0	0.0	0.0	0.0	[a]
Unlinked 1866–80								
Unmarried								
All				19.9	32.4	36.5	18.5	0.0
Without parents				19.9	32.4	36.5	18.5	0.0
Married				58.6	54.2	38.5	38.1	20.1
Widowed				242.0	74.9	43.5	33.2	0.0

Note: Migration at the time of marriage is not included here.

[a] Data have been omitted because the sample was too small to be meaningful.

Table 3.10. Remigration of Unmarried Women, by Years since Entry, in the Linked Random Sample

Number of Years	Observed		Migration Rate (m_x)	Probability of Migration (n_x)	Percent Remaining (l_x)
	Person-Years	Exits			
0	24.4	14	0.5728	0.4242	100.0
1	13.3	9	0.6773	0.4736	57.6
2	9.1	3	0.3282	0.2999	30.3
3					21.2

kind of migration was very common in Verviers. This table is based upon unmarried women in the linked sample who arrived while the 1849–55 population register was open. Table 3.10 uses the life table approach to follow such women in the first three years after their arrival, and it shows that most of them did indeed return home shortly. More than 40 percent of these in-migrants left in less than one year, and almost 70 percent left in less than two years. Only 21 percent of the migrants remained in Verviers longer than three years.

When migrants did leave Verviers, they were not necessarily returning to the place from which they had come. There are 283 cases of women who entered and departed in the same population register. Only 77 reported a destination matching their last residence before in-migrating to Verviers or their place of birth. Return migration was more common among women who stayed for shorter times. Exactly one-third of the migrants who left Verviers in less than three years returned to their previous residence or birthplace (20 out of 60). Although these figures probably underestimate the number of women who eventually returned to their origins after one or more intermediate moves, they do suggest that attachments to places of origin were weak. Many women had been orphaned before they moved, and there was a general redistribution of population from the countryside to the cities and towns. The movement into Verviers was only part of a larger circulation of labor in the region.

Tables 3.8 and 3.9, taken together, emphasize the heterogeneity of the migrant population. There was clearly a stream of labor migrants, reflected in Table 3.10, that was highly mobile and unstable. But these women were only one kind of migrant. Their rapid turnover always kept them a small proportion of the population of migrants at any given time. There is every reason to believe that women who stayed longer than three years became less and less mobile. In examining the next set of tables we can consider several different types of migrants.

Despite the rapid remigration of young women who came to Verviers, the proportion of migrants in the population rose with age, as the unlinked sample shows (see Table 3.2). The lack of a random sample from the 1856–65 population register leaves a gap in this data set, but two mechanisms appear likely. First, even though most migrants stayed only a short time, some did become permanent residents. As the flow of migrants in and out of Verviers continued each year, the number of permanent-resident migrants accumulated.

Second, the character of the unmarried migrants who entered the city appears to have changed. It is likely that older migrants were less able to return home. As their parents died and their siblings married, older migrants were less likely to have a family elsewhere to which they could return. For many of these women migration was part of a career choice. They had decided not to marry, and Verviers offered more employment than rural areas. Older domestic servants, in particular, appear to have been relatively stable.

In Table 3.11 we examine the household patterns of unmarried migrants. This table suggests that the migrants included in the two samples were not really the same kinds of women. The migrants in the linked sample were very likely to have lived with parents, while the migrants in the unlinked sample were very unlikely to have done so. This is due to the timing of different types of migration described above. The linked sample captured young migrants who either came with parents or returned home in a few years. The unlinked sample, on the other hand, captured older

Table 3.11. Household Composition for Migrants, by Marital Status

	Unmarried	Married	Widowed
Linked 1849–80			
Parent present	62.2	4.6	17.0
Sibling present	13.5	3.8	0.0
Other kin	0.0	5.4	42.7
Nonkin	8.1	10.4	8.8
Solitary	4.8	0.6	3.2
Servant	10.6	0.0	0.0
Spouse/own child	0.8	75.2	28.3
	100.0	100.0	100.0
Unlinked 1866–80			
Parent present	13.2	4.4	3.8
Sibling present	11.1	2.3	5.3
Other kin	0.0	4.7	9.1
Nonkin	26.6	10.5	27.5
Solitary	12.0	3.1	10.0
Servant	31.0	0.0	5.5
Spouse/own child	6.0	74.9	38.9
	100.0	100.0	100.0

migrants who came without parents and probably had no families to return to.[6] This difference is examined more closely in the next section, using the information on age at migration in the linked sample.

It is also very interesting to note the proportion of servants among the unmarried migrants, shown in Table 3.12. We saw earlier that very few natives ever lived as domestic servants in an employer's household. However, this pattern was common among migrants, especially among the older migrants in the unlinked sample. Once again the two samples appear to have captured different migration streams. In the linked sample domestic service was most common at ages 25–29, but it disappeared at older ages. The migrants in this sample either married, changed occupations, or left the city. Domestic service was more common at younger ages in the unlinked sample also, but a higher proportion of those women remained in service. These older servants were probably women who had chosen domestic service as a career, while younger women often viewed it as a temporary expedient.

6. Moch (1983) found that migrants who married in Nîmes were much less likely to have had living parents than women born in the city.

Table 3.12. Household Composition of the Unmarried Migrants, by Age

	15–19	20–24	25–29	30–34	35–39	40–44	45–49	50–54
Linked 1849–80								
Parent present	75.8	65.3	56.0	52.5	57.8	56.0	64.7	66.7
Sibling present	12.1	8.4	14.4	18.8	24.3	25.7	2.2	0.0
Other kin	0.0	0.0	0.0	0.0	0.0	0.0	0.0	0.0
Nonkin	6.6	8.0	5.1	6.9	11.5	18.3	33.1	33.3
Solitary	1.2	6.7	6.4	6.1	1.5	0.0	0.0	0.0
Servant	4.4	11.0	17.0	12.9	4.8	0.0	0.0	0.0
Spouse/own child	0.0	0.6	1.1	2.9	0.0	0.0	0.0	0.0
	100.0	100.0	100.0	100.0	100.0	100.0	100.0	100.0
Unlinked 1866–80								
Parent present				19.4	15.8	11.7	9.6	2.1
Sibling present				4.7	5.9	14.6	17.3	7.3
Other kin				0.0	0.0	0.0	0.0	0.0
Nonkin				30.5	27.5	24.8	24.3	41.3
Solitary				4.3	10.3	14.1	14.5	16.3
Servant				36.4	34.7	28.5	26.6	30.8
Spouse/own child				4.6	5.7	6.2	7.7	2.2
				100.0	100.0	100.0	100.0	100.0

AGE AT MIGRATION AND FAMILY OF ORIGIN

In Tables 3.8 through 3.12, migrants are identified as those who were born outside of Verviers. However, the population registers also report the timing of in-migration, which allows us to describe two different streams of migrants. In the linked random sample there are many women who migrated to Verviers before the age of 15.[7] Table 3.13 shows that these women had the same strong attachment to their families of origin as women who had been born in the city.

Table 3.13 compares nonmigrants with those who migrated to the city as children (under age 15) and as adults (age 15 or older).[8] The household patterns of unmarried nonmigrants were even more family oriented than those shown in previous tables, especially at younger ages. Almost 90

7. The 1849–55 population register reported the date of entry into Verviers for all persons born outside the city. The 1866–80 register, from which the unlinked sample was drawn, did not always report the date of entry for persons who had arrived before the register began.

8. A small number of native Verviétoises who had migrated out of the city and then returned are treated as migrants in Table 3.13. These women constitute less than 10 percent of the migrant category.

Table 3.13. Household Composition, by Age and Migrant Status, for Unmarried Women, Linked Random Sample, 1849–80

Age	Parent Present	Sibling Present	Other	Total	Number
		NONMIGRANT			
15–19	85.4	12.2	2.4	100.0	458
20–24	84.6	9.3	6.1	100.0	838
25–29	81.3	11.4	7.3	100.0	589
30–34	75.7	12.9	11.4	100.0	350
35–39	61.0	28.0	11.0	100.0	241
40–44	49.6	31.3	19.1	100.0	217
45–49	34.8	41.8	23.4	100.0	114
50–54	27.6	21.2	51.2	100.0	25
		CHILD MIGRANT			
15–19	79.0	11.9	9.1	100.0	117
20–24	79.4	12.3	8.3	100.0	194
25–29	73.8	18.2	8.0	100.0	179
30–34	50.8	27.2	22.0	100.0	105
35–39	34.3	33.1	32.6	100.0	50
40–44	32.8	43.9	23.3	100.0	32
45–49	0.0	9.1	90.9	100.0	6
50–54	0.0	0.0	100.0	100.0	1
		ADULT MIGRANT			
15–19	70.2	7.7	22.1	100.0	44
20–24	56.8	4.2	39.0	100.0	203
25–29	39.8	11.9	48.3	100.0	180
30–34	52.3	4.9	42.8	100.0	88
35–39	65.9	13.2	20.9	100.0	53
40–44	66.7	4.0	29.3	100.0	38
45–49	52.5	0.0	47.5	100.0	23
50–54	12.5	0.0	87.5	100.0	4

percent of nonmigrant women under age 40 lived with members of their families of origin before marriage. In general, women who migrated as children were very similar to nonmigrants, although the proportion living apart from their families was somewhat higher between ages 30 and 39.

Adult migrants present a completely different picture. Adult migrants between ages 20 and 34 were actually less likely to live with their families than those between 35 and 44. The most likely explanation for this pattern is that the younger ages included more short-term migrants to the city who had been attracted to Verviers by the high demand for female labor in the textile industry and domestic service. These labor migrants were likely to continue their search for work elsewhere or return to their origins

Table 3.14. Proportion of Unmarried Women Residing with One or More Parents, by Migrant Status, Compared with Projected Proportion of Women with One or More Surviving Parents, Linked Random Sample, 1849–80

Age	Observed				Mortality Projection
	Entire Sample	Non-migrant	Child Migrant	Adult Migrant	
	PERCENTAGE OF WOMEN RESIDING WITH PARENTS				
15–19	83.10	85.40	79.00	70.20	97.66
20–24	79.20	84.60	79.40	56.80	95.51
25 29	72.00	81.30	73.80	39.80	91.97
30–34	67.10	75.70	50.80	52.30	86.33
35–39	57.90	61.00	34.30	65.90	77.96
40–44	50.00	49.60	32.80	66.70	66.64
45–49	36.40	34.80	a	52.50	51.44
50–54	25.10	27.60	a	a	33.23
	PROJECTED PERCENTAGE OF WOMEN WHO VOLUNTARILY LEFT PARENTS[b]				
15–19	14.56	12.26	18.66	27.46	
20–24	16.31	10.91	16.11	38.71	
25–29	19.97	10.67	18.17	52.17	
30–34	19.23	10.63	35.53	34.03	
35–39	20.06	16.96	43.66	12.06	
40–44	16.64	17.04	33.84	−0.05	
45–49	15.04	16.64	a	−1.05	
50–54	8.13	5.63	a	a	

Note: The mortality projection was constructed in the following way. First, age-specific mortality rates from the linked random sample were used to estimate the proportion of surviving parents for children who were born when their parents were 25, 30, 35, and 40 years old. It was assumed that mothers and fathers were the same ages, and the combined male and female mortality rates were used. This yielded four estimates of parents' survival for each age of child. These four estimates were combined by assuming that there were twice as many children born to parents who were 25, 30, and 35 than to parents 40 years old. This implies an average age at parenthood of 31.5 years, which is very close to the age difference between women in the sample and their surviving mothers. Finally, the series was converted from exact ages to intervals of age by a two-point moving average.

This projected series underestimates the mortality of parents for several reasons. First, mortality in the observed period, 1849–80, was lower than mortality before 1849. In particular, the high mortality associated with the potato famine in 1846 and the cholera epidemic in 1849 is not included. Second, the average ages of parents used in the projection are less skewed than the actual distribution, so there are fewer births at younger ages. Although the observed average age at parenthood was about 31.5, this average is actually upwardly biased. Mothers who gave birth at younger ages had more exposure to mortality before their daughters were enumerated in 1849.

[a] Data have been omitted because the sample was too small to be meaningful.

[b] Difference between mortality projection and observed.

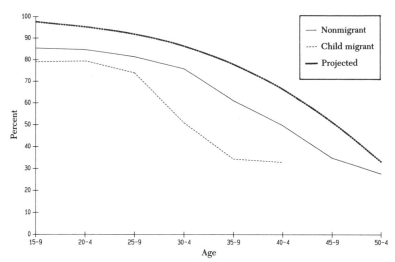

Figure 3.6. Percentage of women living with at least one parent, by age and migrant status, linked sample

to marry. This was the classic pattern of rural women who went to the city to earn money for their own dowries. Women who remained after age 35, however, were a different part of the migration stream. These older women were much more likely to have arrived with their parents and with the intention of settling permanently in the city. At older ages they were even more attached to parents than urban natives.

MORTALITY OF PARENTS AND HOUSEHOLD COMPOSITION

Table 3.14 and Figure 3.6 attempt to show how mortality affected the household patterns shown in previous tables. The last column of the table is a projection of the proportion of women at each age who would have had at least one surviving parent. This projection is based upon the mortality observed in the linked random sample and a distribution of parents' ages at the births of the observed women. The assumptions in this projection tended to overestimate by a small amount the proportion of surviving parents at each age. In the bottom panel of the table the proportions of women who were observed living with parents are subtracted from the proportions with surviving parents estimated by the mortality projection. This yields an estimate of the proportion of women who had voluntarily left the households of their parents. Figure 3.6 compares the projected percentage living with parents with the observed percentages for nonmigrants and child migrants in the linked random sample.

If all women are considered regardless of their migration histories, the bottom panel of Table 3.14 suggests that 15–20 percent of the women at each age were living apart from surviving parents. This proportion is greatest at ages 35–39, and it declines to 8 percent at ages 50–54. This decline was caused more by the rapidly increasing mortality of parents than by any tendency of daughters to return to the family.

As we see in Table 3.14, there are marked differences between migrants and nonmigrants at different ages. At younger ages nonmigrants were much less likely to have left their parents. Only 11–12 percent of nonmigrants under age 35 could have been living with parents but were not. At these ages 27–52 percent of the adult migrants had left their parents. The child migrants were more similar to nonmigrants than to women who migrated at older ages.

After age 35, however, the relative standing of the migration groups changes dramatically. The proportion of nonmigrants and child migrants living away from surviving parents increases by a small amount for the nonmigrants and by a large amount for the child migrants. Older adult migrants, on the other hand, were actually more likely to live with their parents. Between ages 40 and 49 the proportion of adult migrants living with parents is almost exactly equal to the proportion of surviving parents derived from the mortality projection. This underlines the compositional change in the adult-migrant group noted above. After age 35 temporary migrants tended to move on, and the remaining adult migrants were women whose migration to Verviers was a sign of their strong commitment to the parents with whom they had migrated.

CONCLUSION

The evidence presented in this chapter emphasizes the strength of the ties that bound an unmarried woman to her family of origin in the nineteenth century. Only a minority, fewer than one in five, of these women lived apart from their parents and unmarried siblings. There are no signs that these bonds weakened as women grew older; rather the mortality of parents and the marriages of siblings made coresidence with the family of origin demographically less and less possible.

The household patterns of married women show the preference for independent, neolocal residence, which Laslett has identified as a key element of the northwestern European family. Marriage was a distinct break with the family of origin, and married women rarely lived with either parents or unmarried siblings.

One of the consequences of urban employment opportunities appears to have been the elimination of a life course stage between the family of origin and marital household. This pattern is still evident among the young migrants who came to Verviers to work as servants for one or two years. But native women had no need to move away from their families of origin to find work.

This chapter has also tried to describe complexities in migration patterns that have been previously unexamined. In three French cities examined by Moch and Tilly (1985), women most often migrated in family groups. In the Verviers data we see a similar pattern. Women who came before the age of 15 almost always came with their parents. Many older women also arrived in a family group; these migrants were more often married women arriving with husbands and children. The family migrants also made the most important contribution to the city's population, because they were likelier to stay in the city than single women. Nevertheless, the rapid turnover of labor migrants, like that of domestic servants, meant that very large numbers of young women gained some experience in the city.

4

Female Work and Wages

PROBLEMS IN THE STUDY OF WOMEN'S OCCUPATIONS

Few areas show the underlying division between women and men in nineteenth-century society more clearly than the roles assigned to women in the economy. The segregation of occupations by sex was very close to complete, and women were restricted to a small number of occupations, most of which were associated with traditional domestic activities. The roots of this pattern are deep in European culture, and a recent ethnographic discussion of traditional European society reveals that the sexual division of labor was inherent in peasant life and culture (Segalen, 1980). The high female employment in nineteenth-century textile centers, like Verviers, was a cause of great contemporary concern, but sexual segregation was the rule even in textile factories. Certain operations were always identified as female specialties. Employers sometimes used the introduction of new machines to move women into other areas, but this was resisted by male workers and had little overall effect in the nineteenth century.

Although female occupations were few in number, it is possible to discern a social hierarchy among them. These differences appear most clearly in the intergenerational transmission of social status. Daughters from wealthy families usually avoided work entirely, and those who did report occupations tended to be respectable seamstresses. In other classes, we see a clear association between a father's income and his daughter's occupation. Young women from better-off families chose the needle trades in preference to the textile industry, and they preferred the latter in preference to casual day labor.

The responsibilities of marriage and motherhood took women out of the full-time labor force, but the domestic responsibilities of married women were often mixed with income-producing activities. An 1853 survey of workers' family budgets from all of Belgium found that almost all wives

91

contributed some income to the family economy (Alter, 1984a). Countless women took in laundry and sewing, washed floors, cooked for unmarried workers, and so on (Fohal, 1928, p. 34; Poetgens, 1895, p. 25; Lepas, 1844, p. 200; Belgium, Commission du travail, 1887, 1:1050). These makeshift types of work were common in nineteenth-century cities, which had a large informal sector of casual and part-time work. Retailing, in particular, was often a part-time family business (De Camps, 1890, p. 224; Rowntree, 1910, p. 413; Commission médicale, 1847, p. 86). Food was sold in open markets and small shops, and both seller and buyer were usually women. Married women could also find industrial out-work, which they could pursue at their own pace. Although Verviers was a world leader in the mechanization of woolen textile production in the nineteenth century, many manufacturers still used domestic out-workers for certain operations. Female tasks were particularly suitable for this type of organization, and many married women continued on a part-time basis the work they had done before marriage.

Unfortunately, the income-producing activities of married women are very difficult to document. Although a variety of sources suggest that these were important to many nineteenth-century families, official documents systematically underreported these areas of female activity. The woman who added a neighbor's laundry to her own told the census taker that she was a housewife not a laundress. When the wife of a factory foreman ran a shop or cabaret—a notorious abuse of a foreman's power over workers— her husband's name was recorded in the tax register, because a married woman could not make a contract in her own name. The tax registers of Verviers provide a better picture of the small-business activities of unmarried and widowed women, and contemporary observers commented that many of the businesses attributed to married men were run by their wives (Belgium, Commission du travail, 1887, 2:141; Conseil communal, 1836, AV).

The prevalence of female employment was in conflict with the strong emphasis on female domesticity in mid-nineteenth-century European society. Domesticity was the ideal not only of the bourgeoisie, it was also espoused by writers who were influential among workers, like Proudhon, and in the debates of the early socialist movement (Moses, 1984). In the mid-nineteenth century, however, women from working-class families rarely avoided employment of some kind. Whenever possible, daughters were trained as respectable seamstresses rather than engaging in the socially questionable activities in the textile factories or casual labor. After their marriages women continued to earn money in a variety of small ways made possible by the informal structure of much of the urban economy. These makeshifts were particularly important to widows, who often ran shops or cabarets. Near the end of the nineteenth century, rising incomes reduced the need for the earnings of wives, and economic development eliminated and formalized many of the activities that had been available to married women.

TYPES OF FEMALE EMPLOYMENT

Table 4.1 presents the women in the four population register samples distributed among five occupational categories and a sixth category for no occupation or ménagère. The categories are:

1. Proprietary and professional. This category is mostly composed of women who ran businesses or lived from property income. A number of women were listed as *négociantes* (merchants). In the elite sample the most common occupation was *rentière*. There were in fact few professional occupations with the exception of a handful of teachers.

2. Needle trades and skilled. This group is primarily composed of women in the needle trades (*couturières, modistes, lingères*). There were also a few women reported as sales clerks (*filles de boutique*) and occasionally occupations like *boulangère* (baker).

3. Textile industry. Within the textile industry there were some occupations that were exclusively female, such as *nopeuse* (women who cut the knots from woven cloth). Some women were also listed as spinners and some as weavers, but these were predominantly male occupations.

4. Day labor. This category is primarily *journalières* (day laborers), but it also includes a few other unskilled occupations and very low status work in the textile industry.

5. Servants. Most servants lived with their employers. There were also women living with parents reported as servants in the population register. It is not clear whether these women were working as servants during the day, or whether they were in fact living with employers and reported at their *de jure* residence with their parents.

6. No occupation and ménagère. The great majority of married women were listed as ménagère (housekeeper), but this was often used for unmarried women as well. In earlier registers clerks appear to have made a meaningful distinction between women reported as *sans profession* (no occupation) and ménagère. Daughters in elite households were much more likely to be reported as sans profession than other women. Since these women lived in households with servants, they almost certainly did little housework. Reporting practices were changed in the 1866 population register, and many more women were recorded as having no occupation.

93

Table 4.1. Occupational Distribution of Women in the Samples, by Marital Status

	Proprietary and Professional	Needle Trades	Textiles	Day Labor	Servant	None or Ménagère	Total	Number
	ALL WOMEN							
Linked Sample, 1849, 1856, 1866								
Unmarried	1.2	26.1	29.0	6.5	5.7	31.4	100.0	754
Married	3.0	9.3	14.5	3.4	0.6	69.2	100.0	504
Widowed	10.7	25.0	10.7	3.6	0.0	50.0	100.0	28
Entire sample	2.1	19.5	22.9	5.2	3.6	46.7	100.0	1,286
Unlinked Sample, 1866								
Unmarried	9.0	19.7	19.7	8.2	23.8	19.7	100.0	122
Married	2.5	6.9	4.7	2.8	0.0	83.2	100.0	321
Widowed	11.4	14.3	22.9	14.3	8.6	28.6	100.0	35
Entire sample	4.8	10.7	9.8	5.0	6.7	63.0	100.0	478
Elite Sample, 1849, 1856, 1866								
Unmarried	3.1	8.8	0.7	0.0	0.0	87.4	100.0	294
Married	0.9	0.9	0.0	0.0	0.0	98.1	100.0	108
Widowed	66.7	0.0	0.0	0.0	0.0	33.3	100.0	9
Entire sample	3.9	6.6	0.5	0.0	0.0	89.1	100.0	411
Older Women, 1849								
Unmarried	3.8	25.5	29.2	5.7	13.2	22.6	100.0	106
Married	0.6	5.3	14.1	3.1	0.3	76.5	100.0	319
Widowed	9.4	9.4	18.8	12.5	6.3	43.8	100.0	32
Entire sample	2.0	10.3	17.9	4.4	3.7	61.7	100.0	457
	ONLY WOMEN WITH OCCUPATIONS							
Linked Sample, 1849, 1856, 1866								
Unmarried	1.7	38.1	42.4	9.5	8.3		100.0	517
Married	9.7	30.3	47.1	11.0	1.9		100.0	155
Widowed	21.4	50.0	21.4	7.1	0.0		100.0	14
Entire sample	3.9	36.6	43.0	9.8	6.7		100.0	686
Unlinked Sample, 1866								
Unmarried	11.2	24.5	24.5	10.2	29.6		100.0	98
Married	14.8	40.7	27.8	16.7	0.0		100.0	54
Widowed	16.0	20.0	32.0	20.0	12.0		100.0	25
Entire sample	13.0	28.8	26.6	13.6	18.1		100.0	177
Elite Sample, 1849, 1856, 1866								
Unmarried	24.3	70.3	5.4	0.0	0.0		100.0	37
Married	50.0	50.0	0.0	0.0	0.0		100.0	2
Widowed	100.0	0.0	0.0	0.0	0.0		100.0	6
Entire sample	35.6	60.0	4.4	0.0	0.0		100.0	45
Older Women, 1849								
Unmarried	4.9	32.9	37.8	7.3	17.1		100.0	82
Married	2.7	22.7	60.0	13.3	1.3		100.0	75
Widowed	16.7	16.7	33.3	22.2	11.1		100.0	18
Entire sample	5.1	26.9	46.9	11.4	9.7		100.0	175

The samples differ along several different dimensions, and each type of difference affects the distribution of occupations. Table 4.1 shows clearly that the most important factor in female occupational patterns was marital status. Most unmarried women reported occupations, while most married women did not. Widows tended to move back into the labor force, and their occupational pattern fell between unmarried and married women. The proportion of unmarried women reported as housekeepers or without an occupation varied among the random samples from 20 percent to 31 percent. Married women had the opposite proportions in and out of the labor force: from 69 to 83 of the married women in the sample did not report occupations. The proportion of widows with occupations fell between patterns of the married and unmarried with from 28 to 50 percent reported without occupations.

The occupational patterns of women from elite households highlight the social significance of female employment in the nineteenth century. Fewer than 13 percent of the unmarried elite women were reported with occupations, and fewer than 2 percent had occupations after marriage. Widows in the elite were almost as likely to have an occupation as other widows, but the most common occupation among them was rentière. The aversion to work of women from the bourgeoisie is hardly surprising, and these women belonged to families who could afford to keep them idle.

There were three partial exceptions to the ban on female work in the bourgeoisie: teaching, commerce, and the needle trades. Teaching was still an uncommon career for women. The low school attendance in Belgium at this time and the important role of Church schools created few openings for female teachers. Some bourgeois women apparently did engage in commerce. Three unmarried women were recorded as merchants (négociantes). Tax records discussed below show more active participation of women in business. Undoubtedly, many women were actively involved in the enterprises of their fathers, brothers, and husbands, but only a few women ran businesses themselves. In a similar textile region in northern France, Bonnie Smith (1981, pp. 46–47) has noted an increasing exclusion of women from business in the early nineteenth century.

The patterns of elite women show that the needle trades occupied a special place among female occupations. Ten percent of these women were listed as modistes or couturières, the only occupations with a significant number of participants. There are at least three reasons why dressmaking would have been an acceptable profession for these women. First, sewing is a traditional domestic activity. Second, fashion in clothing was an important part of women's lives. Third, and perhaps most important, dressmakers served an exclusively female clientele, and, therefore, the continuation of dressmaking as a female craft preserved the separation of the sexes.

Another major difference among samples appears in the proportion of domestic servants. Among unmarried women only 5.7 percent of the linked sample were reported as servants, compared with 23.8 percent in the unlinked sample and 13.2 percent in the older women sample. This seems to be a consequence of differences in construction of the samples and perhaps also of changes in reporting practices in 1866 and an increase in the number of servants. The linked sample, which follows a sample of women from the 1849–55 register over time, suffers attrition because women continued to move out of Verviers, but migrants to the city were not added after 1856. In Chapter 3 we saw that in this sample a very high proportion of unmarried women lived with their parents. Since domestic servants were often in-migrants, they tend to be undercounted in the linked sample as compared with the unlinked random sample drawn from the 1866–80 register. As stated above, there may also have been a change in recording practices beginning in 1866. The population registers were meant to show the *de jure* population, and short-term residents, like domestic servants, need not have been recorded. It is possible, however, that the 1866–80 register came closer to a *de facto* standard than earlier registers. The comparison of the unlinked sample from 1866 to the older women sample from 1849 suggests that recording practices may have changed.

The bottom panel of Table 4.1 shows the distribution of women who reported occupations among the five occupational groups. An underlying similarity among unmarried, married, and widowed women is apparent in the random samples. One-half to three-quarters of the women with occupations in each of these samples were roughly evenly divided between the needle trades or the textile industry. Between 10 and 20 percent were found in day labor. The main difference was in domestic service, which was primarily an occupation of the unmarried. There was also a tendency for married women and widows to move into proprietary occupations. This is most marked in the linked sample, in which the percentage in the "Proprietary and Professional" category increased from 1.7 among unmarried women to 9.7 among married women and 21.4 among widows. The elite sample is again distinguished by the concentration of unmarried and married women in the needle trades and the high proportion of rentières among widows.

Table 4.2 shows the occupational distribution at different ages of the unmarried women in the random samples. The data are rather sparse after age 35, but the overall impression derived from these data is that there was little change in occupation with age. The unlinked sample has the clearest trends. Between ages 30–34 and 40–44 unmarried women in the unlinked sample moved out of domestic service and into proprietary occupations.

Table 4.2. Occupational Distribution of Unmarried Women in the Random Samples, by Age

	Proprietary and Professional	Needle Trades	Textiles	Day Labor	Servant	None or Ménagère	Total	Number
	ALL UNMARRIED WOMEN							
Linked Sample, 1849, 1856, 1866								
15–19	0.0	22.3	25.1	7.6	2.4	42.6	100.0	251
20–24	1.5	27.2	33.3	4.7	7.9	25.4	100.0	342
25–29	1.2	25.3	36.1	7.2	7.2	22.9	100.0	83
30–34	6.0	40.0	6.0	6.0	6.0	36.0	100.0	50
35–39	0.0	23.8	28.6	19.0	4.8	23.8	100.0	21
40–44	0.0	28.6	42.9	14.3	0.0	14.3	100.0	7
Entire sample	1.2	26.1	29.0	6.5	5.7	31.4	100.0	754
Unlinked Sample, 1866								
30–34	4.7	21.9	20.3	9.4	29.7	14.1	100.0	64
35–39	12.2	18.4	18.4	6.1	18.4	26.5	100.0	49
40–44	22.2	11.1	22.2	11.1	11.1	22.2	100.0	9
Entire sample	9.0	19.7	19.7	8.2	23.8	19.7	100.0	122
Older Women, 1849								
30–34	0.0	31.8	34.1	9.1	13.6	11.4	100.0	44
35–39	8.3	27.8	25.0	2.8	11.1	25.0	100.0	36
40–44	4.3	13.0	26.1	4.3	17.4	34.8	100.0	23
45–49	0.0	0.0	33.3	0.0	0.0	66.7	100.0	3
Entire sample	3.8	25.5	29.2	5.7	13.2	22.6	100.0	106
	ONLY UNMARRIED WOMEN WITH OCCUPATIONS							
Linked Sample, 1849, 1856, 1866								
15–19	0.0	38.9	43.8	13.2	4.2		100.0	144
20–24	2.0	36.5	44.7	6.3	10.6		100.0	255
25–29	1.6	32.8	46.9	9.4	9.4		100.0	64
30–34	9.4	62.5	9.4	9.4	9.4		100.0	32
35–39	0.0	31.3	37.5	25.0	6.3		100.0	16
40–44	0.0	33.3	50.0	16.7	0.0		100.0	6
Entire sample	1.7	38.1	42.4	9.5	8.3		100.0	517
Unlinked Sample, 1866								
30–34	5.5	25.5	23.6	10.9	34.5		100.0	55
35–39	16.7	25.0	25.0	8.3	25.0		100.0	36
40–44	28.6	14.3	28.6	14.3	14.3		100.0	7
Entire sample	11.2	24.5	24.5	10.2	29.6		100.0	98
Older Women, 1849								
30–34	0.0	35.9	38.5	10.3	15.4		100.0	39
35–39	11.1	37.0	33.3	3.7	14.8		100.0	27
40–44	6.7	20.0	40.0	6.7	26.7		100.0	15
45–49	0.0	0.0	100.0	0.0	0.0		100.0	1
Entire sample	4.9	32.9	37.8	7.3	17.1		100.0	82

Occupational Inheritance and Status

The strict definition of female roles was important not only in limiting the activities of women but also in differentiating among female occupations. In a recent analysis of working-class heroines in late nineteenth-century French novels, Marie-Hélène Zylberberg-Hocquard (1981, pp. 613–15) emphasizes the difference between seamstresses and factory workers. Seamstresses tended to be sympathetically treated, whereas factory workers were much more likely to be described in disparaging terms, and they usually suffered miserable fates. The occupational choices of women in Verviers show clearly that needle trades were more highly regarded than work in the textile industry.

Even within the textile industry, occupations tended to be segregated by sex. Women were concentrated in operations like *noppage* (cutting the knots from woven cloth), and relatively few women became spinners or weavers. Male workers resisted the entry of women into skilled occupations. The introduction of new shearing machines provoked machine breaking in 1830, and shearing remained a predominantly male occupation (Desama, 1985; Lejear, 1906). Despite their economic interest in lower-priced female workers, many factory owners shared their contemporaries' prejudice against female factory workers, and some tried to segregate male and female workers in separate rooms.

We get a clear picture of the social ranking of women's occupations by comparing the occupations of unmarried women living with their parents with the occupation of the head of the household. This is presented in Table 4.3 for unmarried women in the linked sample in 1849, 1856, and 1866. As we saw above, among the elite women the most desirable occupation was no occupation at all. In Table 4.3 no occupation or ménagère was reported for 59.7 percent of women from bourgeois households and for 50.9 percent from petty bourgeois households. This proportion drops quickly to 27.0 percent for daughters of skilled workers and 20.9 and 11.8 percent, respectively, for workers in the textile industry and day laborers. The high proportion without occupations in the petty bourgeoisie also reflects opportunities for work in family businesses like bakeries and butcher shops. Domesticity was an ideal that only the better-off could achieve.

It is also apparent that the other common women's occupations were ranked in order: needle trades, textile industry, and day labor. The higher social status of the needle trades emerges in the second panel of Table 4.3, which shows the distribution of occupations among those women who reported occupations. In bourgeois households 68.0 percent of the

Table 4.3. Occupational Distribution of Unmarried Women Living with Parents, by Occupation of Head of Household, Linked Sample, 1849, 1856, 1866

	Proprietary and Professional	Needle Trades	Textiles	Day Labor	Servant	None or Ménagère	Total	Number	Percent
ALL UNMARRIED WOMEN									
Bourgeois	6.5	27.4	6.5	0.0	0.0	59.7	100.0	62	11.6
Petty bourgeois	1.7	31.9	11.2	0.9	3.4	50.9	100.0	116	21.7
Skilled	0.0	27.0	37.0	5.0	4.0	27.0	100.0	100	18.7
Textiles	0.0	31.0	43.4	3.1	1.6	20.9	100.0	129	24.2
Day labor	0.0	11.8	50.0	23.5	2.9	11.8	100.0	34	6.4
None	0.0	19.2	46.2	7.7	0.0	26.9	100.0	26	4.9
Ménagère	3.0	26.9	34.3	11.9	0.0	23.9	100.0	67	12.5
Entire sample	1.5	27.7	30.3	5.2	2.1	33.1	100.0	534	100.0
ONLY UNMARRIED WOMEN WITH OCCUPATIONS									
Bourgeois	16.0	68.0	16.0	0.0	0.0		100.0	25	7.0
Petty bourgeois	3.5	64.9	22.8	1.8	7.0		100.0	57	16.0
Skilled	0.0	37.0	50.7	6.8	5.5		100.0	73	20.4
Textiles	0.0	39.2	54.9	3.9	2.0		100.0	102	28.6
Day labor	0.0	13.3	56.7	26.7	3.3		100.0	30	8.4
None	0.0	26.3	63.2	10.5	0.0		100.0	19	5.3
Ménagère	3.9	35.3	45.1	15.7	0.0		100.0	51	14.3
Entire sample	2.2	41.5	45.4	7.8	3.1		100.0	357	100.0

daughters with occupations were couturières or modistes, and 64.9 percent of the daughters of the petty bourgoisie were in this category. More than a third of the daughters of skilled men and of workers in the textile industry also went into the needle trades, but the most common occupations for these women were in the textile industry. Daughters of unskilled laborers tended to inherit their fathers' low status. In the households of day laborers fewer than 14 percent of daughters with occupations became seamstresses, and 26.7 percent of them became day laborers themselves, compared with only 7.8 percent of all women.

Occupational Mobility

The observations in successive population registers included in the linked sample create an opportunity to examine occupational mobility for these women. Table 4.4 compares the occupations reported in successive enu-

Table 4.4. Occupational Distribution in Successive Enumerations for All Women and for Selected Marital Status Combinations, Linked Random Sample

Occupation at First Enumeration	Occupation at Second Enumeration								
	Proprietary and Professional	Needle Trades	Other Skilled	Textiles	Day Labor	Servant	None or Ménagère	Total	Number
ALL WOMEN									
Proprietary and professional	20.0	0.0	0.0	0.0	0.0	0.0	80.0	100.0	5
Needle trades	0.8	35.7	8.5	3.9	1.6	0.8	48.9	100.0	129
Other skilled	0.0	9.4	21.9	6.3	12.5	0.0	50.0	100.0	32
Textiles	1.0	2.5	2.5	47.5	9.1	1.0	36.4	100.0	198
Day labor	0.0	5.7	8.6	17.1	5.7	2.9	59.8	100.0	35
Servant	0.0	7.4	0.0	3.7	11.1	44.4	33.3	100.0	27
None	8.0	13.8	5.8	11.6	1.4	3.6	55.8	100.0	138
Ménagère	5.6	7.3	1.7	7.3	0.0	0.6	77.4	100.0	177
Entire sample	3.4	12.1	5.0	18.5	4.2	3.0	53.9	100.0	741
Number	25	90	37	137	31	22	399	741	
UNMARRIED AT BOTH ENUMERATIONS									
Needle trades	1.6	53.1	10.9	6.3	3.1	1.6	23.4	100.0	64
Other skilled	0.0	12.5	0.0	12.5	37.5	0.0	37.5	100.0	8
Textiles	0.0	1.6	3.1	71.9	12.5	1.6	9.4	100.0	64
Day labor	0.0	18.2	27.3	27.3	18.2	9.1	0.0	100.0	11
Servant	0.0	13.3	0.0	0.0	6.7	80.0	0.0	100.0	15
None	8.6	17.3	6.2	14.8	2.5	3.7	46.9	100.0	81
Ménagère	0.0	25.9	3.7	3.7	0.0	3.7	62.9	100.0	27
Entire sample	3.0	22.6	6.7	24.8	6.7	7.0	29.3	100.0	270
Number	8	61	18	67	18	19	79	270	
UNMARRIED THEN MARRIED									
Proprietary and professional	0.0	0.0	0.0	0.0	0.0	0.0	100.0	100.0	2
Needle trades	0.0	17.4	6.5	2.2	0.0	0.0	73.9	100.0	46
Other skilled	0.0	14.3	21.4	7.1	7.1	0.0	50.0	100.0	14
Textiles	2.2	3.3	2.2	43.5	7.6	0.0	41.3	100.0	92
Day labor	0.0	0.0	0.0	14.3	0.0	0.0	85.7	100.0	14
Servant	0.0	0.0	0.0	8.3	16.7	0.0	75.0	100.0	12
None	5.3	13.2	2.6	10.5	0.0	0.0	68.4	100.0	38
Ménagère	6.7	26.7	0.0	0.0	0.0	0.0	66.6	100.0	15
Entire sample	2.1	9.4	3.9	21.0	4.3	0.0	59.2	100.0	233
Number	5	22	9	49	10	0	138	233	

Table 4.4. Occupational Distribution in Successive Enumerations for All Women and for Selected Marital Status Combinations, Linked Random Sample *(continued)*

Occupation at First Enumeration	Occupation at Second Enumeration								
	Proprietary and Professional	Needle Trades	Other Skilled	Textiles	Day Labor	Servant	None or Ménagère	Total	Number
MARRIED AT BOTH ENUMERATIONS									
Proprietary and professional	0.0	0.0	0.0	0.0	0.0	0.0	100.0	100.0	2
Needle trades	0.0	7.1	0.0	0.0	0.0	0.0	92.9	100.0	14
Other skilled	0.0	0.0	42.9	0.0	0.0	0.0	57.1	100.0	7
Textiles	0.0	2.5	0.0	20.0	5.0	2.5	70.0	100.0	40
Day labor	0.0	0.0	0.0	10.0	0.0	0.0	90.0	100.0	10
None	0.0	0.0	0.0	0.0	0.0	16.7	83.3	100.0	12
Ménagère	7.6	1.7	0.0	5.9	0.0	0.0	84.7	100.0	118
Entire sample	4.4	2.0	1.5	7.9	1.0	1.5	81.8	100.0	203
Number	9	4	3	16	2	3	166	203	

merations.[1] The rows indicate occupations at the first enumeration, and can be interpreted as the women's origins. The columns indicate occupations at the second enumeration, and can be intepreted as the women's destinations. Since marital status was an important part of occupational choice, Table 4.4 also presents selected combinations of marital statuses. Women who remained unmarried at both enumerations can be compared with unmarried women who married by the next enumeration and with women who were married at both enumerations. There were too few widows to draw conclusions about their occupational mobility, but widows are included in "All Women," the first panel of the table.

The panel showing all combinations is the result of several different trends. First, there was an overall movement toward being reported as ménagères. Much of this tendency was associated with marriage, when many women withdrew from the labor force. Second, the tendency to continue in the same occupation differed across occupations. Workers in the textile industry and domestic servants were the most likely to retain their occupations. However, day laborers (journalières) were unlikely to be reported the same way twice. This may reflect the ambiguity of the term as much as real mobility. Almost any woman could have called herself a journalière, meaning that she was paid by the day, even though she

1. Table 4.4 uses information reported at the enumerations in 1846, 1849, 1856, and 1866, and when new households were started after marriage. Women who migrated into the city between censuses are not included until they were present for a census.

had a specific occupation. This would have been most likely to occur in the textile industry, however, and it is reassuring that textile workers were not especially likely to be reported as day laborers in later censuses. The overall tendency, therefore, was for women to move from other occupations toward housekeeping, much of which was associated with marriage. However, certain occupations were more stable than others. Women in the textile industry were the most likely to report the same occupation at two successive censuses, and day laborers were the least likely to do so.

The second panel shows women who were unmarried at both observations. Women in the textile industry and domestic service were the most occupationally stable. More than 70 percent (71.9 and 80.0, respectively) reported the same occupation twice. Needle workers were the next most likely to retain their occupations (53.1 percent). Day laborers, however, often changed occupations. Among the 11 women reported as day laborers, only 2 (18.2 percent) were so reported the next time observed.

As we would expect, many women changed their occupation to ménagère when they married. The third panel of the table compares occupations of women who were unmarried in one register and married in the next. The proportion of women who were ménagères or who reported no occupation rose from 22.7 percent (38 and 15 of 233 women) in the first register to 59.2 percent after they were married. The only group that showed a strong tendency to retain their occupation was the textile workers. Only 41.3 percent of the textile workers gave up their occupations after marriage, and 43.5 percent remained textile workers.

The tendency to give up their occupations continued even after women married. Among women observed twice after marriage, the proportion of women who were ménagères or had no occupation rose from 64.0 percent (12 and 18 of 203 women) to 81.8 percent. Part of this difference may be due to young wives who continued to work until the birth of their first child. However, El Kefi-Clokers (1975–76) argues that women tended to continue working after their first or second child by placing their children in the care of a neighbor or relative. After the third child this was no longer feasible, and they withdrew from the labor force. Hareven (1982) and Tilly and Scott (1978) also note a tendency for some married women to have continued working or reentered the labor force in response to the family's need for cash.

WAGES IN INDUSTRY

Table 4.5 presents daily wages for major occupations in Verviers from 1836 to 1869 published by the city's Chambre de commerce. Most of

102

Table 4.5. Wages (in francs per day), by Occupation, 1836–69

	1836	1846	1856	1863	1869
MALE OCCUPATIONS					
Serruriers	1.73[a]	2.25[a]	2.50	3.00	3.87[a]
Charpentiers	1.90	2.25	2.65	2.87[a]	3.50[a]
Laveurs et ouvriers teinturiers	1.40	1.46	1.60	2.60	3.37[a]
Fileurs	1.80	1.90	2.90	3.12[a]	3.40
Nettoyeurs de card	1.47	1.75	2.30	3.25	3.30
Corroyeurs	1.83	2.00	2.25	3.00	3.25
Ourdisseurs	0.80	0.95	1.57	1.65	3.25
Tisserands à la main	1.97[a]	1.70	2.85	3.00	3.00
Menuisiers	1.98	2.00	2.25	2.75	3.00
Rameurs	—	1.25	1.40	2.34[a]	3.00
Presseurs	1.47	1.78	1.78	2.15	3.00
Decatisseurs	1.25	1.40	1.45	2.10	2.87[a]
Tisserands à la mécanique	—	—	—	—	2.75[a]
Briseurs	0.84	1.27	1.50	1.75	2.65
Foulons	1.40	1.50	1.75	2.30	2.67[a]
Manoeuvres	—	1.25	1.50[a]	1.87[a]	2.50[a]
Drousseurs	0.91[a]	0.93[a]	1.30	1.50	2.50
Laineurs	1.15	1.25	1.40	1.75	2.25
FEMALE OCCUPATIONS					
Rentrayeuses	0.73	0.80	1.10	1.40	2.25
Trieuses	0.98	1.08[a]	1.70	1.85	2.00
Brosseuses	0.75	0.80	0.80	1.25	2.00
Nopeuses	0.77[a]	1.00	1.20	1.70	1.80
Couturières	0.73	0.80	1.10	1.40	—
Eplucheuses	0.70	0.75	0.85	1.35	1.62[a]
CHILDREN'S OCCUPATIONS					
Rattacheurs		0.70	0.90	1.10[a]	1.60
AVERAGE WAGES					
All adults	1.26	1.36	1.69	2.12	2.72
Male	1.46	1.58	1.93	2.41	3.00
Female	0.77	0.87	1.12	1.49	1.93
Female as percent of male	53.2	55.1	58.0	61.8	64.3

Sources: Chambre de commerce de Verviers. *Rapport général sur la situation du commerce et de l'industrie en 1868.* Verviers: A. Remacle, 1869, p. 69. The rates for couturières, which were not listed in the 1869 report, are from Chambre de commerce de Verviers. *Rapport général sur la situation du commerce et de l'industrie en 1864.* Verviers: G. Nautet-Hans, 1865, p. 11.

[a] This figure is the midpoint of a range given in the source.

the occupations in the list are those of workers in the textile industry, and it is possible that the few exceptions (*serruriers, charpentiers, corroyeurs, menuisiers,* couturières) were also employed by textile factories. The reliability of these figures has been confirmed by examination of the wage books of two firms which are preserved in the Archives de l'etat à Liège.[2] In the wage books it is clear that there was a range of wage rates for each occupation. Individual wage rates reflected differences in experience, productivity, and responsibilities for supervising and training other workers. Furthermore, different occupations were subject to more or less unemployment, and women were particularly likely to work part-time. The figures in Table 4.5 are acceptable as modal wage rates, but small differences or changes in rank from year to year are not always reliable.

The first conclusion that emerges from Table 4.5 is that the wages of women were less than the wages of unskilled males. The most relevant male occupation is *manoeuvre,* which refers to an unskilled worker. Between 1846 and 1869 the daily wages of manoeuvres increased from 1.25 francs to 2.50 francs, while the average for the female occupations went from 0.87 francs to 1.93 francs. The wages of female occupations were occasionally more than those of the two least skilled male textile occupations, *drousseur* and *laineur,* and drousseur was one of the few occupations performed by both men and women.

It is also very interesting to note the small range of wages among female occupations. It is as if they were limited to the small space between children's wages and the lowest skilled males'. The range between the highest and lowest female wage rate is less than 45 centimes, except for the *éplucheuses* after 1846. The low wages of éplucheuses were due to technological changes in the industry, which mechanized this operation after 1850.

Perhaps the most surprising finding in Table 4.5 is that women's wages were actually rising relative to the wages of men during this period. The last line of the table compares female and male wages, and it shows that female wages were rising faster than male wages. Expressed as a percentage of male wages, the wages of women increased from 53 to 64 percent. The averages presented at the bottom of the table treat each occupation equally (i.e., they do not reflect the relative size of occupations), but it is unlikely that the pattern observed was offset by changes in the composition of the labor force (Alter, 1984a).

Surviving wage books also suggest that much of the work done by women in the textile industry was done on a putting-out basis. The records of the David firm show "éplucheuses externes" earning only one or two

2. Fonds David, 1842, 1844, AEL; and Fonds Flagontier et de Thier, 1861–62, 1864–65, AEL.

francs per week. The firm often employed éplucheuses, nopeuses, and *rentrayeuses* in groups of two to four women, who probably worked at home (Fonds David, No. 5144 [1844], AEL). El Kefi-Clokers (1975–76) finds similarly low wages reported by women to the Bureau de bienfaisance. Collier (1965, p. 16) has concluded from the wage books of pickers in the English cotton industry that they were working only to augment the earnings of others in their families, and the same pattern is evident in Verviers (Lepas, 1844; Fohal, 1928).

PETTY COMMERCE

One of the most difficult parts of the female occupational world to evaluate is commerce and retail trade. Selling vegetables and other small produce was usually a female task in preindustrial Europe, just as today markets are still run by women in many less-developed societies (Boserup, 1970). Shopkeeping was often a secondary occupation in the nineteenth century. It was a way of supplementing earnings, rather than being a full-time occupation. There are a variety of sources from nineteenth-century Verviers that give us glimpses of this world and a rough idea of its importance.

The best source for examining retailing and other small businesses in nineteenth-century Belgium are the records of the *patentes*, which were licenses for economic activity. All commercial activity was subject to a patente, and even peddlers and street vendors, *marchands ambulants indigènes*, were recorded. In the patentes we find large numbers of shopkeepers and *cabaretiers* who went unreported in the census. Table 4.6 shows the occupations of women identified in the patentes for 1871 ("Registre des patentables," 1871, AV).

In 1849 the patentes were the basis for a new tax, the Taxe sur la fortune présumée, which was needed to repay city debts incurred during the economic crisis following the potato famine in 1846. The Taxe sur la fortune présumée was a progressive income tax with adjustments for dependents and different tax rates for income from businesses, property, and government salaries. The tax was preceded by a survey in which potential taxpayers were required to declare their annual incomes. These declarations were reviewed by a tax commission which assessed each taxpayer (Alter, 1978). The tax was in force from 1849 to 1855, and the first annual register reports both the declarations and the assessment of the commission. An examination of the declaration forms returned in 1848 shows the part-time nature of many small businesses. There are a number of examples in which a manual occupation was reported, but the tax commission changed the occupation to *boutiquier* or cabaretier (Pièces diverses—fortune présumée," AV).

It is possible to identify four levels of commerce in mid-nineteenth-

Table 4.6. Women with Patentes in 1871, by Occupation and Marital Status

	Unmarried	Married	Widowed	Entire Sample
NUMBER DISTRIBUTION				
Boutiquière, etc.	77	12	92	181
Cabaretière	8	11	22	41
Miscellaneous commerce	8	3	17	28
Marchande ambulante	4	13	3	20
Couturière	10	6	2	18
Miscellaneous manufactures	3	0	6	9
Bouchère and boulangère	1	0	6	7
Institutrice	5	1	0	6
Cassière	1	1	0	2
Coiffeuse	1	0	2	3
"Bals à danse"	1	1	0	2
Blanchisseuse	2	0	0	2
Total	121	48	150	319
PERCENTAGE DISTRIBUTION				
Boutiquière, etc.	63.6	25.0	61.3	56.7
Cabaretière	6.6	22.9	14.7	12.9
Miscellaneous commerce	6.6	6.3	11.3	8.8
Marchande ambulante	3.3	27.2	2.0	6.3
Couturière	8.3	12.5	1.3	5.6
Miscellaneous manufactures	2.5	0.0	4.0	2.8
Bouchère and boulangère	0.8	0.0	4.0	2.2
Institutrice	4.1	2.1	0.0	1.9
Cassière	0.8	2.1	0.0	0.6
Coiffeuse	0.8	0.0	1.3	0.9
"Bals à danse"	0.8	2.1	0.0	0.6
Blanchisseuse	1.7	0.0	0.0	0.6
	100.0	100.0	100.0	100.0

Source: "Registre des patentables," 1871, AV.

century Verviers: wholesale merchants and full-time shops, artisans, part-time shops, and street vendors. In the first category are those reported as marchand or négociant for a wide range of products. It is likely that the relatively small number of men and an even smaller number of women who engaged in commerce full time combined both retail and wholesale functions. Only a few boutiques could have been classified as full-time operations: the 1846 census for Verviers lists only one boutiquier. The fact that this group was small is an indication of the lack of development of the consumer economy. Women who participated in moderate- to large-scale commerce usually did so as the partners of their husbands. Unmarried women were rarely listed in this group of occupations, and very few widows appear to have been successful in continuing their husbands' businesses.

Much of the retail trade in nineteenth-century Verviers was still conducted with artisans. The most common of these were bakers and butchers, but tailors and *fabricants de pains épices* (makers of spiced bread or pastries) were also common. These shopkeeping artisans were the last remnant of the craft organization of industry, and they had become the core of the petty bourgeoisie. We can see these shops today in any Belgian city, and it is clear that they are family enterprises. Wives and daughters typically serve customers at the counter while the husband and son do the baking or butchering. In 1871 there were four widows reported as bakers and two as butchers. While these numbers are small, they do suggest that women were sometimes successful in continuing the businesses of their late husbands.

The most numerous kinds of retailing in the tax records were the boutique and cabaret. Even though the 1846 census recorded only 1 boutiquier and 34 cabaretiers, there were hundreds of each in the 1849 Taxe sur la fortune présumée. The discrepancy between both the numbers reported in the tax register as compared with the census and the ways in which they were reported suggest that these were small-scale enterprises. In the records of the Taxe sur la fortune présumée there are a number of cases in which a man who declared a manual occupation was taxed as a boutiquier or cabaretier. Almost all of these enterprises were assessed at the minimum tax rate. It is also instructive to see how often these occupations were combined with others. In the 1871 patentes there are 94 women listed as boutiquières and an another 79 who were reported as boutiquières plus an additional occupation (Table 4.6; this category in the table also includes 3 *charcuteries* and 5 *fripières*). It was common to combine a boutique with a cabaret or charcuterie. This type of part-time retailing is especially interesting because it created opportunities for married women and widows to make significant contributions to the family economy without abandoning their domestic roles.

At the lowest level of commerce were the street vendors. The 1871 role of patentes ends with a list of marchands ambulants indigènes. In addition to wandering vendors there were also people who simply put a basket of goods on the street in front of their homes. In 1847 a survey was taken of *échoppes et mannes* not in the regular outdoor market ("Echoppes," 1847, AV). The survey counted 160 such vendors. This is certainly a minimum estimate, because the small scale of these operations suggests that many would not be operating every day. Also, the survey was conducted in December, and we may suspect that street life was more active in the summer months. It is clear that most of these vendors were selling a few

Table 4.7. Percentage Distribution of Assessments, by Size of Assessment, Sex, and Marital Status, Taxe sur la fortune présumée, 1849

	Size of Assessment (francs earned per year)					
	0–999	1,000	1,001–1,999	2,000	2,001 +	Total
Male						
Unmarried	0.9	36.8	19.9	13.9	28.6	100.0
Married	0.0	48.4	17.4	13.5	20.8	100.0
Widowed	0.0	39.0	17.1	13.8	30.1	100.0
Female						
Unmarried	12.2	52.0	7.1	16.3	12.2	100.0
Married	0.0	100.0	0.0	0.0	0.0	100.0
Widowed	0.0	52.1	14.6	17.2	16.1	100.0

Source: "Livre aux déclarations sur la fortune présumée," 1848, Vol. 2, AV.

items on the street in front of their houses. Most were selling fruits and vegetables, but others were selling furniture and other used goods (fripiers), children's toys, kegs and tubs, and so on.

Selling in the street was a last recourse for the poor and for those in temporary difficulty because of unemployment (Zylberberg-Hocquard, 1981, p. 615). It is also very interesting to note that while only 15 percent of all women in the 1871 patentes were married, 13 of the 20 female marchandes ambulantes indigènes were married. However, the distance between the marchand ambulant indigène and the small boutiquier was probably not very great. The main difference was that the boutiquier could afford a more spacious apartment on the ground floor in which business could be conducted (Commission médicale, 1847). Table 4.7 shows the size of businesses in the 1849 Taxe sur la fortune présumée. More than half of the women assessed in the tax were at the minimum level, 1,000 francs or less per year.

Table 4.8 examines age patterns of women who ran small businesses recorded in the 1849 Taxe sur la fortune présumée. The table compares the distribution of ages of women linked from the tax register to the 1849 population register with the distribution of ages of women in the 1846 census. The numbers of women in each age and marital status in 1846 only approximate the numbers in 1849, but adjusting these figures without additional information would not improve the accuracy of this procedure.

Overall, Table 4.8 shows that the proportion of women running small businesses increased with age from under 1 percent in their 20s to 12 percent over age 70, but this pattern was the result of movements between and within marital status groups. The differences between marital status groups are very marked. Only one married woman was listed in the tax register in 1849, although many women ran businesses listed under the

Table 4.8. Number of Females in 1846 Census and 1849 fortune présumée, by Age and Marital Status

Age	Unmarried	Married	Widowed	Total
	NUMBER OF FEMALES IN 1846 CENSUS			
20–24	1,063	199	4	1,266
25–29	515	403	15	933
30–34	271	489	31	791
35–39	226	615	33	874
40–44	155	563	55	773
45–49	112	508	80	700
50–54	109	359	117	585
55–59	65	277	126	468
60–64	64	206	166	436
65–69	48	150	163	361
70+	57	73	323	453
Total	2,685	3,842	1,113	7,640
	NUMBER OF FEMALES IN 1849 FORTUNE PRÉSUMÉE			
20–24	3	0	0	3
25–29	5	0	1	6
30–34	12	0	2	14
35–39	8	1	6	15
40–44	10	0	12	22
45–49	13	0	16	29
50–54	14	0	22	36
55–59	9	0	19	28
60–64	5	0	28	33
65–69	5	0	24	29
70+	7	0	48	55
Total	91	1	178	270
	RATIO OF FEMALES IN FORTUNE PRÉSUMÉE TO 1846 CENSUS			
20–24	0.3	0.0	0.0	0.2
25–29	1.0	0.0	6.7	0.6
30–34	4.4	0.0	6.5	1.8
35–39	3.5	0.2	18.2	1.7
40–44	6.5	0.0	21.8	2.8
45–49	11.6	0.0	20.0	4.1
50–54	12.8	0.0	18.8	6.2
55–59	13.8	0.0	15.1	6.0
60–64	7.8	0.0	16.9	7.6
65–69	10.4	0.0	14.7	8.0
70+	12.3	0.0	14.9	12.1
Total	3.4	0.0	16.0	3.5

names of their husbands. Among unmarried women the tendency to run a business increased with age up to 50 and then leveled off between 10 and 14 percent. Widows were the most likely to have businesses, but they were most likely to do so in their 40s. The proportion of widows with businesses jumped from around 7 percent at ages 25–34 to about 20 percent around age 40 and then declined to about 15 percent after age 50. The gradual increase in the proportion of all women with businesses was primarily the result of the increasing numbers of widows at older ages.

Part-time shopkeeping was important to women in two ways: first, as a way that a married woman could make a contribution to the family economy, and second, as an opportunity for unmarried and widowed women with sufficient capital to remain in the petty bourgeoisie. A variety of signs indicate that married women not only worked in these part-time businesses but often initiated them. Since these businesses were conducted in the family's living quarters, wives could hardly have remained aloof, and shops were often open while the husband was away at work. Since the Belgian legal code prevented women from undertaking contracts in their own names, businesses run by married women had to be officially recorded under the husbands' names. In the 1871 list of patentes we have found 48 cases where the business was listed under a husband's name with the designation "épouse" attached (see Table 4.6), and there were undoubtedly many more where the wife was primarily responsible for the business.

Although peddling could be the last resort of the poorest families, boutiques and cabarets were most often run by wives of skilled workers and foremen (Commission médicale, 1847). In the family budgets collected in 1853, income from wives and nonwage sources was highest in families where the husband's income was higher (Alter, 1984a). In later generations the higher wages of these workers was used for domestic consumption, but at midcentury a small amount of family capital was often a path into the petty bourgeoisie.

Small businesses were especially important to widows. It is likely that 15–20 percent of widows obtained income in this way. For widows with small children these businesses had the attraction of being easily combined with child care and other domestic activities. A few widows were apparently able to continue businesses started by their husbands in industries that were not normally female occupations. Thus, in 1871 one woman was reported as a "tailleuse de pierres" (stone quarrier) with four workers, and another was a "marbrier" (marble cutter) with six workers. There are fewer than a dozen cases of this sort, however. More than three-quarters of the small businesses of widows were shops and cabarets; these women must have either converted family capital to this purpose or continued part-time shops begun before their husbands' deaths.

CONCLUSION

The work experience of nineteenth-century Verviétoises was shaped primarily by their family lives. This appears most clearly in the movement out of the labor force at the time of marriage, but even among unmarried women the low labor-force participation of daughters of the petty bourgeoisie shows the importance of family decision-making. Age, on the other hand, was not a major factor in occupational patterns. Older women did not tend to move into the preferred needle trades, nor did they either enter or leave the textile industry. There was undoubtedly some circulation among these occupations, but there was little trend. The main change in occupations at older ages was the tendency to open small businesses, boutiques, and cabarets, and this was related more to the acquisition of capital than age.

Although there were only a few female occupations, they were distinctly ranked in social status, and daughters inherited the occupational status of their parents in the same way that sons did. The social status of female occupations was not based upon differences in wages. Occupational segregation compressed all female wages in the small space between unskilled males' wages and those of children, and the needle trades were paid about the same as textile occupations. Nevertheless, a social stigma was attached to factory work, which daughters of the bourgeoisie and even the petty bourgeoisie were able to avoid.

The withdrawal of married women from the work force tends to conceal their economic contributions to their families. The only survey of workers' incomes from the mid-nineteenth century suggests that married women with children did make a significant monetary contribution to the family economy by working part-time (Alter, 1984a). Can we doubt that a married seamstress turned to her needle when her husband was unemployed, or that textile workers did out-work or even returned to the factories? The married women of Verviers were also found in the myriad of small, part-time shops and cabarets. The Belgian Civil Code made the husband legally responsible, but many of these were female enterprises conducted while husbands were at work. Finally, there was an entire world of casual labor that we will never find reported: women who took in laundry, who cooked meals for unmarried workers, who cleaned kitchens and scrubbed floors.

111

5

Courtship and the Double Standard:
Illegitimacy and Bridal Pregnancy

NONMARITAL SEXUAL ACTIVITY AND FAMILY HISTORY

A puzzling and controversial aspect of family life in nineteenth-century Europe is the prevalence of premarital sexual activity and illegitimacy. Data from a number of western European countries show a rising trend in illegitimate fertility beginning in the eighteenth century and peaking in the last quarter of the nineteenth century (Shorter, Knodel, and van de Walle, 1971; Laslett, Oosterveen, and Smith, 1980). This issue is important for the study of nineteenth-century Verviers, which had a moderately high illegitimacy ratio (about 9 percent of all births were illegitimate) and a very high rate of bridal pregnancy (30–40 percent). Since the regulation of childbearing is a primary function of any family system, rising illegitimacy rates are often considered a sign of social disorganization. One can hardly be surprised that contemporaries were concerned about the large number of illegitimate births and abandoned children, and that they feared a general breakdown in morality and an increase in crimes like infanticide.

The rise of illegitimacy in the nineteenth century poses an important problem for historians of the European family. Most recent work in family history has seen greater strength in the nineteenth-century family than contemporary social observers or later sociologists believed. Louise Tilly and Joan Scott have emphasized the importance of the working-class family as an economic unit and the similarities between early industrial and preindustrial families (Tilly and Scott, 1978). The rise in illegitimacy seems to challenge the views that the family remained important, that parents retained authority over children, and that community standards were important in guiding courtship and marriage. How can the prevalence of premarital sexual activity be reconciled with the view that the family retained its social and cultural importance?

Part of the answer lies in rejecting the common association of illegitimacy with industrialism and urbanization. The parallel between rising illegitimacy and the development of modern industry in some cities fed contemporary concern about the breakdown of morality and the family among the industrial working classes. Illegitimacy was by no means an exclusively urban phenomenon, however. We now know that rural illegitimacy rates were also rising in the nineteenth century, and cities often had less illegitimacy than surrounding rural areas (Laslett, 1980a; Knodel and Hochstadt, 1980). Moreover, most recent historical discussions of illegitimacy trends emphasize the sexual permissiveness of many rural courtship practices. Late nineteenth-century ethnologists, particularly Scandinavians like Eilert Sundt, became aware that rural traditions often allowed sexual intimacy before formal marriage (Sundt, 1980; Myrdal, 1968, pp. 42–44). This cultural pattern is usually associated with higher illegitimacy rates and high rates of bridal pregnancies.

Several authors have suggested that these rural courtship patterns persisted among rural migrants to urban areas and in areas where agricultural change was converting petty proprietors to rural proletarians (Neuman, 1972; Tilly, Scott, and Cohen, 1976; Phayer, 1974; Lee, 1977). In these new situations social control over male behavior was greatly reduced. Women who came to the cities continued to view intimacy as an acceptable part of courtship leading to marriage. But in the cities their expectations of marriage were much more likely to be disappointed. The anonymity and mobility of cities made it much easier for men to renege on their promises of marriage and disappear. Furthermore, many women had come to the cities without families and social support, and they had little protection from sexual exploitation and victimization. Even the rural community could no longer force young men to marry the women that they had impregnated, because men were no longer tied to the village by the need to inherit property. New economic opportunities and an increase in geographic mobility made it easier for local youths to leave, and brought young women into contact with men who had fewer ties to the local community.

This interpretation helps explain premarital sexual behavior in nineteenth-century Verviers, but for several reasons I have attempted to augment and modify it. First of all, the focus on rural courtship patterns has drawn attention away from descriptions of urban working-class cultures with similar behavior. Rural cultures could not simply be carried into urban areas without adaptation and development. It is appropriate to see a continuity between the rural and urban patterns, but there are several good studies from the twentieth century that can add insights to this discussion (see the section "Courtship and the Double Standard," below).

Second, current literature tends to overemphasize the social isolation of women who became unwed mothers. This tendency is particularly clear in an influential article by Louise Tilly, Joan Scott, and Miriam Cohen (1976), which implies that unwed mothers were mostly migrants to urban areas. This may have been true in London and Paris, where legions of domestic servants could be found, but the single women who became pregnant in Verviers, though often socially vulnerable, were isolated neither from the community nor from their parents and kin. The patterns in Verviers can probably be found in other established working-class communities as well.

Finally, the high rate of bridal pregnancy, as well as illegitimacy, raises an apparent paradox concerning the effectiveness of social control. Illegitimacy seems to indicate a weak community, while bridal pregnancy suggests that norms were often enforced. I will try to suggest sources of conflict and ambivalence in the value system that implicate peer group and community pressure in both types of behavior. While most women could count on some social support in bringing a partner to marriage, the community supported gender roles that encouraged men to seek exploitative sexual relations. A woman who fell afoul of the double standard would find that the community had turned against her.

The following section presents an interpretation that emphasizes four aspects of the social context of nonmarital sexual activity. First, the culture of nineteenth-century Verviers was tolerant of premarital sexual activity and its consequences (Christensen, 1960; Pope and Knudsen, 1965). Sexual activity was apparently accepted as a normal part of courtship. Although European cultures have all seemed to prefer female chastity before marriage and to condemn illegitimacy, these values have varied in strength (Segalen, 1980, p. 26). For example, Smout (1980, p. 209) describes the marked difference in behavior between Scots and Irish immigrants living in Scotland. The Irish brought with them a strong moral condemnation of premarital sexual activity, and they had much lower illegitimacy than natives living alongside them in Scottish cities. The patterns observed in Verviers could hardly have existed if the virginity of brides had been deemed indispensible or the stigma of illegitimacy had been too great.

This is not to say that female sexual activity was actually promoted in Verviers or that there was any approval of illegitimacy. The evidence suggests that the former was tolerated primarily because marriage was expected to follow, and illegitimacy was always condemned. Female chastity can be preferred without being considered the sole or predominant virtue in a bride. The behavior observed in Verviers could not have persisted, however, if female virginity had been highly valued or if sanctions against illegitimacy had been very strong.

Second, high levels of bridal pregnancy and illegitimacy do not imply female sexual emancipation or equality, but rather the opposite. Premarital sexual activity is often found in societies in which the "double standard" is firmly entrenched. When the social worlds of the sexes are highly segregated, as they have been in many working-class cultures, the interpretations assigned to male and female sexual behavior are different. Both male and female peer groups can encourage sexual activity, but often with different goals and values. Males acquire prestige from sexual adventures. Females are encouraged to develop a permanent attachment to a male. Premarital sexual encounters are more likely to be characterized by males acting out their cultural domination of women than by women expressing their individuality. In direct contrast to Edward Shorter, I see illegitimacy and bridal pregnancy as the results of one of the least "modern" aspects of European culture. (For a very different view see Shorter, 1972, 1973, and 1977).

Third, the extent to which nonmarital sexual activity results in illegitimacy rather than bridal pregnancy is strongly related to the social and economic opportunities of males. Clearly, the strength and effectiveness of social sanctions against males are important, but the availability of social and economic rewards may be just as important in discouraging males from exploitative sexual behavior. Men with higher expectations are less likely to risk disrupting their personal lives and reputations with socially disapproved sexual conduct.

Finally, in Verviers sexual activity during courtship occurred within a family system in which children acknowledged parental authority and their obligations to their families of origin. The initiation of courtship was subject to constraints set by parents and accepted by children. Obviously, the courtship system was run by children, but parents had more reason for concern about the timing of marriage than about the mate choices of their children. Working children made a significant economic contribution to their families of origin that some parents were reluctant to relinquish. Bridal pregnancy sometimes helped children overcome parental opposition to a marriage, although we cannot be sure that this was a conscious strategy.

This last part of the argument rests on evidence of average ages and household composition of women with nonmarital conceptions in Verviers. Nonmarital conceptions, whether they led to bridal pregnancies or illegitimate births, occurred at about the same ages as marriages without previous conceptions. An average age of first birth in the middle 20s implies a long period of restraint after the age of sexual maturity. Since most of these women were working, many of them in factories, earlier opportunities for sexual encounters were not lacking. Furthermore, unmarried women living with parents were just as likely to become pregnant as those living alone. If parents tried to prevent the sexual activities of their daughters, they were quite ineffective. Courtship and sexual intimacy were apparently postponed until marriage was an acceptable outcome for both parents and children.

There are two kinds of evidence in this chapter. First, a description of the cultural context of premarital sexual activity is assembled from contemporary references. Second, quantitative data from the population registers are used to show the extent of illegitimacy and bridal pregnancy and the backgrounds of women with pre- and postnuptial conceptions. Two samples are examined: the linked random sample and the marriages from 1844 and 1845. It is possible to compare women whose first birth was conceived after marriage with women who married while they were pregnant and with those whose first birth was illegitimate. In both samples the women are separated into three groups: postnuptial conceptions, prenuptial conceptions, and illegitimate births. The two samples differ in the last category, however. The marriage sample includes only those unwed mothers who subsequently married and "legitimated" their children.

While it is impossible to show the motivations of women and men in nineteenth-century Verviers, the available data support the interpretative framework presented here in some key ways. Overall, the similarities among these different groups of women are more striking than their differences. They tended to be about the same age: pregnant brides were slightly younger, unwed mothers were slightly older. Premarital sexual activity was less common in higher social classes, but not totally absent except in the elite. In household composition there was also a basic similarity, although unwed mothers were more often migrants and orphans. Women who were older, fatherless, or lower in social status were more likely to become unwed mothers. They had less bargaining power in courtship and were less able to mobilize the community to bring their partners to marriage. The culture and economy of nineteenth-century Verviers forced women to take risks during courtship, and for women in weaker positions in the marriage market the risks were greater.

COURTSHIP AND THE DOUBLE STANDARD: AN INTERPRETATION OF PREMARITAL SEXUAL ACTIVITY

It is difficult to discuss nonmarital sexual activity without conveying some picture of the personal and social significance of this behavior. Most recent discussions in family history have emphasized the practices of night courting and "bundling," which were common in rural areas of northern Europe (Neuman, 1972; Tilly, Scott, and Cohen, 1976; Kälvemark, 1980; Smout, 1980). These customs show that premarital sexual activity was often an accepted part of courtship. But it may be more helpful here to look at examples of working-class behavior that are associated with frequent bridal pregnancies.

A particularly useful description of the role of sexual activity in courtship is in Richard Hoggart's (1971) description of the English working-class community in which he was born. He describes the frequent references to irregular sexual experiences in the male peer group, and he remarks that men felt "little sense of guilt or sin in connection with their sex-life. . . . In some respects their attitude toward promiscuous sex activity does come from a long way back. But for them it is all rather scrabbily hole-and-corner" (pp. 83–84).

Girls often confronted the crude remarks of the boys around them, but seemed unaffected. "To me the surprising thing is that so many girls are able to remain unaffected, to retain both an ignorance about the facts of sex and an air of inviolability towards its whole atmosphere that would not have been unbecoming in a mid-nineteenth-century young lady of the middle-classes" (Hoggart, 1971, p. 84). Overall, Hoggart concludes:

> My experience suggests, then, that most girls do not move from man to man, picking up fragmentary experience on the way, but that they begin courting early and go on steadily until an early marriage. Some still "get into trouble" from fifteen onwards, but they are the exceptions. Many have some sexual experience before marriage, but usually with the boy they eventually marry; they have not been promiscuous. Nor are they sheltered: from sixteen they are regarded as in most respects adult; they meet the boy they "fall for" and start courting. They are probably almost completely ignorant of the practice of sex. They feel romantically towards the boy; he presses; it does not seem all that important to wait until marriage, and they yield. He will perhaps take precautions, but a proportion of men will not, being unprepared or inexpert. If a baby is conceived, the marriage takes place sooner than was expected, but the girl is unlikely to feel that she has been caught. My impression is that most of the girls who lose their virginity before marriage lose it in this way—with boys they are genuinely fond of, when circumstances conspire—rather than from any deliberate passing from boy to boy "for the fun of it." (pp. 84–85)

Hoggart's description emphasizes the difference between the motivations of men and women, and one can infer that the social importance of sexual activity often exceeded, perhaps even precluded, personal or sexual gratification. The "double standard" under which the same behavior is interpreted differently for men and women is central to this behavior. For the males a sexual conquest provides status within the peer group. Women who behave in the same way, however, are strongly censured and socially stigmatized (Rainwater, 1966, p. 104). Status in the female peer

117

group, presumably, comes from having a steady partner and the expectation of marriage. Chastity has little value for its own sake, however, and at some point a developing relationship with a young man more than offsets the risk to a woman's reputation. These sexual encounters are in a sense public as well as private, and their social implications are more important than any expression of individuality. It is also important to note that the double standard rests in part upon the social segregation of male and female peers[1] (see also Rainwater, 1966; Vincent, 1960; Furstenberg, 1976; Reiss, 1960).

Under the double standard young women must negotiate the differences between the long-run goal of marriage and the immediate demands of their partners. Sexual activity can be used as a way of building commitment, but it can also brand her as the wrong kind of woman. If the woman agrees to sexual intimacy too early in the relationship, her behavior will be interpreted as disreputable, and her partner will be less likely to concede the commitment to marriage that she is seeking. On the other hand, if she refuses too long or too adamantly, her partner may conclude that she lacks commitment to him. Once a woman has had a sexual relationship in a courtship that failed to result in marriage, the sexual bargaining in later courting becomes even more difficult. Her subsequent partners will expect sexual intercourse earlier in the relationship, and they will be less likely to interpret sexual activity as a sign of commitment. Thus, women who have engaged in sexual activity in unsuccessful courtships are increasingly at risk of becoming unwed mothers in later courtships. Sundt (1980) describes this increase in sexual activity in later courtship, but in keeping with the double standard he condemns the morality of the woman:

> One can anticipate, what experience also establishes, that when there is such great freedom it more frequently happens that less modest girls overstep the recognized border of what is decent which, as we have said, is also firmly fixed here. I refer to a case such as that of a girl who, at a young and unsettled age, loses her honour and as a result gives herself up to a more and more wanton life, with the abominable plan that, since the father of her first child deceived her, probably the second or the third child's father will in his turn be caught by her and become her husband. It is just the girl who has lost her character and becomes despised who has a double reason to dread lonely

---

1. Although the double standard in the lower and working classes is a major theme in a branch of sociology (e.g., Rainwater, 1966; Reiss, 1960; Vincent, 1960), there is a minor historical tradition which reserves this term for the upper and middle classes. Thus, Keith Thomas (1959, p. 206) writes, "Among the lowest classes of society the tradition of promiscuity was too strong to allow the emergence of so sophisticated a concept as that of the double standard" (see also Smout, 1980, p. 193). Obviously, I disagree with this evaluation of the sophistication of lower-class culture and with the interpretation that lower-class behavior was promiscuous.

old age. She probably feels, therefore, that she has a kind of right to seek a breadwinner. (p. 161)

Although discussions of illegitimacy often focus exclusively on women, the economic prospects of young men appear to be strongly linked to the occurrence of illegitimacy, as well as to the effectiveness of peer group pressures for exploitative sexual behavior. When young males find it difficult or impossible to fulfill the economic roles prescribed by society, several factors encourage premarital sexual activity. First, social controls are less effective. Parents and authorities who have no rewards to offer or withhold have very little leverage. Second, if other sources of social and self-esteem are impractical, peer group pressure for exploitative sexual relationships becomes more effective. Finally, if economic opportunities are completely lacking, marriage loses its social significance for young men. When failure as a husband is almost a certainty, why should a young man be cautious and circumspect in his courtship and sexual behavior (Vincent, 1960)?

Men who establish permanent relationships with women apparently concede the expectation of marriage, not without affection, but with a sense of the inevitability and the greater importance of marriage and the family. Family is a transcendant value in the community described by Hoggart (1971, p. 32). "'Sin' is any act against the idea of home and family, against the sense of the importance of 'keeping the home together.'" The male culture may joke about marriage, but it also recognizes that the ultimate male status is the head of a household.[2] Arnold Green's (1941) classic study of courtship in an immigrant working-class community in the United States describes male motivation in this way:

> The boy has a reduced success drive. He does not exercise the caution, foresight, and repression of impulse that the middle-class boy must use in courtship, as in all other relationships, to ensure that the channels of vertical mobility be kept open to him. In terms of social and economic betterment, the local Polish boy has little either to gain or lose by marrying . . . thus a passive-resistant, uncalculating attitude is maintained toward marriage. Its coming soon or late means little to the boy's life organization: while contraceptives are always carried during casual dating, he often grows careless in steady dating. Most of the marriages in the Polish Parish are precipitated by premarital pregnancy. (p. 347)

Low expectations and an underlying fatalism in much of working-class culture combine to separate premarital sexual activity from the conscious planning of marriage.

---

2. See also Hoggart, 1971 (pp. 48–51) on the status of father in the family and the socialization of young men.

In addition to the tensions between the man and woman who are court-ing, there are the important potential conflicts between the goals and interests of children and parents. In the nineteenth century, parents often had an economic interest in delaying their children's marriages. Sexual activity may have been used by children as a protest against strong parental authority. If a parent refused consent to a marriage, social pressure due to the pregnancy was probably exploited without having been consciously planned.

Where the surrounding community interpreted sexual intimacy as a prelude to marriage, bridal pregnancies were a common and accepted outcome, but illegitimacy was neither intended nor approved. Neverthe-less, illegitimacy was more likely to occur in this courtship system. First of all, women who permitted premarital intimacy put themselves at risk of illegitimate births. Even if their expectations of marriage were well founded, circumstances sometimes conspired to delay or prevent the mar-riage. Some marriages did not occur before a child was born, because the couple had misjudged their economic resources or encountered un-expected opposition from parents. In other cases, the man simply refused to honor his implied obligation. Since male and female motivations were often different, it would have been easy for each party to hold a different interpretation of their behavior.

Finally, the double standard implies that some women by their conduct give up the protection of society. These women become targets for casual sexual relations. Although some women move into this category intention-ally, more lose their reputations against their wills. Even women whose sexual conduct is within normal limits can acquire bad reputations, and thus become likely candidates for unwed motherhood. A "bastardy prone sub-society" can emerge because young women inherit the reputations of their parents, and their partners tend to impose upon them behavior likely to result in unwed motherhood (Laslett, 1980b). The risk of illegitimacy is greatest for women who are economically and socially weak. They have less bargaining power during courtship and less access to social sanctions later. Thus, the double standard makes illegitimacy more likely, without making it intended or condoned.

The courtship system of Verviers forced women to choose between alternatives involving risks. A woman's goal was marriage, but the risk of becoming an unwed mother had to be weighed against the risk of remain-ing a spinster. If she were to agree to her partner's demand for sexual intimacy, she could perhaps strengthen their relationship and increase the likelihood that they would marry. On the other hand, she risked conceiv-ing a child and becoming an unwed mother. Moreover, even if she did not become pregnant, she might lose esteem in the eyes of her partner, and if she did not marry him, she would have less bargaining power in later relationships. Women who were less attractive in the marriage market or economically or socially deprived had to take greater risks in courtship, and they could have less confidence that a partner would marry. All unmarried women faced these concerns as they grew older and lost bargaining power in the marriage market: the pool of eligible husbands became smaller, and the women were more likely to have had earlier unsuccessful courtships.

This is not meant to imply that all nineteenth-century illegitimacy can be explained in this way. There were some women who had no intention or desire to marry the fathers of their children. At one extreme, an unmeasurable proportion of illegitimate births resulted from rapes. Since the double standard always calls female motivations into question, it tends to increase the likelihood of rape in even legitimate courtships (see also Rossiaud, 1976). Fairchilds (1978) suggests that rape was a ritualized part of some courtships in southern France. At the other extreme, prostitution also made a contribution to illegitimacy. Considering the importance of children as economic support in old age, we should not be surprised if some women chose a future as unwed mothers over the alternatives of an impoverished spinsterhood or an unhappy marriage.

ATTITUDES TOWARD ILLEGITIMACY AND PREMARITAL SEXUAL ACTIVITY

Contemporary references from Verviers and elsewhere in Belgium reflect a toleration of premarital sexual activity with the expectation that pregnancies would be followed by marriage. The prevalence of bridal pregnancy in Wallonia is evoked by the saying "She will win the kettle of the curé." This refers to a story in which a rural curé promised to give a kettle to the first nonpregnant bride to come before him. According to the story, he never had to make an award (Dejardin, 1891–92, 17:215).[3]

---

3. A French official in Liège in the 1780s described the pressure that men applied to women during courtship:

> Une d'elles, au dessus de l'âge de se marier et restée fille, que je connois, dit et répéte souvent que celles qui restent sans se marier de bonne heure sont à coup sûr les plus honnêtes.—Pourqoui! lui dis je.—Pourqoui? C'est qu'elles n'ont pas voulu souffrir certaines gentillesses de la part des hommes qui répondent tout simplement qu'ils en trouveront d'autres.
>
> Ici, m'a-t-elle dit souvent, un homme recherche une demoiselle; si, au premier moment où il sera libre avec elle, elle ne veut pas lui accorder certaines privautés, le lendemain il la quitte et elle sera abandonnée.
>
> (One [woman], past the age of marrying and still unmarried . . . says . . . that those who

A visitor to Verviers in the 1840s observed, "If a girl lets herself be seduced, the child is not abandoned and a legitimate marriage always repairs the first fault" (Appert, 1848, p. 153).[4] A Belgian author writing about poverty in 1870 took the large number of legitimations as evidence of a "relative morality" that could be improved with education and solicitude. "If in general the girl of the factory gives herself, at least she does not sell herself" (Dauby, 1873, p. 44n.).[5]

Another observer describing the miners of Hainaut evokes what Green (1941) calls a "passive-resistant, uncalculating attitude" to explain why they waited until a pregnancy occurred to marry.

> [When the worker marries,] to the cares of his existence are going to be added that of a wife and soon after of a family, for, whatever is said, the association of two miseries is hardly likely to diminish its weight. The calculation thus appears very simple to him and the worker, fearing slavery and indigence, does not marry except at the final extremity. (Vanden Broeck, 1843, p. 59)

The most interesting of these references is the following passage:

> When there were several daughters in a family, the first that wanted to marry often had difficulty obtaining permission; frequently the intended had to carry her off: which was called *él fer biser*. For the rest, the curé united the couple clandestinely, when they were in his good graces, and the parents did not wait to absolve them. (Xhoffer, 1866, p. 20)

In this passage, elopement and presumably premarital pregnancies were

---

do not marry early are certainly the most honest.—Why! I ask her.—Why? Because they did not want to suffer certain kindnesses from men who simply respond that they will find someone else.

Here, she frequently tells me, a man seeks a girl; if, at the first moment when he is free with her, she does not want to accord him certain privacies, the next day he leaves her and she is abandoned.)

Extracted from the journal of Michel-Nicholas Jolivet, sent by him in the form of a letter to Paris, 18 August 1783, and published by Dr. Jos. Alexandre under the title *Description du pays et principalemant de la ville de Liège.* Reprinted by Jean Servais, "Les femmes wallonnes: ce qu'on en dit," *Wallonia* 19(1911): 196.

4. Other comments of this kind can be found in Thomassin, 1879, p. 219; Vanden Broecke, 1843, p. 58; Belguim, Commission du travail, 1887, pp. 1030–33; Henau, 1847, p. 191.

5. "However before tracing the causes, we ought to point out that the sensuality of the factory woman is not prostitution; it is not the same as the dabauchery of servants, seamstresses and many others who belong to small industry. She knows the man to whom she gives herself; he is from her class and she sees her future husband in the father of her child. This explains the considerable number of legitimations of children by marriage which are done each year in Ghent." J. Mareska and J. Heyman, *Enquête sur le travail et la condition physique et morale des ouvriers employés dans les manufactures de coton, à Gand.* Gand: F. et E. Gyselynck, 1845, p. 238.

part of the negotiation between parents and children. The description implies that these conflicts became ritualized.

Premarital sexual activity was, of course, strongly condemned by the Catholic church, but, as Michael Phayer (1974) has argued for Germany, it is likely that this aspect of official morality never replaced local custom. Perhaps more important was the apparent toleration of prenuptial pregnancies and even premarital births followed by the marriage of the parents, which was a long-standing position of the Catholic church and also found in Belgian civil law. The Church considered children legitimate offspring if their parents later married. Under the Belgian Civil Code, as well as French revolutionary and Napoleonic law from which it was derived, a child "legitimated" by the parents' marriage was legally equivalent to children born after the marriage. This is most apparent in the Civil Code's handling of inheritance, under which legitimated children had full rights to the father's succession. The Civil Code also gave limited rights to illegitimate children who had been legally "recognized" by the father. Recognition was not allowed when it implied adultery or another violation of law, however.

The Catholic diocese of Liège had occasion to clarify its priorities concerning illegitimacy and marriage in response to an inquiry from the Société de Saint François Régis of Verviers. The society had become concerned about marriages in which children were being legitimated by men who were not their biological fathers. Was the society committing a sin when it assisted these marriages? The Church replied that there was no sin on the part of the society, since they were not misrepresenting the parentage of the children. Furthermore, the marriages of women with illegitimate children were to be encouraged (Fonds Doutreloux, 1883, ADL). The Church clearly ranked the encouragement of marriages among the poor ahead of condemning illegitimacy, an agenda that the working-class community must have shared.

Nineteenth-century Belgians seem to have assumed that sexual activity was a natural and strong inclination of both men and women, but the double standard of sexual conduct was applied. Harry Peters of Anvers gave the 1887 Commission du travail a remarkably frank assessment of the needs of unmarried workers in his account of the budget of a worker living alone. "If the man is older than 18 or 19 years there are laws of nature which he cannot escape, which cost him, per week (by estimation) . . . 2.00 [francs]." Women were said to have the same needs but with an important difference.

> For the woman, there are also the inevitable laws of nature, but the satisfaction of these costs her nothing. But she is, with regard to expenses, in possible danger, because alas! the woman is exposed to having a child, and being

alone, she is triply unhappy and ten times miserable. (Belgium, Commission du travail, 1887, 1:501)

It is also noteworthy that the official approach to prostitution was regulation rather than suppression. The police, in particular, took the position that it was better to license brothels so that persons suspected of leading girls into prostitution could be watched more easily.[6]

Although sexual activity was to some extent tolerated, women ran the risk of acquiring a bad reputation. Folklorists confirm that illegitimacy was censured (van der Linden and Pinon, 1978, p. 41), and the quantitative evidence from Verviers also shows that unwed mothers were much less likely to marry. A rare female writer in the newspaper of the First International in Verviers, *Le Mirabeau*, emphasized the double standard.

> When a young man has seduced a girl and abandoned her, the latter falls into disrepute, her reputation is lost, fingers are pointed at her. The boy, on the contrary, goes his way and finds other girls who have no scruple about receiving him, it even seems that he has acquired a certain notoriety that makes him sought after. (*Le Mirabeau*, 24 October 1873, BV)

This writer blamed other women for spreading rumors about each other and not supporting their less fortunate sisters.

Men did not escape their responsibilities without social censure, however. A man who failed to marry the mother of his child risked public ridicule in the form of a *charivari* (Yernaux and Fievet, 1956, pp. 34–35). Again, it is easy to underestimate the power of communities in early industrial cities. Labor markets in these cities were often highly personal, and family and social contacts were still very important in finding desirable jobs. Although cities offered some degree of anonymity, the community could still impose economic as well as social sanctions on males.

The double standard tends to be supported by societies in which males and females are segregated both in cultural symbols and in their everyday social interactions. Male socialization in nineteenth-century Belgian cities centered on the cabaret. Writers often accused husbands of seeking refuge in the cabaret, while their wives faced the hardships of raising children on low wages in an overcrowded apartment (Ducpetiaux, 1855). The

6. In official correspondence from the mid-nineteenth century the *commissaire de police* of Verviers repeatedly favored granting licenses for brothels. The commissaire preferred to have persons suspected of promoting prostitution in fixed locations, where they could be watched more easily ("Pièces diverses," 16 January 1852, AV). A liberal discussion circle in Verviers also viewed prostitution as immoral but necessary. Since prostitution was impossible to eliminate, they thought it should be regulated and subjected to sanitary inspections. Opinion was divided on whether the *"tenants de maisons de débauches"* should be allowed to vote ("L'Etude cercle," Fonds de la Ville, 1867, BV).

Table 5.1. Numbers and Rates of Illegitimate First Births and Marriages, by Age, Linked Random Sample

Age	Woman-Years of Exposure	Illegitimate First Births	Marriages	Rates (per 1,000)	
				Illegitimacy	Marriage
15–19	601.9	1	8	1.7	13.3
20–24	1,182.3	9	91	7.6	77.0
25–29	909.4	13	72	14.3	79.2
30–34	531.1	4	31	7.5	58.4
35–39	325.0	0	3	0.0	9.2
40–44	272.2	2	2	7.3	7.3

Note: Exposure of unmarried women with illegitimate children has been excluded.

relationship between the culture of the cabaret and marriage patterns is evoked by the Napoleonic prefect.

> The men, after having fulfilled their occupations, live, as it were, separated from the women, and reunite in the estaminets, and other places, where relieved of respect and of discretion which is required by their [the women's] presence, the choice of subjects and of expressions is as lax as the desire to please. This desire does not even seem to influence the marriages. Despite the great liberty which exists among young people of both sexes and which ancient local laws still favor, the unions have seemed and still seem to be more the work of the conveniences of fortune, or the invincible attraction which brings the two sexes together, rather than of any careful consideration. (Thomassin, 1879)

In the eyes of this bourgeois observer, the social segregation of men and women supported a courtship system in which sexuality expressed neither personal nor romantic sentiments, "the desire to please."[7]

Marriage and Illegitimacy in the Population Register, 1849–1880

If marriage and illegitimacy are two different consequences of courtship behavior, they should occur at the same ages. Table 5.1 shows the similarity in ages at which marriage and illegitimacy occurred in Verviers. In this table illegitimacy and marriage rates are constructed by dividing the number of illegitimate first births and the number of marriages by the number of "woman-years" at risk in each age group. At each age under

7. "L'Emancipation de la femme" (*Le Mirabeau*, 17 April 1870, BV) describes women who worked during the day and did household chores at night while their husbands went out.

Table 5.2. Mean Age at Marriage or First Birth, by Type of
First Birth, Linked Random Sample, 1849–80

	Mean	Std. Dev.	Number
Age at marriage:			
Postnuptial conception	25.8	4.34	69
Prenuptial conception	24.9	3.17	38
Age at illegitimate			
first birth	27.2	4.97	29

Table 5.3. Age Distribution at Marriage or First Birth, by Type of First Birth, Linked
Random Sample, 1849–80

Age	Postnuptial Conception	Prenuptial Conception	Illegitimate First Birth	Total	Illegitimacy as Percent of All Nonmarital Conceptions
	PERCENT BY AGE				
15–19	66.7	0.0	33.3	100.0	100.0
20–24	52.5	32.8	14.8	100.0	31.0
25–29	46.3	29.6	24.1	100.0	44.8
30–34	60.0	13.3	26.7	100.0	66.7
35–39	100.0	0.0	0.0	100.0	0.0
40–44	0.0	0.0	100.0	100.0	100.0
Entire sample	50.7	27.9	21.3	100.0	43.3
	PERCENT BY TYPE OF FIRST BIRTH				
				Entire Sample	
15–19	2.9	0.0	3.4	2.2	
20–24	46.4	52.6	31.0	44.8	
25–29	36.2	42.1	44.8	39.7	
30–34	13.0	5.3	13.8	11.0	
35–39	1.4	0.0	0.0	0.7	
40–44	0.0	0.0	6.9	1.5	
	100.0	100.0	100.0	100.0	
Number	69	38	29	136	

40 an unmarried woman was much more likely to marry than to become
an unwed mother. Both events occurred primarily in the lives of women
between the ages of 20 and 34. Also, the rates peaked for both at ages 25–
29, but this peak was much more pronounced for illegitimate first births,
leading to a higher average age for unwed mothers than for brides.

Tables 5.2 and 5.3 compare the ages of unwed mothers with those
of brides with post- and prenuptial conceptions. Again, in Table 5.2 we
see that the unwed mothers tended to be older, and also that marriages

Table 5.4. Distribution of Migrant and Age Groups, by Type
of First Birth, Linked Random Sample, 1849–80

Migrant Status/ Age Group	Postnuptial Conception	Prenuptial Conception	Illegitimate First Birth
Nonmigrant	73.9	71.1	41.4
Child migrant	14.5	21.1	27.6
Adult migrant	11.6	7.9	31.0
	100.0	100.0	100.0
Number	69	38	29

with bridal pregnancies tended to involve younger women.[8] The most dramatic figures are those in the last column of Table 5.3. This column expresses illegitimate first births as a percentage of illegitimate first births and prenuptial conceptions combined. This percentage rises from 31.0 at ages 20–24 to 66.7 at ages 30–34. In other words, younger women who became pregnant outside of marriage were much more likely to marry than older women. Illegitimacy was not, in general, a problem related to youth. Rather, women were more likely to be abandoned as they grew older. The interpretation offered here is that older women had less bargaining power in the marriage market and a greater need to take risks.

The following tables examine the backgrounds of these three groups. Table 5.4 shows their migrant status and general age at migration to Verviers. Women who became unwed mothers were much more likely to have been migrants, and they were especially likely to have been adult migrants. While more than 70 percent of the brides had been born in Verviers, only 41 percent of the unwed mothers were natives. Furthermore, the women who migrated after age 15 constituted 31 percent of the unwed mothers compared with 12 and 8 percent of the brides with post- and prenuptial conceptions.

Table 5.5 shows the household composition of these women in two ways. The first panel presents household composition at the time of marriage or first birth, while the second panel displays all of the exposure observed before the marriage or birth. In this table it appears that women without parents were at greater risk of an illegitimate birth. At the time of their illegitimate births, only 48 percent of the unwed mothers lived in a household with at least one parent, compared with 74 and 71 percent, respectively, for the brides with post- and prenuptial conceptions. On the other hand, even those unwed mothers without coresiding parents

8. Table 5.2 tends to underestimate average ages, but the relative bias is likely to be small.

Table 5.5. Household Composition at the Time of Marriage or First Birth and Earlier, by Type of First Birth, Linked Random Sample, 1849–80

Household Composition	Postnuptial Conception	Prenuptial Conception	Illegitimate First Birth
AT THE TIME OF MARRIAGE OR FIRST BIRTH			
Parents	73.9	71.0	48.2
Mother only	33.3	13.2	20.7
Father only	2.9	28.9	10.3
Both	37.7	28.9	17.2
Siblings	11.6	15.8	31.0
Other kin	4.3	0.0	0.0
Nonkin	2.9	5.3	10.3
Solitary	4.3	2.6	6.9
Servant	0.0	2.6	3.4
Spouse/own child	2.9	2.6	0.0
	100.0	100.0	100.0
Number	69	38	29
ALL PRIOR OBSERVATION			
Parents	75.2	85.1	70.4
Mother only	25.6	26.5	46.1
Father only	4.8	21.9	1.9
Both	44.8	36.7	22.4
Siblings	15.4	13.3	20.8
Other kin	2.4	0.0	0.0
Nonkin	2.4	0.3	1.1
Solitary	3.6	0.6	4.4
Servant	0.7	0.6	2.9
Spouse/own child	0.2	0.0	0.3
	100.0	100.0	100.0
Number of person-years	556	201	140

were usually not isolated from their families: 31 percent had siblings living with them. Only a small minority of the unwed mothers lived with nonkin (10.3 percent), alone (6.9 percent), or as servants (3.4 percent). Among the brides the differences in household composition between those with post- and prenuptial conceptions were very small.

Although all three groups were likely to live in a household with at least one parent, there were interesting differences in which parents were present. Women whose first births were postnuptially conceived were much more likely to live with both parents at the time of marriage. About 38 percent of this group had two coresiding parents at marriage, com-

Table 5.6. Occupational Distribution of Women, by Type of
First Birth, Linked Random Sample, 1849–80

Occupation	Postnuptial Conception	Prenuptial Conception	Illegitimate First Birth
Bourgeois	7.8	0.0	0.0
Needle trades	12.5	12.9	25.0
Skilled	7.8	6.5	3.6
Textiles	39.1	58.1	50.0
Day labor	6.3	0.0	7.1
Servant	1.6	12.9	7.1
None	12.5	9.7	0.0
Ménagère	12.5	0.0	7.1
	100.0	100.0	100.0
Number	64	31	28

pared with 29 percent of the pregnant brides and 17 percent of the unwed mothers. The pregnant brides stand out in an unusual way. They were much more likely to live with widowed fathers than nonpregnant brides or unwed mothers. Pregnant brides came from households with widowed fathers (28.9 percent) more than twice as often as households with widowed mothers (13.2 percent), whereas widowed mothers were much more common in both other groups.

When we turn to the second panel of Table 5.5, showing all the observation before marriage or birth, we see even more similarity in the household composition of these three groups. The unwed mothers were still less likely to have lived with parents, but even this group had at least one parent 70 percent of the time they were under observation before their first birth. However, almost half (46 percent) of the group lived in households without fathers. Among the brides it was actually those who conceived prenuptially that lived with parents more of the time before their marriages. Fully 85 percent of the women who later conceived prenuptially had lived in households with at least one parent, but again we see that it was often a widowed father.

Table 5.6, which examines the occupations of the brides and unwed mothers, shows a strong relationship between sexual activity and social status. The women who conceived after marriage were much more likely to report the occupations that were associated with higher social status. One in four of the postnuptially conceiving brides reported themselves as ménagères or without occupations, and all of the women who reported bourgeois occupations, like rentière, were in this group. The pregnant brides and unwed mothers were most likely to work in the textile industry, 58 and 50 percent, respectively. The needle trades were found in all

129

Table 5.7. Occupational Distribution of Heads of Households,[a] by Type of First Birth, Linked Random Sample, 1849–80

Occupation	Postnuptial Conception	Prenuptial Conception	Illegitimate First Birth
ALL HEADS OF HOUSEHOLDS			
Bourgeois	5.7	4.9	0.0
Petty bourgeois	21.4	8.1	1.2
Skilled	23.6	11.8	11.5
Textiles	27.7	37.0	29.7
Day labor	2.2	13.7	10.8
None	1.9	0.0	7.2
Ménagère	17.5	24.5	39.6
	100.0	100.0	100.0
Number of person-years	423	159	111
ONLY HEADS WITH OCCUPATIONS			
Bourgeois	7.1	6.5	0.0
Petty bourgeois	26.6	10.7	2.3
Skilled	29.3	15.6	21.6
Textiles	34.4	49.0	55.8
Day labor	2.7	18.1	20.3
	100.0	100.0	100.0
Number of person-years	341	120	59

[a] Only heads of households who are parents of the women in the sample are included.

three categories, but they were overrepresented among unwed mothers—25 percent compared with 13 percent of the brides.

Table 5.7 presents the occupations of the heads of households of women who lived with parents at some time before marriage or their first birth. The first panel of the table shows the distribution of all occupations of heads of households, and the second panel shows only those with reported occupations, which excludes most female heads. The table shows that bridal pregnancy was found in all social classes, but both bridal pregnancy and illegitimacy were most often associated with lower social origins. Some bridal pregnancy was found in the bourgeoisie as defined in these occupational categories, but it is worth noting that this category is broader than the social elite examined in a separate sample. It also is clear that sexual activity was less common among the daughters of the petty bourgeoisie. This social origin was twice as common among the post- than the prenuptially conceiving brides (26.6 versus 10.7 percent), and unwed mothers rarely came from this class (2.3 percent). Premarital sexual activity was common among the daughters of skilled workers, and especially among the daughters of textile workers and day laborers.

When viewed together these tables fit the picture of sexual activity and courtship presented above. Little sexual activity could have occurred before couples had reached an age when marriage was feasible. Pregnant brides were about a year younger than those who conceived after marriage, but unwed mothers tended to be more than a year older. The presence of at least one coresident parent seems to have done little to prevent premarital sexual activity, although fathers may have been successful in bringing about marriages rather than illegitimate births. Women who conceived before marriage were as likely to have at least one coresident parent as those who conceived after marriage. Women who became unwed mothers had more likely been orphaned, but often this had happened relatively recently and 48 percent lived with at least one parent. If we compare the pregnant brides with the unwed mothers, the former were more than twice as likely to have had a coresident father.

Illegitimacy appears to have been less the result of social isolation than of a variety of disadvantages in the marriage market. Women who became unwed mothers had migrated to Verviers more recently than brides, but almost all of them had come with parents and siblings. They were more likely to have lower social origins, and at the time of their first births more likely to be older and to have been orphaned. None of these factors made illegitimacy inevitable, but they all made it more difficult to find a partner, more difficult to refuse his sexual advances without jeopardizing the relationship, and more difficult to apply social pressure to bring him to marriage.

BRIDAL PREGNANCY AND LEGITIMATION, 1844–1845

Table 5.8 shows the distribution of first-birth intervals for the 295 marriages between bachelors and spinsters in 1844 and 1845. This information was collected by searching for births in the birth registers and also by linking these couples to the 1846–48 population register. Among these couples 13 percent could not be located, presumably because they had left the city, and 5.4 percent had no birth listed in the population register. Almost half of those whose first births were found were premaritally pregnant, and an additional 7 percent had premarital births that were legitimated at the marriage.

The births in these marriages are displayed by months after marriage in Figure 5.1. The clear bimodal pattern in this figure is usually taken

Table 5.8. Distribution of First-Birth Intervals,
Marriages 1844–45

First-Birth Interval	Number	Percent of:	
		Marriages	Births
13+ months	32	10.9	13.3
12–8 months	72	24.4	30.0
7–0 months	119	40.3	49.6
Legitimation	17	5.8	7.1
No birth	16	5.4	
Not found	39	13.2	
	295	100.0	100.0

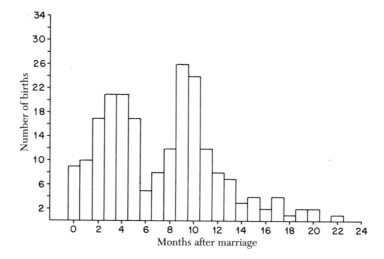

Figure 5.1. Number of first births, by months between marriage and first birth, Marriages 1844–45

as an indicator of a society with permissive attitudes toward premarital sexual activity. One peak represents births following prenuptial conceptions, which tended to occur 3 or 4 months after marriage, and a second peak at 9 and 10 months after marriage shows the concentration of postnuptially conceived first births. Christensen has argued that prenuptial conceptions tend to produce a bimodal pattern, such as the one in this figure, in societies that are tolerant of premarital sexual activity. He found very different patterns of first-birth intervals in data from Denmark and the United States. In the United States before the sexual revolution of the 1960s, parents of prenuptially conceived children tended to marry

Table 5.9. Mean Ages of Husbands and Wives, by First-Birth Interval, Marriages 1844–45

First-Birth Interval	Number	Husbands	Wives
13+ months	32	29.3	25.8
12–8 months	72	27.7	26.0
7–0 months	119	26.2	25.4
Legitimation	17	23.6	25.5
Entire sample	240	26.9	25.6

three months after conception, compared with five months in the Danish sample (Christensen, 1960, pp. 35–36). Christensen attributes the United States pattern to a desire to conceal the premarital pregnancy. American norms regarding premarital sex were much stricter and the disapproval of illegitimacy was much stronger than in Scandinavia. In the United States, couples hurried into marriage to conceal the pregnancy, while Scandinavian couples, subject to less social disapproval, were less motivated to marry quickly.

Table 5.9 shows the average age at marriage of husbands and wives by first-birth interval. None of these categories is far from the average age for all wives of 25.6 years. Women with postnuptial conceptions were about a half year older than others, and wives with prenuptial conceptions were almost exactly the same age as wives who legitimated a child. The average ages of husbands were much more distinctive, however. Husbands with postmarital conceptions were a year or more older than the average age for all husbands, which was slightly less than 27 years. But husbands with first-birth intervals of 8–12 months and 13 or more months averaged 27.7 and 29.3 years old, respectively. It is particularly interesting to note that long first-birth intervals, 13 months or more, were associated with older husbands rather than older wives. The husbands in marriages with legitimations were particularly young. These men averaged 23.6 years of age, compared with 26.2 for husbands with prenuptial conceptions.

It is important to note that the relative age of brides who legitimated a child suggests that they were a special subgroup among women who bore illegitimate children. In the preceding section we found that unwed mothers tended to be older than brides, but brides who legitimated children were the same age as other brides, and, of course, they were younger still when their first births occurred. Marriages with legitimations stand out for the young ages of the husbands, as discussed above. These age patterns and the household patterns discussed below suggest that legitimations identify the part of illegitimacy due to delayed marriage. The women

133

Table 5.10. Percentage of Marriages with a Birth, by Length of First-Birth Interval and Husband's Occupation, Marriages 1844–45

First-Birth Interval	Bourgeois	Petty Bourgeois	Skilled	Textiles	Laborers	Total
Number	21	53	61	69	36	240
Entire sample	8.8	22.1	25.4	28.8	15.0	100.1
PERCENT BY LENGTH OF FIRST-BIRTH INTERVAL						
						Total
13+ months	6.3	31.3	31.3	21.9	9.4	100.0
12–8 months	18.1	27.8	16.7	26.4	11.1	100.0
7–0 months	4.2	17.6	26.9	33.6	17.6	100.0
Legitimation	5.9	11.8	41.2	17.6	23.5	100.0
PERCENT BY HUSBAND'S OCCUPATION						
						Entire Sample
13+ months	9.5	18.9	16.4	10.1	8.3	13.3
12–8 months	61.9	37.7	19.7	27.5	22.2	30.0
7–0 months	23.8	39.6	52.5	58.0	58.3	49.6
Legitimation	4.8	3.8	11.5	4.4	11.1	7.1
	100.0	100.0	100.0	100.0	100.0	100.0

in these marriages apparently had miscalculated the couple's ability to marry, but not the intentions of their partners. In most respects they were more like other brides than other unwed mothers, who were at a greater disadvantage in the marriage market.[9]

Tables 5.10 and 5.11 show the marriages of 1844 and 1845 broken down by first-birth interval and the occupations of husbands and wives. Both tables show that bridal pregnancies and legitimations came from all social classes in Verviers, but they were more common among the poor. Bridal pregnancies were most common for husbands who worked in the textile industry or as day laborers and for wives who were day laborers (journalières). Legitimations came disproportionately from skilled workers and laborers.

Table 5.12 shows the household of the wife before marriage for each category of the first-birth intervals. This table shows the same predominance of residence with parents as in the population register sample.

9. As mentioned earlier, the Société de Saint François Régis feared that some legitimations were undertaken by men who were not the child's biological father. In many cases, however, legitimated children had already been recognized by their fathers at the time of birth. It is unlikely that more than a small minority of children were legitimated by men other than their biological fathers.

Table 5.11. Percentage of Marriages with a Birth, by Length of First-Birth Interval and Wife's Occupation, Marriages 1844–45

First-Birth Interval	Sans	Ménagère	Couturière	Textiles	Journalière	Other	Total
Number	18	35	41	38	81	27	240
Entire sample	7.5	14.6	17.1	15.8	33.8	11.3	100.0
PERCENT BY LENGTH OF FIRST-BIRTH INTERVAL							
							Total
13+ months	9.4	12.5	15.6	15.6	37.5	9.4	100.0
12–8 months	13.9	12.5	20.8	18.1	19.4	15.3	100.0
7–0 months	4.2	15.1	13.5	15.1	42.0	10.1	100.0
Legitimation	0.0	23.5	29.4	11.8	29.4	5.9	100.0
PERCENT BY WIFE'S OCCUPATION							
							Entire Sample
13+ months	16.7	11.4	12.2	13.2	14.8	11.1	13.3
12–8 months	55.6	25.7	36.6	34.2	17.3	40.7	30.0
7–0 months	27.8	51.4	39.0	47.4	61.7	44.4	49.6
Legitimation	0.0	11.4	12.2	5.3	6.2	3.7	7.1
	100.0	100.0	100.0	100.0	100.0	100.0	100.0

Even though 16 percent of the wives were not located in a household before their marriages, 64 percent were found living with parents. There is little difference among these categories in the tendency to live with parents. The wives with legitimated children were actually slightly more likely to have lived with parents (70.6 percent) than the entire sample (64.4 percent). It is also noteworthy that only two consensual unions were found. Consensual unions appear to have been a way of life among Parisian workers, but Belgian observers differed in their evaluations of the prevalence of consensual unions in the 1840s.[10]

In Table 5.13 we see the first household in which these couples were recorded after their marriages. The table shows a variety of living arrangements that reflect the recording practices at the time. More than half (53.0 percent) of the couples were found living completely independently. There were an additional 71 couples (30.1 percent) who were listed

10. The 1846 inquiry on working conditions and child labor specifically asked about concubinage. It was reported as rare except in Mons and Liège (Belgium, Ministère de l'intérieur, 1846, pp. 37–219). Frey (1978) estimates that concubinage was very common in Paris, but his calculations may overestimate its prevalence. Frey takes recognition at the time of birth as an indicator of cohabitation. In Verviers population registers, however, men who recognized illegitimate children are rarely listed in the same household as the mother.

Table 5.12. Composition of Wife's Household before Marriage,
by Length of First-Birth Interval, Marriages 1844–45

Wife's Household before Marriage	13+	12–8	7–0	Legitimation	Total
Number	32	71	116	17	236

PERCENT BY COMPOSITION OF
WIFE'S HOUSEHOLD BEFORE MARRIAGE

					Entire Sample
Parent	71.9	63.4	62.1	70.6	64.4
Kin	3.1	7.0	4.3	0.0	4.7
Nonkin	6.3	5.6	9.5	0.0	7.2
Own head	6.3	7.0	7.8	0.0	6.8
Consensual union	0.0	0.0	0.9	5.9	0.8
Not found	12.5	16.9	15.5	23.5	16.1
	100.0	100.0	100.0	100.0	100.0

PERCENT BY LENGTH OF
FIRST-BIRTH INTERVAL

					Total
Entire sample	13.6	30.1	49.2	7.2	100.0
Parent	15.1	29.6	47.4	7.9	100.0
Kin	9.1	45.5	45.5	0.0	100.0
Nonkin	11.8	23.5	64.7	0.0	100.0
Own head	12.5	31.3	56.3	0.0	100.0
Consensual union	0.0	0.0	50.0	50.0	100.0
Not found	10.5	31.6	47.4	10.5	100.0

as living separately in houses that contained another household headed by a parent. These households are labeled "conjugal, supported" in the table. About 10 percent of the couples were listed as the primary couple in a household that also contained parents or other kin (labeled "conjugal, extended"). Only 13 (5.5 percent) of the 236 couples located after marriage were found living as subfamilies in a household headed by another individual.

These household patterns identify the legitimation couples as the ones who were economically unprepared for marriage. When we examine the postmarital households of couples by their first birth intervals, we find little difference between the pre- and postnuptial conception couples. The likelihood of bridal-pregnancy couples to live independently was almost exactly the same as the two categories of postnuptial conceptions taken together. The couples with legitimations, however, were noticeably less likely to be independent. Only 35.3 percent of the legitimation couples

Table 5.13. Composition of Household after Marriage, by Length of First-Birth Interval, Marriages 1844–45

Household after Marriage	13 +	12–8	7–0	Legitimation	Entire Sample	Number
Conjugal, independent	64.5	49.3	54.7	35.3	53.0	125
Conjugal, supported	29.0	23.9	32.5	41.2	30.1	71
Conjugal, extended	6.5	14.1	8.6	5.9	9.8	23
Subfamily	0.0	9.9	4.3	5.9	5.5	13
Widowed/spouse absent	0.0	2.8	0.0	11.8	1.7	4
	100.0	100.0	100.0	100.0	100.0	236
Number	31	71	117	17	236	

lived independently, compared with 53.0 percent in the entire sample. Legitimation couples were 10 percent more likely to live in the same house as parents (41.2 percent compared with 30.1 percent), and 2 of the 17 wives with legitimations were found living without their husbands.

CONCLUSION

This chapter has presented an interpretive model of premarital sexual activity that attempts to account for the high levels of both bridal pregnancy and illegitimacy in nineteenth-century Verviers. Like most recent writers on this subject, the account given here emphasizes courtship behavior and the toleration of sexual activity in anticipation of marriage. Migrants to rapidly growing cities like Verviers carried with them rural courtship practices, like bundling and other forms of night courting. We can also gain insights from more recent descriptions of working-class courtship, however. This literature emphasizes the ambivalence and conflict in sexual behavior in a way that is often missing in descriptions of rural customs. By drawing our attention to the double standard, these descriptions help explain how both bridal pregnancy and illegitimacy can result from the same courtship pattern. It is not simply that social pressure succeeds in forcing the young man to marriage in one and not the other, although that is an important part of the story. Behavior associated with the double standard also increases the likelihood that women who fail in the marriage market will be forced into unwed motherhood and prostitution.

In some ways this interpretation attempts to go beyond previous historical discussions of illegitimacy. It accepts the contention of Tilly, Scott, and Cohen (1976) that urban illegitimacy patterns evolved from rural courtship patterns, but it modifies their emphasis on the social isolation of women in cities. The empirical evidence from Verviers suggests that unwed mothers

137

were not isolated from the urban community, although they were more likely to be migrants and orphans. The urban working-class community also played an important role in supporting the double standard by maintaining the cultural, social, and economic segregation of men and women. Thus, illegitimacy does not imply that men and women were free of all social control, but that community and peer groups influenced them in conflicting ways.

Similarly, I am less interested in showing the existence of the "bastardy prone sub-society" suggested by Laslett (1980b) than in asking why illegitimacy would tend to be perpetuated in certain families. Under the double standard, women who are born out of wedllock become targets for sexual exploitation. The expectations that men bring to relationships with these women make it likely that they will become unwed mothers themselves.

The scattered references of contemporaries generally indicate a tolerant attitude toward premarital sexual activity in nineteenth-century Belgium and a culture conducive to the double standard. Descriptions of the permissive attitude toward premarital sexual activity usually link this toleration to the assumption that the couple would later marry. In most respects the culture of the Belgian working class seems to have followed the classic pattern of the double standard. The roles of males and females were clearly separated, and the ubiquitous cabarets were primarily a male form of leisure. The most direct account of the double standard comes from Hubertine Ruwette in the local organ of the first International Workingmen's Association, who rebuked women of her class for tolerating and even supporting it.

The quantitative evidence from the marriage and population registers of Verviers is consistent with the courtship interpretation of bridal pregnancy and illegitimacy. The similarity in the ages of unwed mothers and pregnant and nonpregnant brides suggests that all three outcomes were part of the same pattern. Most important, of the women who conceived outside of marriage, the younger were more likely to marry than the older. This is the expected pattern in a courtship system in which sexual activity is related to bargaining position and risk-taking in the marriage market. Furthermore, the high average age of all three groups of women implies a long period of self-restraint.

The marriages with legitimations seem to identify a subgroup of unwed mothers. While the average unwed mother was slightly older than the average bride, women who legitimated children became mothers at a slightly younger age. This component of illegitimacy appears to be due to postponed marriages rather than the severe disadvantage in the marriage market, which most unwed mothers experienced. We should also note that less than a third of all illegitimate children were later legitimated.

The household patterns of women in nineteenth-century Verviers shed a little light on the role of parents in the courtship system. Since all women tended to live with parents before marriage, it is apparent that parents were not effective in preventing their daughters from being sexually active. While it is doubtful that parents accepted such behavior with equanimity, there probably was little reason for them to intervene. Parents did make a difference, however. Women living with parents were more likely to be pregnant brides than unwed mothers, and parents assisted couples who married after a child had been born.

Evidently, parents allowed their daughters to choose their own spouses, but this does not mean that parents gave up the right to approve the choices. Since the age at marriage was high and courtships were often lengthy, daughters undoubtedly knew their parents' views before they reached the stage of intimacy. Premarital pregnancy did put pressure on some parents who were obstructing marriages, but we cannot know how often this was a conscious strategy.

When we view nineteenth-century courtship as a process of personal and social bargaining, it is possible to see several paths that led to illegitimate births. First, there were cases in which both partners were committed to marriage. Children who were later legitimated by marriage appear to have resulted from sexual unions that were premature in terms of the economic resources of the couple but not in terms of their commitment to each other. These couples were younger than couples with bridal pregnancies and more likely to live with parents after the marriage. Illegitimate births resulted from miscalculation rather than lack of intention to marry. Some additional illegitimate births were due to marriages that were permanently obstructed. In these cases the intention to marry was present, at least at the time of coition, but the marriage was prevented by insurmountable economic difficulties, the death of one partner, or the unalterable opposition of parents.

Second, some young women were mistaken or misled about the intentions of their partners. There were many opportunities for misunderstandings in these relationships. Women who lacked the social resources to force their partners to marry them were more likely to be exploited, and possibly more likely to deceive themselves about the level of commitment their partners felt toward them.

Finally, we may suppose that some proportion of women chose unwed motherhood as an alternative to spinsterhood without children. Although such a woman would suffer social disapproval and economic distress when her child was young, the economic support of a child in later years may have more than offset these hardships.

In the end, I would like to return to the ambivalent role of the community in this story. Sexual activity in courtship occurred without community approval but without condemnation either. The community's primary interest was in the maintenance of the family system and the male dominance implicit in it. Premarital sexual activity did not violate these principles, especially if couples waited until they were in a position to marry. Unwed motherhood challenged both the social and economic foundations of this system, and the double standard assured that women were aware of the consequences. The father of an illegitimate child suffered disapproval, but his fate hardly compares with the burden of the unwed mother.

6

Family Economy and the Timing of Marriage

This chapter is concerned with the relationship of young women to their families of origin, in particular with their decision to marry. European marriage patterns involved the separation of young people from their families of origin and the creation of a new household. This is a critical point in the life course where the roles of young women in their families of origin may be revealed, and this chapter will look at factors affecting the timing of marriage for clues to the relationships between young women and their parents. Many writers have argued that the factory system in the nineteenth century weakened the family and undermined parental authority. If women were in fact emancipated from their parents by the urban industrial economy, the characteristics of their families of origin should have had little effect upon the timing of their marriages. If they were still deeply committed to a system of mutual family obligations, however, we should be able to see evidence of the web of obligations tying daughters to their parents and siblings.

Chapter 3 revealed the strong attachment of young women to their households of origin. Few women left their parents' homes, except by marriage, and spinsters seem to have stayed until their parents died. In this chapter a hazard model will be used to examine how household characteristics affected the likelihood of marriage. This model attempts to separate the economic characteristics of the family from the social obligations between parents and children. The results show that family considerations had important effects upon the timing of marriage. On one hand, some women postponed marriage when their mothers were widowed, and, on the other hand, older brothers helped their sisters to marry. Overall, the nuclear family placed demands upon its members which tended to delay marriage.

Late Marriage and the Social Position of Young Adults

The European pattern of late marriage creates a large number of unmarried young adults not found in other family systems. Since the full status of adulthood has traditionally been achieved only with marriage, unmarried young adults have always been in an ambiguous position. There is increasing evidence that young adults in preindustrial Europe occupied a special status between childhood and adulthood with a measure of independence and often institutions of their own. In the twentieth century the stages of life have been redefined by the formalization of education and other institutions that segregate adolescents and young adults. Nineteenth-century society was in transition between these two systems: the older institutions of youth had largely disappeared, but modern education was not yet in place.

Several writers have recently emphasized the importance of the discovery that young men and women often left their parents' homes to live and work as servants or apprentices in the homes of others (Hajnal, 1983; Wall, 1983b). John Hajnal (1983) has revised his description of the "European marriage pattern" to emphasize the importance of the movement of young adults among households. Although preindustrial households were not more likely to include extended families than modern households, they were more likely to include servants. Servants were by no means restricted to the households of the wealthy, and a high proportion of young people went into service between the ages of 15 and 20.

This system served important economic and social functions. It provided a mechanism for the redistribution of labor among families. Young people moved from families that were either too numerous or too poor in land or capital to need their labor to households that could better employ them. Servants were socialized in the behavior appropriate in a society that emphasized hierarchy and deference, and it has even been suggested that parents sent their children away because they believed that others would be more likely to discipline them (Morgan, 1966; Demos, 1970). They were also separated from their parents at the time that conflict over the transmission of property would have been most acute.

The institutions of service in rural areas and apprenticeship and journeymanship in urban areas created a stage of life and a social group between children and adults. The servants in preindustrial households were evidently quite different from the domestic servants of the nineteenth century. They were more integrated into the master's family, participating in the family meal and being subject to the moral supervision of the head of the household *in loco parentis*. Youth was defined by a role in

142

society rather than age, and the youth group often functioned as a semi-autonomous group in community festivals and rituals (Davis, 1971).

During the nineteenth century this preindustrial form of service largely disappeared. As guilds and the craft organization of production disappeared, apprentices and journeymen no longer lived in the homes of their masters. In urban areas the domestic servant became an employee, and the activities of this outsider in the home were closely watched (see Fairchilds, 1984). The older form of service persisted longer in rural areas, but there too it was replaced by wage labor. Later in the century the expansion of education imposed the rhythm of schooling on the life course and segregated young people in formal institutions (Modell, Furstenberg, and Hershberg, 1976).

Nineteenth-century writers and subsequent sociologists often concluded that industrialization, the factory system, and urbanization weakened parental authority and emancipated children from the family (see Mitterauer and Sieder, 1983, pp. 24–27). In preindustrial society the father's authority over his children was enforced by his control over the means of production. Both the peasant and the urban artisan controlled property that their children would need to establish themselves as economically self-sufficient adults. The development of wage labor removed the economic basis of patriarchal authority by making family capital in either land or craft skills irrelevant to the earning power of young people. Contemporaries, like the early sociologist of the family Frédéric Le Play (1878), feared that the basis of stable family life had been fatally weakened. Observers were particularly concerned about the moral consequences of the employment of young women in factories.

Edward Shorter is the most noted recent writer to emphasize the disruptive effects of industrialization and to focus on the importance of female participation in the wage labor force. Shorter (1973, 1977) has argued that the rising illegitimacy rates in the nineteenth century were the result of a revolution in female sexual attitudes. Their economic emancipation from the family freed women to indulge in expressive sexuality of which illegitimacy was the result. Shorter's account differs from earlier writers about family breakdown mainly in his scorn for the traditional village society and his preference for the emancipation of the individual from the family.

Most historians are skeptical of the attitudes that Shorter attributes to young women in the nineteenth century, and he has been criticized for accepting uncritically the statements of middle-class observers. Indeed, the trend in historical work has been to emphasize the continued importance of the family as an economic and social unit. The family often continued to be a unit of production in the early factories (Smelser, 1959), and the

143

opportunities available in urban areas actually increased the coresidence of children with parents. Tilly and Scott (1978) have characterized the family system of nineteenth-century workers as a "family wage economy." Under this system parents and children pooled their income in a common family fund and pursued a joint economic strategy even when the family was not the unit of production. This is presented as a historical stage between the family economy of peasant farming and craft production, when the family was a unit of production, and the "family consumer economy," when the family no longer relies upon income from children. Studies of family budgets have underlined the importance of children's income to nineteenth-century workers, especially when the father had passed the age of peak earnings (Modell, 1978; Haines, 1979b; Goldin, 1979; Alter, 1984a).

Michael Anderson (1971) suggests that the decisions of young adults in the nineteenth century were characterized by more short-run calculative self-interest than in previous generations. Although his evidence from the Lancashire textile center of Preston shows the enormous importance of the family as an economic and social unit, Anderson cites contemporary observers who pointed to growing feelings of independence among young factory workers. Children continued to be committed to the family because of the need for family assistance in critical situations, like unemployment and illness. Nevertheless, the earning power of children changed the nature of the bargain within the family toward one in which children negotiated with their parents as equals.

Anderson's interpretation involves an apparent paradox: the attitudes of young people were becoming more individualistic and calculative at the same time that their behavior was becoming more familial. He shows that children in the city of Preston were much more likely to continue to live with their parents than their counterparts in surrounding rural areas. While the young people of Preston could have interpreted this behavior differently from their rural cousins, Anderson's interpretation rests upon the comments of middle-class observers, not on the observed behavior itself. Furthermore, as Michael Katz (1975) has pointed out, Anderson approaches this issue with a theoretical framework that emphasizes transactions among family members, which may predispose him to see calculation in urban areas and normative behavior in rural areas.

In light of the higher incomes of young people and potential independence from parents, it is surprising that the age at marriage in nineteenth-century cities remained relatively high. Ages at marriage were sometimes but not always lower in urban than rural areas, at least for males, but they were still in the middle or late 20s (Knodel and Maynes, 1976). These are very late ages at marriage by almost any comparison, even twentieth-century Europe and nineteenth-century United States. European workers never fulfilled the worst fears of the Malthusians.

One nineteenth-century observer of marriage ages in Verviers offered an explanation of the late age at marriage that echoes Anderson's reports of calculative behavior, but with an important difference. A representative from the Société de Saint François Régis of Verviers told the Belgian Commission du travail in 1886: "In the working class, often egoism, the desire to conserve the earnings of children, prevents parents from consenting to the marriage of their children" (Belgium, Commission du travail, 1887, 1:1024). Thus, rather than the individualism of children, this observer emphasized the selfishness of parents. The Société de Saint François Régis was in a good position to observe this kind of behavior. They had been established to encourage the marriage of the poor, and their activities consisted primarily in assisting poor couples in gathering the legal documents needed to marry. Under the Belgian Civil Code parents could hinder their children from marrying by refusing to give consent. In the absence of parental consent a long and expensive formal procedure had to be followed before children could marry. Even so, it is hard to believe that parents could have benefited much from preventing their children's marriages if those children would simply have left home.

The evidence presented below suggests that the behavior of unmarried women was still very strongly affected by their obligation to participate in their families of origin. There may indeed have been a great deal of overtly calculative behavior, but young women appear to have deferred to their parents' wishes more often than not. In part, this occurred because female wages were too low to make them economically independent. But the evidence also suggests that women delayed their marriages because of noneconomic obligations to their parents and siblings.

Marriage for Interest and the Authority of Parents

If bourgeois contemporaries believed that workers in the nineteenth century formed liaisons with little thought for the future, they accused members of their own class of too much calculation. The conflict between sentiment and interest in marriage was the central theme in much of the literature circulating in Verviers and published in its newspapers (Alter, 1978; Evans, 1930). Liberals and Catholics agreed that wealth and fortune played too great a role in forming marriages, and even the bishop of Liège rebuked young men for treating marriage as a mercantile speculation that repairs the dissipation of youth (de Montpellier, 1867, 4:50). Books of advice urged young women and their families to pay more attention to personal qualities. As one wrote:

> Yes, a name, a fortune, decides a marriage; these sorts of alliances are the order of the day, they are even good form. It is the goods, the dignities which one seeks to unite: two families decide themselves so easily after having superficially examined and weighed a few expediencies! . . . Most men marry absolutely like one buys rents on the Bourse: for the money. (Landais, 1847, p. 41)

As well as implying the dominance of economic motives in the marriage behavior of the wealthy, this literature also reflects the control of parents over the marriages of their children. Parents played an active role in selecting spouses for their daughters, and even young men required the permission of their parents.

Although many writers condemned the selfishness and shallowness of marriage for interest, there was also a belief that equality of fortune would lead to better marriages. The most common character in fiction was the young man of fashion seeking a wealthy father-in-law, but other writers described honest doubts about unequal marriages. In one story a bankrupt merchant rejected his daughter's wealthy suitor because their inequality in wealth would lead to resentment and contempt (*Nouvelliste*, 14 August 1844, AV). In another story a law student, returning home to tell his parents of his engagement to a poor girl, worried about their response:

> Before and during his voyage, the young clerk had regarded the consent which he was going to solicit from his parents as something easy to obtain; but no sooner had he arrived in Issartieux, than his ideas changed on this point. In several discussions which he had with his father, he perceived well that his family had made sacrifices for him only in the hope that they would be recompensed one day, and that the education of their son had cost these poor people so dearly, that they would want to sell it at the same price; now, what would they say when Robequin exposed to them that all this education, all these sacrifices, he aspired to set at the feet of a girl without a dowry, if not without virtue. (*Nouvelliste*. 16 November 1844, AV)

The social convention that marriage should unite fortunes of equal size was not a new theme in the nineteenth century, nor was it limited to the bourgeoisie. A popular pamphlet, containing advice and humor for young men and women, offered this:

> When you have someone pleasing in your eyes, inform yourself of her parents, her state and her quality, so that you do not lose your time and your efforts in loving and serving her.
> Many are often fooled in this, because they look more at the beauty and at the good grace of a girl than at the comfort of her father and mother, relatives and friends, who have or should always have the will of their daughter in their hands. You ought therefore before all else to consider this and to know the

honor, condition and comfort of her parents, and if they want her to marry; think well on yourself if you are as rich as she and capable of loving her; because when the horses are equal, they pull equally and the coach advances much better. (*Nouveau trésor*, n.d., MVW; also found in *Le Catéchisme*, [1896], MVW)[1]

Marriage for love had become the ideal in the nineteenth century, but personal attraction was still regularly subordinated to material interests (Borscheid, 1986).

As the last quote implies, young women were expected to follow the advice of their parents. Parental authority was embodied in the Belgian Civil Code, which made it very difficult to marry without approval. Minors (women under age 21 and men under 25) were strictly prohibited from marrying without parental consent. Even after the age of majority, a costly and time-consuming formal procedure was required to show that parental consent had been "respectfully" requested.[2]

The presumption of parental authority in marriage among the bourgeoisie of nineteenth-century Verviers emerges clearly in the history of a young man from one of its wealthiest families. In 1856 Henri Peltzer, then living in Buenos Aires, married without the consent of his father, Henri-Edouard Peltzer. Henri had been sent to Argentina to purchase wool for the family firm, and he later wrote his brother Edouard that loneliness and isolation caused him to seek a wife (Entreprises Peltzer, letter dated 29 November 1856, No. 116, AEL). Henri married without the approval of his father, who disinherited his son for this disobedience. For the next 10 years Henri remained in Buenos Aires, in commercial correspondence with his family in Verviers but out of favor with his father. Writing to his brother in 1859, Henri reported that his father threatened "que s'il me voyait il me donnerait son pied au cul," and he asked Edouard to help him recover his inheritance (Entreprises Peltzer, letter dated 28 December 1859, No. 116, AEL). The father did eventually relent, reinstating his son's inheritance. In 1866 on the eve of his return to Europe, Henri responded with these lines:

1. The popular pamphlets of this type were reprinted many times in nineteenth-century Liège. For popular satire of the marriage for interest, see the poem in Walloon dialect "Li Mariège d'intérêt," in J. J. Dehin, *Les P'tits moumints d'plaisir* (Liège: Max Ghilain, 1848, pp. 35–36).
2. A man or woman past the age of majority could marry without parental consent only after a notary had been employed to make a formal *acte respectueux* to the parent. This presentation was repeated three times, separated by one month, and marriage was allowed one month after the third acte respectueux (Bruno, 1842, p. 215). This provision of the Civil Code was not relaxed until 1887 (De Paepe, 1887, pp. 361–70).

> I would like to finish these lines with a prayer, and that is to grant a little of your goodwill to my wife, it is now more than ten years that we have lived together and never have I reproached myself for having taken her as a companion, her only fault was to be poor and I have supplied that; Grant me, my prayer dear father, we will have nothing else to truly desire, and we will be so happy, in the meanwhile I embrace you
> with all my heart
> your son Henri
> (Entreprises Peltzer, letter dated 25 March 1866, No. 87, AEL)

Despite these touching words, Henri Peltzer's offense was probably not the poverty of his wife but his independent decision to marry. Another brother, August, advised Edouard that wealth was not the primary quality he should seek in a wife.

> One thing certain my dear Edouard is that if you marry a wealthy woman, papa will be, perhaps flattered at first, but if she is not able to make agreeable conversation he will soon find that it is not so beautiful! On the contrary, the good qualities of his daughter-in-law will soon pardon the lack of a fortune, especially if these qualities contribute to making his life enjoyable.
> It seems to me, then, that there is not so much to hesitate about regarding the fortune as far as this might upset papa. Papa who loves us so much at heart will find great satisfaction in our happiness. (Entreprises Peltzer, letter dated 19 March 1857, No. 116, AEL)

In linking parental authority and marriage for interest, I do not mean to suggest that parents were solely motivated by economic gain or that overt conflict necessarily arose between parents and children. However, parents took a less romantic view of future sons-in-law than did their daughters, and they could be expected to examine the economic impact of a marriage on the entire family. It is reasonable to suppose that most daughters acknowledged the authority of their parents in this important decision. After all, young women shared the values of their parents and believed, like August Peltzer, that their parents would find satisfaction in their future happiness.

Marriage and Departure from the Family of Origin

Judith Blake has argued that most parents would prefer to delay the marriages of their children (Blake-Davis, 1967). As long as parents benefit from the labor of their children, they will resist relinquishing that labor to another household. Blake argues that religious considerations often outweigh the benefits that parents derive from their children, as in Asian societies where ages at marriage are very low. We might add that parents would be less likely to oppose the marriage of a child who would continue to live with them in a joint family household. In nineteenth-century Europe, however, parents had little to gain from the marriages of their children; they lost not only the labor of their children but also the family capital given as dowries.

Robert Roberts (1973) remembers that working-class parents in Salford, England, were reluctant to lose their adult children.

> Teenagers in the slums could find courtship extremely difficult. Too early an interest in sex might be condemned by parents just feeling the benefit of a new wage-earning son or daughter. Most Edwardian elders in the lower working class, taking over still another prerogative unchanged from the previous century, looked upon it as a natural right that children after leaving school, should work to compensate parents for all the "kept" years of childhood. Early marriage robbed them, they felt, of their just rewards. (p. 52)

We may assume that children chafed at this control, but Roberts emphasizes their strong attachment to family life.

Parents with marriageable children would have been very much aware of the economic contributions of their children. Nineteenth-century family budget studies show that families with working-age children were in a very favorable economic position. The incomes of children more than compensated for the declining earning power of the father (Haines, 1979b). We might expect that the amount of available family labor would have affected the willingness of parents to relinquish a woman at her most productive age. They would have found it easier to release her when the household included other children of working age and harder when other children were too young to work. Paul Spagnoli (1983, p. 239) has written: "Families which were barely making ends meet had every incentive to retain at home as many producers as possible as long as they could. This is the essential explanation of the pattern of late marriage in the Lille region."

The obligation to provide dowries would also have tended to make heads of households delay the marriages of their daughters. Dowries were the first step in the division of the capital accumulated by a couple over the course of their married life. Indeed, under the Belgian Civil Code, which was derived from the Napopleonic Code, a dowry was legally part of a child's inheritance. The longer daughters and sons contributed to the accumulation of family capital by working for the family rather than to the dispersion of its capital by their marriages, the larger the shares to be divided among the children and the parents in their old age. Both parents and siblings had an interest in delaying this division.

The effect of dowering on marriage probably varied considerably among social classes. Although we have little information about the size of dowries in nineteenth-century Verviers, they were undoubtedly important among the bourgeoisie. Daughters of the working classes probably earned their own dowries, however, and this factor may have been less important for them. Guillaume's evidence from nineteenth-century Bordeaux, where marriage contracts were common in all social classes, shows that many brides brought small amounts of personal property to their marriages (P. Guillaume, 1972). Daumard (1970, p. 132) found that even among Parisian boutiquiers 30 percent had received no property from the family of either husband or wife.

The most dramatic change in the family economy occurred when one parent died, and this could have greatly affected the social contract between a daughter and her remaining parent and siblings. On one hand, she would have been under increased pressure to forego her own marriage to help provide income to a widowed mother or to provide domestic services to a widowed father. On the other hand, the death of a parent might hasten the dissolution of the household. The surviving family might not be economically viable, and children would be encouraged to leave by the division of the inheritance.

We should also consider noneconomic obligations within the family of origin. A common theme in the folklore about marriage warns fathers that they should not allow the *cadette* to marry before her older sister (Monseur, 1892; Vandereuse, 1940–48). A marriage out of birth order was assumed to reflect badly on the elder sister and reduce her chances of ever marrying. Daniel Scott Smith (1973) detected evidence of this kind of behavior in his study of Hingham, Massachusetts, in the eighteenth and nineteenth centuries. He found a marked increase in the proportion of daughters marrying out of birth order in the late eighteenth century, which corresponds to other indicators that parental control over the marriages of their children was declining at that time. Bonnie Smith (1981, p. 60) also found that daughters rarely married out of birth order in the tightly controlled marriage system of the bourgeoisie in northern France.

Finally, the timing of a woman's marriage was also affected by the availability of suitable spouses. European marriages have always been subject to the condition that spouses should be roughly equal in wealth and social standing. Women from different social classes were in different marriage markets and responded to the availability of marriageable men with appropriate social positions. We should remember that social endogamy is usually considered something that parents demanded from their children.

FEMALE EMPLOYMENT AND THE DECISION TO MARRY

Textile cities like Verviers offered a young woman more employment opportunities than other nineteenth-century communities, and her ability to find outside employment must have affected her decision to marry. A simple economic framework is helpful in relating employment opportunities to the decision to marry. Like many economic models it predicts two contradictory tendencies. On one hand, young women could have decided that their earning power made them more independent of men. On the other hand, employment before marriage could have been used to accumulate the capital needed to start a new household at an earlier age.

Most of the writers in the "New Home Economics" have described the decision to marry as a choice between the costs and benefits of marriage and those of unmarried life (Becker, 1973, 1974; Preston and Richards, 1975). In this view marriage involves a bargain in which the woman typically withdraws from the labor force to specialize in home production and rely upon her husband for money income. This is usually advantageous because his wage rate is higher than hers, whereas she has been trained for higher productivity in the home. Consequently, marriage becomes more attractive as the differential between male and female incomes increases. When female wage rates approach male wage rates, the incentive to marry is reduced, and marital instability is likely to increase. Other things being equal, women with jobs ought to find marriage less attractive than those who are not in the labor force.

This model is in obvious contradiction to a common feature of marriage patterns for the last two centuries: the positive correlation between male income and ages at marriage of both men and women. In Verviers the average age at marriage for the daughters of the economic elite (27.4) was more than a year older than the average for all women (26.1).[3] Since women from bourgeois families, like the elite in Verviers, did not work before or after marriage, the differential between the male and female incomes in this social group was at a maximum, but these women married later than women from the working classes, who did work. This comparison underlines the importance of separating economic factors from the consequences of social endogamy in a stratified society.

While most recent economic models of marriage view female earnings as a factor reducing the tendency to marry, nineteenth-century writers more often linked women's work to earlier marriage. From Malthus onward, writers worried about the early marriage of the poor, argued that employment opportunities for women encouraged them to marry (Tilly, 1978). For example, a Belgian legislator told the Chambre des représentants in 1849: "The ease that women have in earning their livelihood in cities is the determining motive in a crowd of marriages. . . . Each shuttle, each wheel, each hammer constitutes a sort of petty capital employed to nourish a family" (Coomans, [1849]). In this view women who worked

3. Estimates were computed by the life table method from the linked samples for the elite and random samples. See Table 6.1.

were likely to marry earlier, because it was easier for them to accumulate the capital needed to start a new household (see also Ogle, 1890). In other words, working women were better able to dower themselves. There is an overtone of Malthusian fear of improvident marriages in these writers, but it seems likely that young women did save their earnings to build the capital of the household that they would form.

Thus, we have two opposing tendencies linking female employment to marriage. In one view, female employment makes marriage a less desirable alternative. In the other view, female employment makes it easier for women to build the savings needed to start a household.

The Timing of Marriage

The problem of censored observations in the population register makes it necessary to use life table techniques to reconstruct the timing of marriage in the linked samples. Table 6.1 shows the reconstruction of marriage rates and the number unmarried at each age. The second and third columns of the table show the number of person-years of observation and marriages of unmarried women derived from the population register. The ratio of marriages to person-years is the marriage rate shown in column four. The life table probability of marriage (q_x) in the next column is a transformation of the marriage rate into the cohort model of the life table. This probability is the proportion of women entering each age group who marry in the next five years. Column six follows a cohort of 100,000 women from age 15 to age 55 by showing the number of women who are still unmarried at each age.[4]

The last column of Table 6.1 shows the movement from unmarried to married for the part of a hypothetical cohort that eventually marries. This column was derived by subtracting the number unmarried at age 55, in the previous column, from the population under consideration. This transformation is useful in computing an expected age at marriage, which is 26.06 years for this population.

The life table procedure tends to overestimate the proportion of women who never married, because it includes young migrants who had come to Verviers to work, but returned to their homes to marry. These women are included in the denominator of the marriage rate, but their marriages are not counted in the numerator. The estimate that 29.6 percent of all women would be unmarried at age 50 is higher than the observed proportions unmarried at older ages. In the linked sample 26.0 percent of person-years between ages 45 and 50 were spent unmarried, and in a random

4. See Watkins and McCarthy, 1980, for a similar analysis of the village of La Hulpe.

Table 6.1. Life Table Estimates of Number Married, by Age, and Expected
Age at Marriage, Linked Random Sample, 1849–80

					Life Table Estimates	
					Number Unmarried:	
	Observed			Probability of Marriage (q_x)	of All Women (l_x)	of Ever Married (l_x)
Age	Person-Years	Marriages	Marriage Rate			
15	615.46	8	0.0129	.0640	100,000	100,000
20	1,235.08	91	0.0736	.3078	93,600	90,902
25	947.44	72	0.0759	.3149	64,789	49,950
30	542.05	32	0.0590	.2521	44,387	20,949
35	343.15	3	0.0087	.0425	33,197	5,043
40	286.91	2	0.0069	.0342	31,786	3,037
45	142.18	1	0.0070	.0342	30,699	1,492
50	29.85	0	0.0000	.0000	29,649	0
55					29,649	0

Expected age at marriage: 26.06

sample from the 1866–80 register this proportion was 23.1 percent. The
census of 1866, however, reported only 17.2 percent of this age group as
unmarried. The population register samples appear to be biased toward
the inclusion of spinsters, who were apparently less mobile than women
who married. Since the number unmarried at age 55 is subtracted before
age at marriage is calculated in Table 6.1, the expected age at marriage is
not very much affected by this bias.

Marriage in nineteenth-century Verviers was similar to the "European
marriage pattern" described by Hajnal and others: marriage was late and a
high proportion never married (Hajnal, 1965; Knodel and Maynes, 1976).
The average age at marriage estimated from the population register data is
lower than the average age at marriage of 28.6, which Lesthaeghe provides
at the same time for all of Belgium. But his estimates are based upon
proportions unmarried in censuses rather than on actual cohorts, a method
that yields a higher age at marriage in Verviers as well[5] (Lesthaeghe, 1977,
p. 46).

5. Singulate mean ages at marriage for Verviers estimated from proportions single, by
age, in the censuses for 1846 and 1866—27.83 and 27.16, respectively—are also higher than
those estimated from the population register samples (Belgium, Ministère de l'intérieur,
1849, 1872). The average age of women in the marriages that took place in Verviers in
1844 and 1845 was 25.9. This suggests that the singulate mean age at marriage tends to
overestimate the age at marriage, probably because of the inclusion of unmarried migrants at
younger ages. Since these women are not present at older ages, the effect of their presence
is not corrected by subtracting the proportion unmarried at older ages, as is done with the
population register data.

It is also interesting to note that marriages in Verviers were spread widely between ages 20 and 35 and not strongly clustered at a few modal ages. Fewer than 10 percent of all marriages took place before age 20, and at age 25 half of those who would ever marry were still single. Women between the ages of 30 and 35 were still very much in the marriage market. The chance that a 30-year-old woman would marry in the next five years was 25 percent. This is not much lower than the peak probability of 31 percent five years earlier (cf. Watkins and McCarthy, 1980).

HAZARD MODEL OF MARRIAGE

The hazard model presented here attempts to capture the factors affecting marriage discussed above. These estimates were constructed by following unmarried women over time, and using the characteristics of their households to explain their propensity to marry. Each life history is divided into intervals of different lengths.[6] The statistical procedure estimates how different variables affected the probability that an interval would end in marriage (Alter, 1984b). The variables in the model examine the effects of age, occupation, unwed motherhood, migration, and family composition.[7] Table 6.2 shows estimates for two subpopulations in the sample: unmarried women aged 15–39 and unmarried women aged 15–29. Although there are very few differences between these two sets of estimates, both are presented to show that they are not sensitive to differences in the behavior of younger and older women. In the text that follows I shall refer to the coefficients estimated for unmarried women aged 15–39. A positive estimated coefficient indicates that the variable in question tended to increase the probability that a woman would marry.

The first group of variables in the model examines changes in the probability of marriage with age. The variable identifying women aged 15–19 has been omitted from the model, so that this category serves as a reference group. The coefficients estimated for older women compare them with women aged 15–19. The estimated coefficients show that the probability of marriage increased after age 20 (1.808, 1.884, and 1.612 for ages 20–24, 25–29, and 30–34, respectively) and remained high until age 35 was reached (− 0.332 for ages 35–39). The pattern in these coefficients re-

6. See Chapter 2 for an introduction to hazard analysis. The data set used in the analysis presented here did not use changes in household composition to mark the boundaries of intervals, but subsequent analysis, in which the death or migration of a parent was added as an event, produced substantially the same results.

7. The coefficients in the estimated hazard model represent independent effects in a multiplicative model.

Table 6.2. Estimated Coefficients and Standard Errors for a Hazard Model of the Determinants of Marriage in the Linked Random Sample, 1849–80

	Unmarried 15–39		Unmarried 15–29	
	Coeff.	S.E.	Coeff.	S.E.
Grand mean	−5.407*	0.603	−5.126*	0.737
Age				
(15–19 omitted)				
20–24	1.808*	0.382	1.764*	0.384
25–29	1.884*	0.405	1.810*	0.409
30–34	1.612*	0.441		
35–39	−0.332	0.709		
Occupation of household head				
(Textiles and Skilled omitted)				
Bourgeois	−0.426	0.344	−0.407	0.397
Petty bourgeois	0.152	0.229	0.223	0.247
Journalier	0.386	0.303	0.473	0.308
NA	−0.222	0.200	−0.263	0.217
Occupation of woman in sample				
(Ménagère omitted)				
Bourgeois, none	0.174	0.306	0.076	0.369
Couturière, skilled	−0.302	0.244	−0.257	0.267
Textiles, journalière	0.225	0.221	0.302	0.244
Servant	−0.129	0.265	−0.224	0.298
Own children	−0.861*	0.398	−1.846*	0.722
Migrant	−0.084	0.209	−0.285	0.249
Kin in household, by age				
Siblings, 0–14	0.048	0.146	−0.037	0.157
Male, 15–64	0.348	0.193	0.575*	0.232
Female, 15–64	0.228	0.180	0.013	0.258
65+	0.447*	0.212	0.584*	0.249
Parents present				
(Both parents present omitted)				
Father only	0.390	0.289	0.204	0.354
Mother only	0.309	0.256	0.480	0.290
None	0.949*	0.275	0.950*	0.370
Adult siblings in household				
Brothers, ages 15+				
Older	−0.196	0.208	−0.379	0.251
Younger	−0.344	0.221	−0.576*	0.260
Sisters, ages 15+				
Older	−0.303	0.203	−0.064	0.286
Younger	−0.146	0.210	0.084	0.283

* Coefficient is twice its standard error.

155

produces the transition rates from unmarried to married that we observed in the life table analysis of marriage above (Table 6.1).

The second group of variables examines the effect of the occupation of the head of household on a woman's age at marriage.[8] In this case women are compared with those who lived in households headed by a skilled worker or a person employed in the textile industry. As we would expect, women from the bourgeoisie were less likely to marry (-0.426), although the estimated coefficient is not statistically significant. There is also some evidence that women in the households of day laborers were more likely to marry (0.386).

The effect of the woman's own occupation was considerably more complex. The reader will recall that an economic model predicts two opposing effects of female employment. On one hand, female employment might have made women more independent and reduced the likelihood of marriage. On the other hand, women who worked were in a better position to accumulate savings so that they could marry earlier. The estimated hazard model compares women with different occupations with women who were reported as ménagères. None of these results are statistically significant, so they do not merit a high degree of confidence, but they are sufficiently interesting to deserve comment.

Employment in the main working-class occupations tended to lead to earlier marriage. Women who worked in the textile industry or as unskilled day laborers (journalières) were more likely to marry than women who worked in their homes. (The coefficient is 0.225 in Table 6.2.) This positive effect probably resulted from their ability to save toward marriage. Other female occupations provide interesting contrasts, however, and at least one type of occupation, couturière, was associated with later marriage.

The category of bourgeois occupations includes women who reported themselves as négociantes (merchants) or rentières as well as those who reported themselves as without an occupation (sans profession). The hazard estimates indicate that these women were more likely to marry (0.174) than ménagères. Women who reported themselves as négociantes were probably daughters who had succeeded to the family business. They would have been more likely to marry for three reasons. First, their wealth made them attractive marriage partners. Second, women were at a considerable disadvantage in the business world, and they must have encountered many difficulties in running their businesses (see also Smith, B. G., 1981, pp. 46–47). Finally, women in the bourgeoisie acquired social standing

8. An individual's occupation was recorded only once in each population register, either when the register was opened or when the person migrated into the city.

as wives, not through their own efforts in the marketplace (cf. Daumard, 1970, p. 185). The positive effect of these occupations is interesting in light of the general tendency of the bourgeoisie to marry later.

The category of female occupations most similar to the male petty bourgeoisie is predominantly composed of courturières (82 percent) and modistes (11 percent), although it also includes women who were boutiquières, cabaretières, etc. The occupations in this category were socially equivalent to male artisans and shopkeepers, like butchers and bakers. The estimated hazard coefficients indicate that these women were less likely to marry than ménagères (-0.302). Perhaps, these occupations gave women a degree of economic independence. Wages were not necessarily higher than factory work or day labor, but because these women were potentially self-employed, the occupations held a unique place in the female economic order.

Servants also tended to be less likely to marry than other women (-0.129). This is the kind of effect that we expect, given the social position of servants. But we are also less confident about these results, because the servants in this longitudinal sample were not necessarily representative of all servants in the city. Furthermore, servants were rarely drawn from the native population of Verviers, and women from rural areas may have returned to their homes to be married. Their marriages would not have been recorded in the registers in Verviers.

The "own children" variable identifies women who had given birth to one or more illegitimate children. Chapter 5 discussed the frequency of premarital sexual activity in Verviers and its implications. Unwed mothers were not rejected by their families. Nevertheless, the double standard of male and female morality was deeply embedded in the culture, and unwed mothers were clearly disapproved. Mothers of illegitimate children were apparently at a significant disadvantage in the marriage market (-0.861). We know from other evidence that they often did marry, usually to the fathers of their children. It seems likely that those who eventually married did so quickly, and that women who could not marry the fathers of their children were much less likely to marry later.

Women who migrated to Verviers as adults also were less likely to marry, as the "migrant" variable shows (-0.084). This variable identifies those who entered Verviers after age 15. The effect is not particularly strong, however. Many adult migrants came with their families, and they were assimilated into the city's social system. Women who came by themselves, like servants, were at more of a disadvantage, but they often returned home after a short stay.

The variables showing the effects of family structure on marriage have been divided into three groups. First, a group of variables describes the number of coresiding kin by age. Second, variables describe whether the woman's parents were present in her household. Third, older and younger adult siblings are identified by sex. These three types of variables attempt to distinguish the characteristics of the household as a labor force from the social obligations among parents and children and siblings.

The first group of variables describes the coresident kin within the household by age and sex. These variables were included to measure the labor force potential of the household. In the prime working ages, 15–64, males and females were separated to reflect differences in their earnings and work roles. All of the estimated coefficients for these variables are positive, indicating that every type of kin tended to increase the probability of marriage. It was particularly surprising to find that the coefficient for siblings under age 15 is positive (0.048). Children in Verviers usually entered the labor force between ages 12 and 14, but experiments with other variables did not reveal a negative effect even for children under 10 years old. If young children were an economic burden to the family, they should have delayed the marriages of their older sisters. It seems that young children were not a major drain of resources. Overall, these estimates suggest that women found it easier to leave large households, and crowding in large families may also have encouraged them to marry.

The variables describing residence with parents compare women who lived with both parents with those who lived with widowed fathers or mothers and those who had no coresident parents. The estimates suggest that the death of either parent tended to make marriage more likely. Women living without parents were most likely to marry (0.949), followed by women with widowed fathers (0.390), and then women with widowed mothers (0.309).

It is important to remember, however, that the hazard model entails a comparison between women who lived with widowed mothers and women who lived with both parents as though the two different households had the same labor-force potential. In effect, this comparison adds another male relative to the household of a widowed mother to replace the late father. Since the father's labor was lost when he died, we may want to subtract the labor of an adult male from the households of women with widowed mothers. In other words, the total effect of the father's death consists of both the effect of living with a widowed mother and the loss of the father's earnings. This total effect is computed by subtracting the coefficient for a working-age male (0.348) from the coefficient for living with a widowed mother (0.309) (see Table 6.3). The result of this computation is negative (-0.039), which suggests that a father's death would indeed have tended to reduce his daughter's chance of marrying. The same computa-

Table 6.3. Estimated Effects of Widowed Parents on Marriage in the Estimated Hazard Model of Marriage

	Widowhood Effect	Labor-Force Effect	Total Effect
Unmarried women, 15–39			
Surviving father	0.390	0.228	0.162
Surviving mother	0.309	0.348	−0.039
Unmarried women, 15–29			
Surviving father	0.204	0.013	0.191
Surviving mother	0.480	0.575	−0.095

tion for a mother's death has a positive result (0.162), however, suggesting a lower level of obligation to widowed fathers than widowed mothers. Thus, the loss of family labor when a parent died was enough to keep a daughter in the household after her father's death, but not after the death of her mother.

These estimates seem to show the strength of attachments within the nuclear family. Women married earlier when released from these obligations by the death of a parent. Widows were probably more in need of help than widowers, and we find that daughters of widowed mothers were less likely to marry than daughters of widowed fathers. Although daughters were undoubtedly called upon to assume the domestic responsibilities of their late mothers, widowers often remarried. A father who remarried would not only replace the domestic labor of his late wife, he would also create a new family situation which would tend to release his daughters from their obligations to him. Similarly, a young woman might have felt a strong obligation to her widowed mother, but her earnings alone would not have made the household economically viable. Ultimately, her mother would have been better off as part of the household of a married child.

The last two pairs of variables examine the effects of siblings of marriageable ages (15 or older). The estimates show that women living with older sisters or younger brothers tended to delay marriage (−0.303 and −0.344). Women with older brothers or younger sisters were also less likely to marry, but these effects were smaller (−0.196 and −0.146). These coefficients tell only part of the story, however. Since adult siblings also enter the hazard model as family labor, they have two ways to affect the probability of marriage: as older or younger siblings and as alternative sources of family labor. Table 6.4 shows the effects of both siblings and the total effect calculated by adding them together. It reveals that the total effects of siblings vary by both sex and birth order. Older brothers facilitated marriage (0.152), because they increased the family's

Table 6.4. Estimated Effects of Siblings on Marriage in the Estimated
Hazard Model of Marriage

	Sibling Effect	Labor-Force Effect	Total Effect
Unmarried women, 15–39			
Older brother	−0.196	0.348	0.152
Younger brother	−0.344	0.348	0.004
Older sister	−0.303	0.228	−0.075
Younger sister	−0.146	0.228	0.082
Unmarried women, 15–29			
Older brother	−0.379	0.575	0.196
Younger brother	−0.576	0.575	−0.001
Older sister	−0.064	0.013	−0.051
Younger sister	0.084	0.013	0.097

labor resources. Older sisters hindered marriage (−0.075), because their labor-force effect was smaller than the effect of birth order, but younger sisters increased the likelihood of marriage (0.082).

Table 6.4 shows that both economic and social obligations governed the relationships among siblings. Women appear to have obtained support from older brothers. In the case of sisters, however, economic considerations were subordinated to an overall family strategy in which sisters married in birth order. The young woman who deferred her marriage in favor of an older sister made a considerable sacrifice to the values of family and parental authority.

CONCLUSION

In contrast to the individualism and independence that Michael Anderson and others have attributed to young people in nineteenth-century cities, the evidence from Verviers emphasizes the persistence of parental authority (Anderson, 1971; Shorter, 1977). Observers often said that workers considered large families a source of prosperity. The desire to retain the earnings of adult children could easily have aroused the *égoïsme* of parents who refused to consent to marriages (Belgium, Commission du travail, 1887).

There is some evidence in the estimated hazard model that brothers helped their sisters and vice versa, but the marriage patterns of women in nineteenth-century Verviers did not evolve primarily from the balancing of needs and services among parents and children. Rather, the moral obligations within the family often overshadowed its economic functions. The family seems to have operated as a joint enterprise which was dissolved when one of its founders died. How else do we interpret the finding that women living with both parents were less likely to marry than those who lived with a widowed father or on their own? Furthermore, one is inclined to doubt that the cadettes would have deferred to the marriages of their older sisters without parental pressure.

The evidence presented here does not suggest that delayed marriage was primarily a response to demographic crises within families caused by the high level of mortality in nineteenth-century Verviers. There is some evidence that family hardship delayed marriage, since women from larger families were more likely to marry. For example, a woman who lived with both parents would have been less likely to marry after her father's death because of the loss of his earnings. However, the death of a mother tended to increase the likelihood of marriage, and in families with equal resources women were less likely to marry if both of their parents were alive.

In contrast to the picture painted by Anderson and most previous authors, the families of Verviers seem to have been characterized by strong parental authority and the deference of adult daughters to the wishes of their parents. The results presented here cannot preclude the possibility that a new sense of individualism and calculation entered the relationships between daughters and parents in nineteenth-century Verviers. Indeed, the subjective interpretation of family behavior probably did change when families entered the cities, although the calculation and self-interest in rural families is often underestimated. The important point is that adult daughters acted as if their parents had first claim on their labor and their actions were subject to parental approval. This stands in sharp contrast to the situation today, when parents pay for advanced educations and expect little in return from unmarried children. In the terms that John Caldwell (1982) has recently introduced, the "net intergenerational flow of wealth" in nineteenth-century Verviers went from adult children to their parents. This does not mean that daughters ever repaid the expenses of their childhood or that the relationship should be viewed as primarily economic, but it does suggest that their families were neither individualistic nor child-centered.

The women of nineteenth-century Verviers seem remarkably similar to the working daughters in Hong Kong interviewed by Janet Salaff. Salaff (1981) has recorded how these young women delay their marriages in order to make economic contributions vital to the social strategies of their families—strategies that revolve around the education and prospects of sons not daughters. While Salaff notes that outside earnings give daughters both an increase in personal freedom and more prestige within the family, these gains are closely circumscribed. The loyalty of these young women is particularly noticeable because they face both the attractions of modern life encountered at work and Hong Kong's patrilineal culture with its unequal treatment of sons and daughters. Salaff writes, "Each woman reconciled her obligations to her family with the pull of nonfamilial opportunities in a different manner, yet each did so in favor of the family" (p. 120).

7

Fertility and Family Limitation

In all societies in the past the life of a married woman was structured by the rhythm of childbearing. From marriage to menopause married women gave birth at regular intervals and structured their lives around the demands of pregnancy and childrearing. The regularity of childbearing was punctuated by the deaths of children and stopped short by the deaths of spouses. In the late nineteenth century this biological regularity yielded to human control, creating a new area of personal control and freedom. In the 1870s beginnings of family limitation are discernible among the women of Verviers.

Research in historical demography has been important in redefining the way in which we think about the demographic transition. Historical research on Europe, especially the European Fertility Project (Coale and Watkins, 1986), has rejected theories that describe fertility decline as a direct response to economic and social development. In nineteenth-century Europe there was no clear association between regional patterns of fertility decline and industrialization or urbanization (Knodel and van de Walle, 1979). Socioeconomic development does help describe differences within regions. For example, rural areas usually lagged behind cities. But similar populations in different cultural regions began the fertility transition many years apart, as Ronald Lesthaeghe (1977) has shown in Belgium. These results have pointed toward theories of cultural diffusion, in which fertility decline follows the spread of new attitudes about the family or the feasibility of contraception.

While patterns of geographic diffusion have been well documented, there are still few studies of transitional populations describing the diffusion of fertility decline at the community level, and most of the available community-level studies have focused on rural populations. The population register samples from Verviers allow us to examine differential fertility in an urban population during the first stage of the fertility transition. An additional sample from the cohort of women born 1805–19 makes it possi-

163

ble to compare the patterns of this transitional cohort with patterns before the fertility transition had begun.

This chapter will address several different issues. First, what was the distribution of fertility across the woman's life course? Sophisticated techniques are needed to identify subtle changes in childbearing behavior related to deliberate family limitation, but they may detract from our appreciation of the importance of childbearing in individual and family lives. The chapter begins, therefore, with an examination of the number of children per woman by age. This draws our attention to the continued importance of the Malthusian checks on population growth, high mortality and late marriage, even in the mid-nineteenth century.

Next we turn to the relationship between childbearing and the economic goals of the family. A continuing theme in the study of declining fertility has been the economic contribution of working children to the family. John Caldwell (1982) has recently revived this line of argument in the framework of a general theory of changing attitudes and behaviors associated with the fertility transition. These arguments seem to be particularly relevant to Verviers, where large numbers of children were employed in the textile factories.

This issue is considered here in a life course framework, in which it is recognized that childbearing does not take place immediately and that earlier and later children may play different economic and social roles. Considering the ages at which children began to work, it seems unlikely that children's earnings actually offset the investments that parents made in their early years. Nevertheless, the timing of children's labor-force participation suggests another perspective. The earnings from children began to be important as a couple neared the end of the childbearing years, and the extended coresidence of unmarried children could continue these benefits into the parents' old age. Thus, large families might have appeared economically beneficial across the life course, because high-parity children were subsidized by their older siblings and later prevented family income from declining as the parents aged.

In the next section the nature of the fertility decline is examined directly by comparing the fertility of women born 1805–19 with the transitional cohort born 1826–35. We find that the level of fertility in Verviers was actually rising at the time that family limitation began to be practiced, and the evidence suggests that breastfeeding had less effect on birth intervals in the later cohort. The origins of fertility decline are then sought in differences among groups defined by occupation, literacy, and age at migration to the city. Each of these variables has a long career in demographic history. Contrary to expectations, however, neither occupation nor literacy are important in identifying couples in the vanguard of the fertility

Table 7.1. Mean Number of Children Ever Born, by Age and Marital
Duration, Linked Random Sample

Age	Marital Duration (in years)						
	0–4	5–9	10–14	15–19	20–24	25–29	30+
15–19	0.52						
20–24	1.02	2.46					
25–29	1.23	2.98	4.12				
30–34	1.12	2.96	4.58	6.32			
35–39	1.40	2.87	4.21	5.95	7.28		
40–44	1.68	2.50	4.10	5.04	7.00	10.00	
45–49		2.24	2.86	4.11	5.60	9.33	
50–54			2.53	3.77	5.38	7.86	13.00
Entire sample	1.15	2.91	4.23	5.21	6.28	8.71	13.00
Number of							
Person-Years	795	792	698	527	344	47	3

transition in Verviers. Urban background, however, was a very important characteristic of couples practicing family limitation. This finding is remarkably similar to the "two generation urbanite" pattern observed in the United States (Goldberg, 1959, 1960; Duncan, 1965). Goldberg shows that rural migrants to urban areas in the U.S. continued to have higher fertility than urban natives living in the same cities. This suggests that socialization in a new cultural pattern emerging in the city was the most important factor in spreading the small-family pattern.

AGE AND FAMILY SIZE

Although fertility control was beginning to be practiced in Verviers in the 1870s, this practice was by no means the only factor affecting family sizes in mid-nineteenth-century Verviers. To a large extent the Malthusian "positive" and "preventive" checks, high mortality and late marriage, were still the factors most responsible for family sizes as the demographic transition began. Some women did bear and rear eight or more children, but only when they married relatively early and were fortunate in escaping early deaths. More often, early widowhood and high infant and child mortality prevented families from becoming large.

Malthus's *Essay on the Principle of Population* set the tone for the population debate for most of the nineteenth century, and the call for late marriage as a prudential response to the economic demands of parenthood was often repeated in Belgium. There is no evidence that couples consciously delayed their marriages in order to have smaller families, but late marriage did substantially reduce family sizes. The effect of late marriage

165

Table 7.2. Mean Number of Births, Child
Deaths, and Surviving Children,
for Currently Married Women in
the Linked Sample

Age	Births	Deaths	Survivals
15–19	0.47	0.00	0.47
20–24	1.18	0.15	1.03
25–29	2.11	0.24	1.88
30–34	3.13	0.55	2.59
35–39	4.28	0.88	3.40
40–44	5.16	1.28	3.89
45–49	5.13	1.37	3.79
50–54	6.17	1.34	4.83

is apparent in Table 7.1, which examines average numbers of children ever born, by age and marital duration. There was a strong relationship between number of children ever born and marital duration at each age. The average birth interval was about 27 months, so each additional five years of marriage increased family size by about two children. (See Table 7.6 below.) The decline of fertility at older ages is also apparent. After age 35 the pace of childbearing slowed, and women who married late did not recapture the time that had been lost. At ages 45–49 women who had been married for 10–14 years averaged only 2.9 children, while those who reached the same marital duration by ages 30–34 had 4.6 children.

High mortality also conspired to reduce family size in nineteenth-century Verviers. Crowded and unsanitary conditions made the city a particularly unhealthy place for most of the century. In 1846 the expectation of life at birth was only 32 years with particularly high infant and child mortality (Alter, 1978). Mortality began slowly improving after 1850, and the expectation of life at birth was 42 years in the families of women in the sample from the 1866–80 population register. But it was not until the 1870s, when clean water from the new dam at Gilleppe reached the city, that mortality decline began to accelerate. The consequences of high mortality for family size are apparent in Table 7.2. The average married woman had experienced more than one child death by age 40.

As a consequence of late marriage and high mortality, achieved family sizes were by no means large in the 1870s. The average married woman over age 40 had fewer than four surviving children (see Tables 7.2 and 7.3). Figure 7.1 shows that families of seven and eight survivors were not uncommon, but they were far from the rule. It is also significant to note in Table 7.3 the similarities in family size across the four samples. The average number of coresident children per married woman aged 45–49

Table 7.3. Number of Surviving Children, by Age,
for Currently Married Women in the
Samples

Age	Cohort of 1805–19	Cohort of 1826–35		
		Unlinked	Linked	Elite
15–19			0.5	0.9
20–24			1.0	1.8
25–29			1.9	2.5
30–34	2.5	2.5	2.6	3.1
35–39	2.6	2.9	3.4	3.3
40–44	3.3	3.2	3.9	2.9
45–49	3.0	3.1	3.8	3.0
50–54		2.8	4.8	[a]

[a] Data have been omitted because the sample was
too small to be meaningful.

was close to three in the unlinked sample of the 1826–35 cohort as well as
in the elite sample and the sample from the 1805–19 cohort. The linked
cohort shows slightly larger family sizes at older ages apparently becuase
of selectivity among the small number of women linked to older ages.

Although family size appears relatively unchanged between the 1805–
19 and the 1826–35 cohorts, the analysis below will show that this similarity hides significant differences in behavior between these groups. The
small family size achieved by the earlier cohort reflects both lower fertility
and higher mortality earlier in the century. Age-specific fertility rates were
lower and birth intervals tended to be longer. The mortality observed in
this sample in the years 1850–54 was relatively low, but this period of
observation follows the cholera epidemic of 1849. Women in this sample
undoubtedly lost children in that epidemic, which was particularly serious for children. In the samples from the 1826–35 cohort higher fertility
was offset by the beginning of fertility control.

CHILD LABOR AND THE FAMILY ECONOMY

The woolen mills of nineteenth-century Verviers made extensive use of
child labor, and most contemporaries stressed the essential contribution
that children made to the family economy. It is natural to ask whether
couples considered a child's potential earnings in their fertility decisions.
Most nineteenth-century observers believed that they did, and writers
sometimes remarked that working-class couples desired large families and
viewed children as a form of wealth. A medical investigator wrote: "It is
a recognized principle in the working class, to have the greatest number

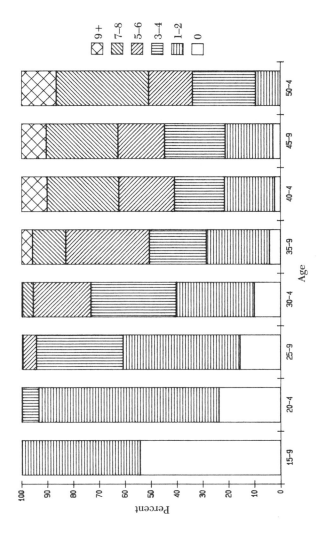

Figure 7.1. Percentage of married women, by number of surviving children and age, linked sample

of children possible. The worker considers the birth of an infant a very happy event: this will be in the future a worker who will help to support the family" (Fossion, 1845, p. 94; also Lepas, 1844).

However, the extensive employment of children does not mean that large families were economically beneficial or that parents viewed children as profitable investments. Contemporaries were also well aware of the costs of children, and frequently emphasized the poverty of families with children too young to work; it will be useful to examine this point in terms of the development of the family over a woman's life course. Young children could be given some tasks in domestic production, but we can only guess when these activities offset their costs. Factory owners were not interested in children before age 12, and at this age they earned less than one-fourth the wages of an unskilled adult male. Children were certainly not an economic benefit to the family before age 4, and they may well have been net consumers until 13 or 14. Although adult children made substantial contributions, these benefits were preceded by years of outlays. Indeed, the pressure that parents felt to bring their children into the mills was created by the economic burdens of having families with young children.

The economic costs and benefits of children figure prominently in the current debate over fertility control in developing countries in Africa and Asia. A number of researchers have pointed to the very young ages at which children assume valuable roles in household production as evidence of the economic utility of large families. Caldwell (1982) argues strongly for a net "flow of wealth" from children to parents, but his concept of "wealth" includes noneconomic benefits of children, such as deference and the social status of fathers of large families. Other researchers, however, have pointed to the costs of young children and the time lag between birth and even the most minimal productive roles (Mueller, 1976). When future costs and benefits are discounted to a present value, the near-term costs of children heavily outweigh their earnings in the future.[1] When one considers not only the direct costs of a child, but also the labor invested by its mother, it is unlikely that children were a good investment. One

---

1. It might be objected that it is inappropriate to impose sophisticated financial calculations on poor workers, who might be expected to have little understanding of credit, discount rates, and present values. But there are good reasons to take the opposite view. Nineteenth-century workers had frequent recourse to credit from grocers, neighborhood moneylenders, and pawnbrokers. Furthermore, they were willing to pay high interest rates. The mont-de-piété (municipal pawnbroker) in Verviers charged 15 percent on its loans. Since these loans were often for very short durations and always involved the loss of the services of the security, the effective interest rate was much higher than the nominal rate (*Exposé*, 1860, AV).

observer reported that mothers in nineteenth-century Verviers sent their children to school as early as possible to free themselves for domestic industry (Poetgens, 1895, p. 2).

The economic calculation is not incorrect, but it may misrepresent the kind of decisions that parents were making. The costs and earnings of children were experienced at different stages of the family life cycle and the parents' life course. Young families did experience serious economic distress, but child labor began to support the family economy at the time when the wages of its male earner were declining. Thus, the timing of children's contributions was an important consideration. Children could fulfill economic functions in a family strategy not reflected in the present-value calculation, and the economic considerations surrounding children of different birth orders changed significantly as the family developed over time.

Rowntree (1903) was the first to emphasize the economic cycle of the family and to show the changing economic importance of children. His budget surveys in late nineteenth-century York reveal a now familiar life cycle of family income. Young families became progressively impover-ished as their first children were born, and older families became increas-ingly well off as these children matured and entered the labor force. Therefore, both views on the economic benefits of children—that they were costly and that they were income producers—were true, but at dif-ferent stages of family development. Families moved through an early crisis caused by the costs of young children, and they also experienced prosperity later in life when these children entered the labor force. The discounted value of a child at birth does not account for the role that child played in the family's economic strategy later in life.

These life course patterns in the family's potential income are illustrated in Table 7.4, which shows the average number of coresident kin in three broad age groups: 0–14, 15–64, and over 65. The dependency ratio sum-marizes the balance between producers and consumers as the women in the sample grew older. The peak period of economic stress in the 1826–35 cohort occurred when wives were aged 35–39 and had three children. At this age the years of highest fertility had been passed, but the oldest chil-dren were not yet ready to enter the labor force. After age 40, however, the balance swung in the other direction as children became old enough to work. Even women aged 50–54 had one underage child, however, so the late age at marriage promised them support from children into their old age.

In a life course perspective we can point to two economic roles for chil-dren that would have supported high fertility. First, there is widespread agreement that children in less-developed societies are valued as a form of

170

Table 7.4. Mean Number of Related Coresident Persons,
by Age, and Dependency Ratio for Women in
the Samples, by Age, Married Women Only

Age of Woman	Age of Coresident Kin			Dependency Ratio
	0–14	15–64	65+	
Linked, 1826–35 Cohort				
Entire sample	2.55	2.29	0.05	1.13
15–19	0.73	2.08	0.00	0.35
20–24	1.36	1.99	0.03	0.70
25–29	2.13	2.02	0.03	1.07
30–34	2.68	2.02	0.03	1.34
35–39	3.13	2.14	0.06	1.49
40–44	3.07	2.56	0.05	1.22
45–49	2.09	3.20	0.13	0.69
50–54	1.54	4.14	0.08	0.39
Unlinked, 1826–35 Cohort				
Entire sample	2.49	2.47	0.05	1.02
30–34	2.55	1.94	0.04	1.34
35–39	2.92	2.10	0.05	1.42
40–44	2.69	2.39	0.04	1.14
45–49	1.97	2.98	0.06	0.68
50–54	1.09	3.50	0.04	0.32
1805–19 Cohort				
Entire sample	2.57	2.50	0.08	1.06
30–34	2.78	2.15	0.03	1.30
35–39	2.58	2.24	0.09	1.20
40–44	2.79	2.68	0.08	1.07
45–49	1.90	2.91	0.07	0.68

social insurance for old age. Eva Mueller (1976), who argues that children are expensive, sees the desire for assistance from children in old age as an important economic support for high fertility. Historical budget studies reveal that the earnings of male industrial workers usually peaked before age 50 and declined at older ages. The earnings of children more than offset this decline, and they provided the prospect of continued high family incomes into the parents' old age.

The second way that child labor supported high fertility was by creating income transfers from older to younger children. The decision to limit family size in nineteenth-century Europe was primarily a decision to avert later births, not a decision to postpone early births within marriage. In transitional cohorts, fertility control is most evident among women 35 and older. This means that the decision to practice family limitation was most likely to occur at the same time the oldest children in the family

171

entered the labor force. However, the incomes contributed by working children reduced the economic motivation for smaller families and delayed the onset of fertility decline. This interpretation of child labor differs from the more common argument that child labor made children less costly. In this view, children's earnings did not offset the costs of their upbringing, but later children were financed by the earnings of earlier children. Thus, parents could decide to continue childbearing, not because additional children were cheap, but because earlier children had raised the family's current income.

David Levine (1983) has suggested that working-class couples had an incentive to compress their childbearing into the early years of marriage. In this way they would have passed the expensive dependency period as soon as possible and reaped the benefits of child labor. We might also point out that high mortality made postponing childbearing a very risky strategy. If parents delayed early births or increased the spacing between births, they risked entering the stage of income decline without children ready to enter the labor force.

Neither family budget studies nor school enrollment patterns indicate a major change in family behavior that we can associate with declining fertility in the 1870s. A comparison of family budget surveys from 1854 and 1891 suggests little change in child labor at the national level (Alter, 1984a). At both dates the normal age of entry into the labor force seems to have been between 12 and 14, although we cannot be sure that it did not increase within this age group. School enrollment patterns from Verviers indicate that parents normally did not depend upon earnings from their preteenage children. In both 1860 and 1880 the ratio of children in primary schools to all children aged 5–14 was between 50 and 55 percent. This suggests that children were allowed to continue in school until they were admitted to the factories at about age 12. The city administration's annual report noted that a number of students quit school about the time of their first communion. (*Exposé*, 1860, p. 51, AV). Since the enrollment pattern does not appear to have changed significantly between 1860 and 1880, it seems unlikely that schooling was directly related to the fertility transition.[2]

Nevertheless, by the 1870s a certain ambivalence toward child labor

2. The annual reports of the city administration (*Exposé*, 1850, 1860, 1870, 1880, AV) provide a less-than-complete picture of school enrollments, because they do not consistently report enrollments in the free Catholic schools in the city after 1860. There was a gradual rise in the proportion of children in public primary schools from about 30 percent in 1860 to 34 percent in 1880. This appears to have been offset by a decline in the proportion enrolled in Catholic schools, however. Although the number of boys enrolled in day classes with the Frères de la doctrine chrétienne increased from 753 in 1859 to 860 in 1879, this represents a decline in proportions from about 30 percent to about 22 percent of boys aged 5–14.

had begun to appear. When the working-class leaders of Verviers debated the question of child labor, one of them criticized his peers for not giving enough consideration to the education and welfare of their children. But this view was attacked by others who stressed the poverty that forced their children to work ("Procès verbaux," n.d., pp. 70–80, BV). Workers and factory owners balanced the undesirability of child labor against the family's need for income, and neither side was willing to endorse legislation to restrict the employment of children. An employer attending the forum of working-class leaders in Verviers emphasized the costs of large families, and suggested that workers follow the good example of the bourgeoisie by not having more children than they could afford ("Procès verbaux," p. 71).

Ambivalence is evident in the ways in which both working-class leaders and employers condemned child labor but resisted legislation. When the workers of Ghent circulated a petition supporting restrictions on the employment of children, the Verviétois refused to lend their support. At a public meeting in Verviers representatives of the workers in Ghent heard local leaders denounce child labor but insist that it would be useless to petition a bourgeois parliament for legislation (Bertrand, 1927; J. Guillaume, 1910, p. 119). Heavily influenced by the anarchist wing of the First International, the Verviétois argued that the reform of child labor would have to await revolution and the reorganization of society (Piette, 1876). Employers, on the other hand, agreed that child labor was bad, but that the consequences of idleness would be worse. According to them, the only way to abolish child labor would be to enact compulsory education (Houget, 1875). In view of the bitter division in the Belgian Parliament between the advocates of secular and Catholic education, compulsory education must have appeared almost as utopian as proletarian revolution.

Thus, it does not seem likely that changes in child labor patterns hold the key to the fertility transition in Verviers in the 1870s. There are signs that attitudes, if not behaviors, were beginning to change, but those seeking to limit child labor were still in the minority. Moreover, children continued to make substantial contributions to the family after they began to work. In a life course perspective these contributions appear to have provided considerable support for high fertility. The timing of these contributions and the ways in which they alleviated economic distress later in the family life cycle appear far more important than their character as a return on earlier investments in childrearing.

FERTILITY AND FAMILY LIMITATION IN HISTORICAL POPULATIONS

An influential body of opinion in historical demography holds that populations before the fertility transition are characterized not by the absence of all behavior affecting fertility, but by the absence of parity-dependent behavior. This view was first advanced by Louis Henry with the awkward term *natural fertility* (Henry, 1961, 1977). Henry's pioneering work with historical European populations has revealed a greater variation in levels of fertility than had been anticipated. We now know that the duration of breastfeeding, for example, varies significantly among populations and can lead to major variations in average birth intervals and fertility rates. Henry also argues that a number of common customs also affect the level of fertility even though they are not practiced for that reason. Some cultures require sexual abstinence during breastfeeding, for example, but view this as a measure protecting the welfare of the infant rather than a way of limiting family size.

The problem, then, is to separate behavior that is intended to limit family size from other behaviors that unintentionally affect family size, like extended breastfeeding. Most previous research has done this by focusing on age patterns of fertility. A number of family-reconstitution studies have shown that during the fertility transition fertility rates at older ages are the first to decline. Thus, attention has been drawn to the average age at last birth and the length of the last birth interval. As fertility declines the average age at last birth tends to decline and the length of the last birth interval increases. Birth intervals at earlier ages do not show signs of fertility control and even became shorter in some nineteenth-century European populations. This is usually taken as evidence that couples were attempting to limit family size by averting later births.

Coale and Trussell (1978) have used these observed patterns to develop a statistical index of fertility control. Their procedure compares a set of age-specific fertility rates with a standard schedule to detect larger-than-expected declines in fertility at older ages. The Coale-Trussell procedure begins with a "natural fertility" schedule based on an average of observed patterns in pretransition populations. This pattern is adjusted for differences in the level of fertility by estimating a parameter, M, which increases or decreases the overall level of fertility without changing the relative level of fertility rates at different ages. A second parameter, m, is used to estimate changes in the shape of the fertility curve. This parameter reflects the degree to which fertility at older ages is lower, relative to the younger ages, than expected from the standard natural fertility schedule. The Coale-Trussell index of fertility control, m, has been found to reflect the onset of family limitation in a number of historical examples of fertility transitions.

The main drawback of the Coale-Trussell approach is that it does not directly address the question of whether fertility control is related to family size. Age patterns, which are the basis of the Coale-Trussell index, are related to family size, but they are also affected by variations in age at marriage. The population registers include detailed information about parity and surviving children which is not utilized by the Coale-Trussell index. For this reason, it is also useful to examine the determinants of birth intervals with life table and hazard models. This analysis identifies the sources of change in fertility rates and comes closer to depicting the actual sequence of events and decisions that are involved in family limitation.

The hazard analysis does offer a direct measure of the relationship between family size and fertility, but this relationship is not a simple one. In transitional populations, in which only part of the population is practicing fertility control, the population at high birth orders is disproportionately composed of couples not practicing fertility control. As explained below, the couples who limit their fertility selectively stop at lower birth orders. This leads to a nonlinear relation between fertility and birth order in the aggregate. It is not yet possible to identify fertility control confidently in this type of analysis, so the Coale-Trussell model is used to examine the effects of independent variables (occupation, literacy, and age at migration) on fertility control.

THE FERTILITY TRANSITION IN VERVIERS

The contrasts afforded by the samples from Verviers show some of the complications involved in describing a fertility transition. Although there is strong evidence that the cohort of 1826–35 had initiated fertility control, this new behavior was partly offset by a rise in the level of fertility. Verviers experienced a secular increase in the level of fertility from about midcentury to 1870, when the fertility transition began (see Figure 1.3, above). John Knodel (1986) has noted a similar rise in the level of fertility in a sample of German villages during the nineteenth century. Thus, when we look at family size by age in Table 7.3 there is little to distinguish the pretransition 1805–19 cohort from the transitional 1826–35 cohort. The two cohorts experienced almost identical numbers of surviving children at every age, and we might be tempted to conclude that fertility was lower in the earlier cohort.

Examination of the age-specific marital fertility rates in Table 7.5 helps clarify the problem. Fertility at younger ages was lower in the earlier cohort, but it was higher at ages 40–44 and 45–49. The interpretation of these differences offered by the Coale-Trussell model is that both the level of fertility and the level of fertility control were rising. (See the section "Covariates of Fertility Control," below, for a discussion of this model.) Since the model assumes that earlier ages are less affected by efforts to

175

Table 7.5. Age-Specific Marital Fertility Rates, by Age, and Estimated Parameters of the Coale-Trussell Fertility Model

| | Cohort of | Cohort of 1826–35 | | |
Age	1805–19	Unlinked	Linked	Elite
AGE-SPECIFIC MARITAL FERTILITY RATES				
20–24			0.413	0.392
25–29			0.378	0.340
30–34	0.241	0.266	0.303	0.270
35–39	0.175	0.195	0.208	0.188
40–44	0.136	0.080	0.094	0.050
45–49	0.040	0.016	0.011	0.000
COALE-TRUSSELL PARAMETERS				
M	0.3419	0.8892	0.9698	0.9131
m	− 0.6001	0.3934	0.3776	0.5330

Table 7.6. Life Table Analysis of Birth Intervals, Linked Random Sample

Months since Last Birth[a]	Observed		Birth Rate (m_x)	Probability of a Birth (q_x)	Number without a Birth (l_x)	Number Who Did Give Birth
	Person-Years	Births				
0–8	708.1	62	0.088	.0638	100,000	100,000
9–17	653.9	150	0.229	.1638	93,617	92,736
18–26	474.9	304	0.640	.3851	78,283	75,287
27–35	275.5	210	0.762	.4313	48,139	40,985
36–47	227.5	65	0.286	.2415	27,375	17,356
48–59	186.5	36	0.193	.1753	20,763	9,832
60–71	42.5	14	0.329	.2920	17,124	5,691
72 +					12,123	0

Expected interval between births: 27.0 months

[a] Months since last birth or marriage.

stop childbearing, low rates at ages 30–34 reduce the parameter measuring the level of fertility, M, in the earlier cohort. The estimated value for M in the earlier cohort is 0.34, compared with estimates around 1.0 for the samples from the 1826–35 sample. On the other hand, the relatively high level of fertility after age 40 is interpreted as evidence of the lack of fertility control. The estimated value for m in the 1805–19 cohort is − 0.60 compared with values ranging from 0.38 to 0.53 in the later cohort. Since values of m rarely exceed 0.2 in natural fertility populations, these estimates confirm that the 1826–35 cohort was beginning the fertility transition.

Table 7.7. Probability of a Birth, by Months since
Last Birth, and Average Birth Interval
(in months)

Months since Last Birth[a]	Cohort of 1805–19	Cohort of 1826–35		
		Unlinked	Linked	Elite
0–8	.0103	.0147	.0638	.0297
9–17	.0265	.1638	.1041	.2968
18–26	.2161	.3851	.2711	.3945
27–35	.2547	.4313	.2472	.2533
36–47	.2948	.2415	.1591	.1237
48–59	.1758	.1753	.1260	.1214
60–71	.3940	.2920	.1853	.2817
Average birth interval	37.9	27.7	27.0	22.0

[a] Months since last birth or marriage.

Table 7.8. Percentage without a Birth after Six Years,
by Age

Age	Cohort of 1805–19	Cohort of 1826–35		
		Unlinked	Linked	Elite
Entire sample	19.8	29.0	12.1	17.1
20–24		.	4.6	10.4
25–29			6.8	3.6
30–34	11.6	5.4	6.9	13.2
35–39	15.6	17.9	16.4	20.5
40–44	25.7	41.8	33.7	45.2

A more detailed comparison of the fertility patterns in these samples suggests that the increase in fertility described above was probably due to changes in infant-feeding practices. This is examined in Tables 7.6, 7.7, and 7.8, which are based upon a life table analysis of the intervals between births. The first two of these tables were constructed by dividing the fertility histories derived from the population registers into time intervals (in months) since the previous birth. The total numbers of observed births and person-years were computed for each interval, and these totals were used to construct life table functions for birth intervals comparable to the life table functions in a mortality table. The technique is illustrated in Table 7.6, which shows a life table constructed from all of the birth intervals in the linked random sample of women born 1826–35. This table follows the general form for life tables discussed in Chapter 2. The life table functions l_x and q_x show, respectively, the number of women still awaiting a birth and the probability of a birth at each time interval since

177

the previous birth. The expected length of a birth interval was computed by considering only those who had a birth, as shown in the last column of the table.

Table 7.7 shows the probability of a birth at each time interval since the last birth for each of the four population register samples. These probabilities are comparable to the q_x probabilities in a mortality table.[3] This table shows a very marked difference between the two cohorts in the probability of a conception in the first nine months after a birth. The probability of a birth interval at between 9 and 18 months in the 1805–19 cohort was far less than that in the later cohort. In the earlier cohort this probability was .03, compared with .10 to .16 for the random samples and .30 in the elite sample from the 1826–35 cohort. The earlier cohort was also less likely to conceive in the second nine months after a birth, but this difference was smaller (.22 compared with a range of .27–.39). Overall, women in the earlier cohort were less likely to conceive in the first two years after a birth, but they did tend to catch up in the third year.

Table 7.8 reconstructs the cumulative effects of the probabilities in Table 7.7 by showing the proportion of women who had still not given birth at the end of six years. This proportion was taken from the l_x columns in the life tables for birth intervals in each duration category. (Life tables like Table 7.6 are not shown for other samples.) Although the earlier cohort tended to have longer birth intervals, the proportion who remained childless was not dramatically higher. At ages 30–34 about 12 percent of the earlier cohort had not closed their birth intervals within six years, compared with 5–7 percent in the random samples from the 1826–35 cohort. The percentage of the earlier cohort was very close to the percentage of childless among elite women, some of whom were already beginning to control their fertility at this age. Thus, the main difference between the fertility patterns in these two cohorts was in the average length of a birth interval, not in the proportion who eventually had a birth.

Of course, longer birth intervals do produce smaller family sizes. Since the childbearing years end between ages 40 and 49, women whose child births are more widely spaced will have fewer births. Nevertheless, the higher fertility in the later cohort was partly offset by a tendency to stop childbearing at older ages. The effect of fertility control is particularly noticeable at ages 40–44. In this age group the earlier cohort was more

3. The probabilities in Table 7.7 show a tendency to rise in the last duration category, 60–71 months. The timing of this upturn suggests that it may include births to women who had experienced a miscarriage earlier. It should also be recognized, however, that most women experienced births at shorter durations and the amount of experience observed between 60 and 71 months is small. (See Table 7.8.)

Table 7.9. Probability of a Birth in the Interval 9–17 Months,
by Status of the Previous Infant

	Cohort of 1805–19	Cohort of 1826–35		
		Unlinked	Linked	Elite
Probability of a Birth				
Surviving infant	0.0315	0.1183	0.1482	0.3829
Infant death	0.1270	0.5007	0.7724	0.5189
Number of Observed Person-Years				
Surviving infant	127.2	312.9	546.6	94.0
Infant death	7.9	16.0	45.3	3.9
Number of Births				
Surviving infant	4	37	81	36
Infant death	1	8	35	2

likely to experience a birth within six years than the later cohort (26 percent childless compared with 34–45 percent in the later cohort). Since the
transitional cohort was apparently more fecund at younger ages, there is
good reason to attribute this difference to voluntary control.

The most likely explanation of the increase in fertility described in
Tables 7.5 and 7.7 is a change in the effect of breastfeeding on fertility.
It is apparent in Table 7.7 that the cohorts differed most in the first year
after a birth. Breastfeeding tends to delay the return to ovulation, and its
effects on the likelihood of conception are greatest in the first year after a
birth. Since the differences among the samples from Verviers were greatest in these months, breastfeeding seems to be implicated. The internal
evidence in the samples shows that breastfeeding in the later cohort had
not been completely abandoned, however.

Table 7.9 examines the effects of infant mortality on the probability
of a birth for women in the interval 9–18 months since the last birth.
Since an infant's death would have ended lactation, it would also have
increased the probability of a birth nine months later for women who were
breastfeeding. If there had been no breastfeeding, there would be little
difference between women whose infants had survived and those whose
infants had died. We see in Table 7.9 that an infant death had a strong
effect upon the probability of another birth in both cohorts. In the later
cohort an infant death raised the probability of a birth from .15 to .77 in
the linked sample and from .12 to .50 in the unlinked sample. The increase
was less in the earlier cohort (from .03 to .13), but there it is based on very
few infant deaths. Infant deaths also increased the probability of a birth
in the elite sample, but there the probability of a birth was much higher
even when the previous infant survived.

179

We can conclude from this that breastfeeding had not ceased in the 1826–35 cohort, but its effects appear to have diminished. The difference between these cohorts may have had either behavioral or physiological origins. First, the length and intensity of lactation may have differed among samples. It is possible that elite women weaned their children earlier, were more likely to supplement breastfeeding with other milk, or made use of wet nurses. Similarly, the age at weaning may have been growing younger between the earlier and later cohort, and even if infants were not completely weaned, they may have been given more supplements in addition to mother's milk in the later cohort.[4]

Second, there may have been a relationship between poorer nutritional status in the earlier period and longer lactation amenorrhea, the anovulatory period caused by breastfeeding. Women in very poor countries and women who have lived through famines tend to resume ovulation much later after a birth than women in prosperous developed countries today. There is a controversy regarding whether this effect is due to nutrition or some other factor, but unfortunately this data set cannot distinguish among the competing interpretations (Menken, Trussell, and Watkins, 1981).

Third, it is possible that some other behavioral pattern was partly or fully responsible for the shortening of birth intervals in nineteenth-century Verviers. For example, many cultures advocate sexual abstinence for lactating women. In earlier centuries it was commonly believed that sexual intercourse would spoil the mother's milk and endanger the child. It is possible that a practice of this kind was beginning to disappear in Verviers at this time.

A Hazard Model of the Birth Interval

A hazard model of the birth interval provides a way of expanding the life table analysis to include additional variables. As in the life table, in Table 7.10 the months since last birth were divided into six categories: 9–17 (the omitted category), 18–26, 27–35, 36–47, 48–59, and 60–71. The hazard model includes the mother's age, the status of the previous infant, the spacing of earlier births, and measures of family size. For reasons explained below, the model presented in Table 7.10 is estimated for married women with three or more children. The variable of most interest

---

4. Courtois (1828, pp. 161–62) reported that breastfeeding of 14 months or longer was common in the early nineteenth century, but Fossion (1845, p. 95) described supplementary feeding at midcentury. If children were given supplements to mother's milk, it would have reduced the effect of breastfeeding on ovulation.

Table 7.10. Estimated Coefficients of the Hazard Model, for
Married Women with Three or More Children

	Cohort of 1805–19	Cohort of 1826–35	
		Unlinked	Linked
Grand mean	− 3.781*	− 1.276*	− 1.660*
Months since last birth (9–17 months omitted)			
18–26	3.273*	1.165*	1.293*
27–35	3.682*	1.233*	1.712*
36–47	3.626*	0.658*	0.792*
48–59	3.072*	0.629*	0.652*
60–71	2.506*	− 0.651*	− 0.386
Mother's age (under 35 omitted)			
35–39	− 0.197	− 0.325	− 0.366*
40–44	− 0.417	− 1.065*	− 1.165*
45–49	− 1.770*	− 1.930*	− 2.572*
Infant death (9–17 months)	3.397*	1.314*	1.001*
Interval from first to third birth	− 0.102*	− 0.035	− 0.011
Children ever observed (3 omitted)			
4	0.547	− 0.210	− 0.090
5	0.164	− 0.457*	− 0.279
6	− 0.076	− 0.008	− 0.085
7 or more	0.939	− 0.206	− 0.257
Observed child deaths (0 omitted)			
1	− 0.232	0.525*	0.299*
2	0.614	0.186	0.235

* Estimated coefficient is at least twice its standard error.

in this exercise is the effect of a child death, because it shows whether
parents increased fertility to "replace" the deceased child.

The coefficients for categories of months since the last birth reproduce
the pattern observed in Tables 7.6 and 7.7. The probability of another
birth was lower in the first period (9–17 months), because nursing the
previous child tended to delay return to ovulation. Births were also less
likely at longer intervals. The more fecund couples had their births at
shorter intervals, and only those with lower fecundability or those practicing contraception remained at the longer intervals. The probability of
another birth, therefore, rose quickly and then declined as time elapsed

since the previous birth. This pattern can be observed in all of the samples. The coefficients in the 1805–19 cohort are larger than those in the other samples, but this is apparently an artifact of the estimation process. The grand mean in the 1805–19 cohort is also much larger. It is the difference between the grand mean and the coefficients for the categories of months since last birth which is important.

The coefficients for categories of age indicate that fertility declined with age, as we would expect. There is a noticeable difference here between the two cohorts, however. The decline at ages 40–44 was much larger in the later cohort, and the coefficients for this age are statistically different from the under-35 age group in the later but not the earlier cohort. The hazard model shows here the transformation of age-specific fertility rates on which the Coale-Trussell marital fertility schedule (M and m) is based. During the fertility transition women were most likely to reduce family size by trying to stop childbearing at older ages than by trying to space earlier births.

The infant death variable was included in the model to capture the earlier return to ovulation of women whose infants died (Knodel, 1975, 1981). As we observed in Table 7.9, an infant death ends the lactation amenorrhea that normally lowers fertility after childbirth. The infant death variable in the hazard model was given a value of one during the period 9–17 months since the previous birth if the child of that birth had died more than 9 months earlier; otherwise, the variable equals zero. For example, when an infant died at age 4 months, the infant death variable was set to one for months 14–17. (The nine-month difference is the time between conception and birth.) This limits the variable's effect to the period when lactation would have affected the mother's fertility. The large effect of lactation in this population is reflected in the statistically significant coefficients in all three samples.

The interval from first to third birth has been included in the model to control for differences among couples in fecundability and lactation practices. These differences cannot be measured directly, but they should persist through each individual fertility history. This variable is used in preference to other birth-interval measures like the average birth interval or the previous birth interval. Variables that include information about the previous birth interval may also include information about parity-dependent fertility control. Since it is the purpose of this model to detect such behavior, the variable for the interval from first to third birth was based on the earliest birth intervals in which a few couples would have controlled their fertility. The use of this variable does restrict the samples to women with at least three children, but this is the most relevant subpopulation for this analysis.

The reader should also note that the interval between the first and third children was computed from children observed in the population register. Most of the fertility histories in the linked sample are complete, but in the unlinked samples some children had died before observation of the family began. The omission of unobserved births in these incomplete histories increases the average interval between the first and third children in the unlinked samples. Ideally, we would want complete birth histories, and we would also want to inflate those intervals in which the death of an infant interrupted lactation.

If the earlier birth intervals were longer, the later intervals should be longer as well. We expect the coefficients of this variable to show this relationship by being negative. All three estimated coefficients are negative, but this variable is statistically significant in only the 1805–19 cohort. The weaknesses of this variable in the later cohort may be due to the beginnings of fertility control, which would be unrelated to interpersonal differences affecting earlier birth intervals.

The estimated coefficients for family size are the most difficult to interpret.[5] Any biological tendency for successive births to reduce subsequent fertility is offset by selection effects, which make more fecund women likelier to reach higher parities. At the highest parities the influence of family size becomes confounded with the end of the reproductive period. In general, we would expect a positive association between number of children and the probability of another birth. This tends to occur because couples with short birth intervals are likelier to reach higher parities. Thus, there will be a higher proportion of relatively more fecund women with larger than with smaller family sizes. This pattern may be offset when some couples practice family limitation, however. If some couples stop at a target family size, fertility will be lowest at the target family size and higher at both lower and higher parities. In this case the effects of fertility control are concentrated near the target. On one hand, none of the couples will be averting births at lower parities. On the other hand, couples practicing family limitation will stop before reaching higher parities, and the fertility rates for large family sizes will reflect only those couples with unrestricted fertility.[6]

The most interesting result that emerges from the estimated coefficients

5. The measures of family size and child deaths used in Table 7.10 include only those children recorded in the registers, but children who died before the registers began are not observed. In the linked samples this is equivalent to children ever born for most women. In the unlinked samples, however, this variable includes only children who were living with the couple when the register began or were born after it started.

6. A pattern of this sort is noted by David Weir (1982) in his work on eighteenth-century French fertility. Parity progression ratios computed from his work tend to show a greater fertility among couples with from three to five children than among those with from six to eight children.

associated with different family sizes in Table 7.10 is the suggestion of a U-shaped pattern in the unlinked sample from the 1826–35 cohort. In this sample couples with four or five children were less likely to experience another birth than those with from three to six or more children. Since this sample also has a slightly higher Coale-Trussell index of fertility control (m), it is plausible that this pattern reflects the practice of family limitation by a part of the population.

The observed child deaths variable is an attempt to measure the "replacement effect" in these samples. If parents were aiming for a particular family size, those who experienced a child death would be less likely to practice contraception than those who had not lost a child. This effect differs from that associated with lactation discussed above. While an infant death will affect fertility only during the time when the child would have been nursed, a replacement effect will operate at all durations of the birth interval. Furthermore, a replacement effect will follow the death of a child of any age. In the hazard model these two effects are clearly distinguished. The infant death variable includes only deaths of children less than 9 months old and affects fertility only 9–17 months since the previous birth. The child death variable reflects all observed deaths and affects fertility at all durations.

John Knodel (1975, 1981) has examined evidence of the replacement effect in historical studies. There is some evidence in the reconstitution studies of Meulan and the Genevan bourgeoisie that fertility was higher after a child death (Knodel, 1975). In nineteenth-century German village genealogies Knodel has found that evidence of a replacement effect was considerably stronger among cohorts practicing family limitation than among natural fertility cohorts. He argues that the weak evidence of replacement among the natural fertility cohorts may be due to biases inherent in the data or introduced by the method of analysis (Knodel, 1981).

In a natural fertility population a child's death will have no effect on fertility because family size is not related to decision-making on the part of the parents. A replacement effect should appear only when some couples who are controlling their fertility respond to the death of a child by relaxing that control. The estimated coefficients for the two cohorts show the kind of change that we expect to occur during a fertility transition. In the earlier cohort the coefficients for both child-death variables are not statistically significant, and the coefficient for one child death is actually negative. In the 1826–35 cohort, however, the coefficients for one child death are both positive and statistically significant.

This evidence of a replacement effect is particularly noteworthy, because it is based upon a sequential approach to fertility histories rather than the aggregation of fertility rates. The sequential approach ties the replacement effect more closely to a decision-making process exercised by couples. At any given time couples in the later cohort were in the process of deciding whether or not to have an additional child. While the results cannot show whether they had a target family size in mind *ex ante*, they do suggest that couples responded when they had too few children as well as when they had too many. Moreover, the methodology of the hazard model differs substantially from the Coale-Trussell approach employed more extensively below, and the two approaches complement each other. The Coale-Trussell model measures only fertility reduction, while the replacement effect is the result of a deliberate increase in fertility. Thus, the existence of a replacement effect suggests that in conditions of high mortality the degree of effective fertility control may be higher and the desired family size may be lower than aggregate measures like the Coale-Trussell model would lead us to believe.

Covariates of Fertility Control

This section uses an adaptation of the Coale-Trussell model of marital fertility to examine three of the most commonly cited covariates of lower fertility: occupation, literacy, and migrant status. The Coale-Trussell model is in fact an application of Louis Henry's natural fertility hypothesis. The model assumes that age-specific patterns of marital fertility are common to all populations, but that the level of fertility may vary considerably. Coale and Trussell derived a standard schedule of marital fertility from a number of studies of historical populations in which family limitation is believed to have been absent. Their model adjusts this standard schedule to match the observed behavior of a population of interest by moving the level of the schedule up or down without changing its shape. An index of the level of fertility, called M, indicates the proportionate change in the level of fertility. Thus, when $M = 1.0$, the level of fertility in the observed population matches that in the standard schedule. Values of M below 1.0 indicate lower fertility, above 1.0 higher fertility.

The Coale-Trussell model assumes that fertility control takes the form of "stopping" rather than "spacing" behavior. This implies that during a fertility transition marital fertility rates will decline at older ages before younger ages are affected. This pattern should be most apparent at ages over 35. The index of fertility control, m, calculates the degree to which the shape of marital fertility has been transformed by movements away from the natural fertility model at older ages. An m value of zero means that the observed pattern matches the shape of the model schedule. Values of m greater than zero suggest disproportionately lower fertility at

185

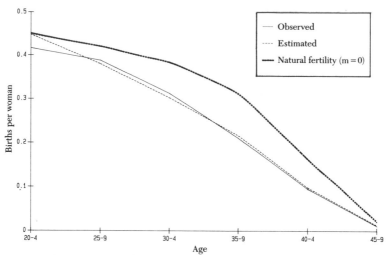

Figure 7.2. Observed and Coale-Trussell model age-specific fertility rates, linked random sample

older ages, but values of m below 0.2 are usually not considered reliable. Thus, while M measures shifts up or down in the level of fertility, m measures a specific kind of transformation in the shape of the marital fertility curve.

Figure 7.2 illustrates the application of the Coale-Trussell model to the fertility of the linked random sample. The three curves in the figure represent the observed marital fertility rates in this sample, the estimated rates predicted by the Coale-Trussell model, and the natural fertility curve corresponding to the estimated rates. The model matches the observed rates very well. The figure shows that the estimated rates are almost identical to the observed rates at every age except 20–24, where the estimate is slightly higher. The natural curve was calculated by using the estimate for the parameter measuring the level of fertility, M, but setting the fertility control parameter, m, to zero. This produces a curve representing the marital fertility rates that would have been reached if no family limitation had been practiced. The natural fertility curve exceeds the estimated curve at every age group after 20–24, but the proportional differences are greatest between 35 and 44. The fertility control parameter, m, measures the area lying between the natural fertility curve and the estimated curve.

The application of the Coale-Trussell model used here extends their original work in two directions. First, a procedure for estimating maximum likelihood is used to calculate M and m. The early articles by Coale and Trussell (1974, 1978) propose two different ad hoc procedures for

186

doing these calculations. Recent work by Trussell and by Goran Brostrom (1985) has shown that maximum likelihood estimates are possible and that they have desirable statistical characteristics.[7] The maximum likelihood estimation procedure also produces estimates of the standard errors of M and m, which make formal hypothesis testing possible. Second, this procedure easily allows us to add covariates into the Coale-Trussell model. This means that intergroup comparisons are possible and that we obtain statistical tests of the differences between groups.[8]

OCCUPATIONAL GROUPS

One of the first surprises in this data set is the pervasiveness of fertility control throughout the occupational hierarchy. We have come to expect an inverse relationship between social status and family size, with high status, high income families being smaller. It is natural to assume that in the twentieth century these cross-sectional differences might also appear in longitudinal data, that is, that in today's population fertility control emerged later in groups that have larger families.

Some of the limited information available on nineteenth-century fertility by occupation does point in this direction. Retrospective fertility histories by occupation collected from the 1911 census of England and Wales show an inverse relationship between social status and fertility in the last half of the nineteenth century. Joseph Banks (1981) has recently argued that the values underlying family limitation developed among the middle classes and diffused downward in the social structure. On the other hand, Michael Haines (1979a) has found very little difference in fertility among occupational groups in the English towns of Durham, Easington, and Merthyr Tydfil between 1851 and 1871. It is also noteworthy that the textile workers of Verviers had lower fertility than other occupational groups of the same socioeconomic status in the 1911 English census (Banks, 1981).

The spread of fertility control through the social structure in the 1826–35 cohort is examined in Table 7.11. This table shows estimates of the parameters of the Coale-Trussell model in samples from the transitional Verviers cohort. Each of the three groups of working-class occupations

7. Trussell (n.d.) has developed a computer program for performing the maximum likelihood calculation ("Program Mm," Office of Population Research, Princeton University). In a personal communication Brostrom showed me how these estimates could be performed with a general-purpose statistical package, GLIM, which facilitates the addition of covariates to the model.

8. The formal model is presented in the appendix to this chapter. I am grateful to both Goran Brostrom and James Trussell for their advice on this model.

Table 7.11. Estimated Parameters of the Coale-Trussell Fertility Model, by Husband's Occupation

Husband's Occupation	Cohort of 1826–35	
	Unlinked	Linked
FIVE-CATEGORY CLASSIFICATION		
M index of the level of fertility		
Bourgeois	1.64	0.96
Petty bourgeois	0.52	1.02
Skilled	1.16	0.99
Textiles[a]	0.83	1.11
Laborers	0.95	0.96
None or not classified	0.21	0.88
m index of the fertility control		
Bourgeois	0.92	−0.01
Petty bourgeois	−0.13	0.38
Skilled	0.60	0.95
Textiles[a]	0.32	0.61[b]
Laborers	0.54	0.52
None or not classified	−0.10	0.49
TWO-CATEGORY CLASSIFICATION		
M index of the level of fertility		
Bourgeois, petty bourgeois	0.88	0.9841
Textiles, skilled, laborers[a]	0.97	1.0468
None or not classified	0.21	0.8755
m index of the fertility control		
Bourgeois, petty bourgeois	0.35	0.32
Textiles, skilled, laborers[a]	0.45[b]	0.45[b]
None or not classified	−0.10	0.49

[a] Omitted category.

[b] Difference from zero greater than twice standard error.

(skilled workers, textile workers, and day laborers) appears to have controlled their fertility. The results for the bourgeois occupations are inconsistent across samples because of the smaller numbers of observations in this category. When bourgeois and petty bourgeois occupations are combined in the bottom panel of the table, however, they also show evidence of fertility control in both samples.

The results in Table 7.11 do not point clearly to a higher degree of control in higher social strata, but we have already seen that fertility control was more advanced among the elite (Table 7.5). The difference between the results shown in Tables 7.5 and 7.11 seems to be due to a social division between the high bourgeoisie and the petty bourgeoisie. The membership of the high bourgeoisie was more clearly identified for the elite sample by using tax assessments than it was for the random sample by using occupations. The same tax data for the random sample also produce higher estimates of fertility control. Women whose fathers paid taxes on more than 2,000 francs in 1849 had a higher value of m than the rest of the sample, but women whose fathers paid 1,000–1,999 francs did not.

The results for occupational groups derived from these samples suggest a more complex relationship between social structure and fertility than a simple inverse correlation. Although the fertility transition seems to have affected manual workers at about the same rate that it affected small shopkeepers, a more restricted group within the bourgeoisie may have begun controlling its fertility earlier than the rest of the population. Thus, the occupational patterns from Verviers do not support a simple diffusion model in which the practice of family limitation spread gradually down the social scale. We see instead a small wealthy elite, in their own words the "bonne bourgeoisie," which began restricting its fertility a generation before the rest of the population. I have shown elsewhere that the social distance between this group and the rest of society was greater than the social distances between any other social groups in nineteenth-century Verviers (Alter, 1978). When fertility control spread outside this restricted circle, it affected almost all occupations equally. The petty bourgeoisie, shopkeepers, and shopkeeping artisans like butchers and bakers were actually somewhat behind manual workers, such as the spinners and weavers in the textile industry.

LITERACY

Education, especially female education, is a key variable in most research on fertility. Education spreads attitudes conducive to lower fertility, and it also increases the opportunity costs of large families. It is not possible to measure the level of education of individuals in the Verviers sample, but it has been possible to use signatures in official documents to identify the literate and illiterate. Belgium was one of the last western European countries to require the education of all children. In the mid-nineteenth century almost half the population of Verviers was completely illiterate. These people can be identified in the civil registers of marriages and births. The Napoleonic Code, from which Belgian law was derived, required the signatures of all parties on official documents. Marriage registers were signed by both the bride and groom as well as their parents and witnesses. In the birth register we usually find the signature of the infant's father, who was

Table 7.12. Estimated Parameters of the Coale-Trussell
Fertility Model, by Literacy

	Cohort of 1805–19	Cohort of 1826–35	
		Unlinked	Linked
HUSBAND'S SIGNATURE			
M index of the level of fertility			
Signed or NA[a]	0.46	1.27	1.05
Did not sign	0.30	0.84	0.84
m index of fertility control			
Signed or NA[a]	−0.49	0.34	0.41[b]
Did not sign	−0.65	0.41	0.35
WIFE'S SIGNATURE			
M index of the level of fertility			
Signed or NA[a]			1.09
Did not sign			0.90
m index of fertility control			
Signed or NA[a]			0.48[b]
Did not sign			0.32

[a] Omitted category.

[b] Difference from zero greater than twice standard error.

expected to report his child's birth. Literacy data have been added to the Verviers data set from these two sources. In the two unlinked samples we have information on the literacy of fathers from the birth register. In the linked sample literacy for both the husband and wife was taken from the marriage register.[9]

Estimates of the Coale-Trussell parameters by husband's literacy are presented in Table 7.12. There is little support for an influence of education on fertility in these results. None of the random samples show a substantial difference in the index of fertility control between literate and illiterate husbands.

9. Literacy information in the linked random sample was taken from 192 marriages. The following table shows the proportion of women and their husbands who were able to sign the marriage register.

	Woman in Sample		Husband	
	Number	Percent	Number	Percent
Signed	99	51.6	149	77.6
Did not sign	93	48.4	43	22.4
Entire sample	192	100.0	192	100.0

Table 7.13. Estimated Parameters of the Coale-Trussell
Fertility Model, by Wife's Migrant Status
and Age at Migration

	Cohort of 1826–35	
	Unlinked	Linked
	M index of the level of fertility	
Nonmigrant[a]	1.27	1.07
Migrant, 0–14	0.76	0.98
Migrant, 15+	0.79	0.60[c]
	m index of fertility control	
Nonmigrant[a]	0.77[b]	0.48[b]
Migrant, 0–14	0.37	0.46
Migrant, 15+	0.07	−0.23[c]

[a] Omitted category.

[b] Difference from zero greater than twice standard error.

[c] Difference from omitted category greater than twice standard error.

MIGRANTS AND NONMIGRANTS

Population registers give us unusual opportunities for studying the process of migration and the differences between migrants and nonmigrants. The effects of migration on fertility have received little attention in historical demography, because it has usually been impossible to reconstruct the fertility histories of migrants. The results presented here show how important this distinction can be in an urban setting like Verviers.

Table 7.13 divides the samples by age at migration and migrant status. This results in a clear and statistically significant difference between migrants and nonmigrants. Furthermore, the timing of migration was important. Women who migrated to the city before age 15 were more similar to natives than to migrants who arrived later. Women who migrated to Verviers after age 15 show no evidence of fertility control.

Table 7.14 reexamines the effect of literacy when migrant status is controlled. Table 7.12 showed no effect of literacy on fertility control, but Table 7.14 shows whether literacy had an effect when the stronger effect of migration is controlled. This is not the case. There is no difference between literacy groups among those born in Verviers, and literate migrants show no evidence of fertility control.

Rural-urban migration has a long history as an explanatory variable in studies of twentieth-century fertility differentials. Goldberg (1959, 1960) and Duncan (1965) have shown that migrants from rural areas had higher fertility than urban natives in some of the earliest U.S. fertility surveys. More recent work on less-developed countries finds similar effects

191

Table 7.14. Estimated Parameters of the Coale-Trussell Fertility Model, by Husband's Literacy and Wife's Migrant Status and Age at Migration

| Husband's Literacy/ | Cohort of 1826–35 | |
Wife's Migrant Status	Unlinked	Linked
	M index of the level of fertility	
Signed/nonmigrant or migrant, 0–14	1.5780	1.0585
Did not sign/nonmigrant or migrant, 0–14	0.9213	0.9870
Signed/migrant, 15+	0.8386	0.5704
Did not sign/migrant, 15+	0.7527	0.8664
	m index of the fertility control	
Signed/nonmigrant or migrant, 0–14	0.5802	0.4852
Did not sign/nonmigrant or migrant, 0–14	0.5301	0.4260
Signed/migrant, 15+	−0.0827	−0.3166
Did not sign/migrant, 15+	0.0401	0.4645

(Hervitz, 1984; Entwisle and Mason, 1985). This difference points to the importance of the city as a cultural influence on fertility behavior. The effect of migration on fertility has received little attention in historical demography, however, because the methods and data of most historical studies cannot identify migrants or must exclude migrants entirely.

Conclusion

The women of the 1826–35 birth cohort were the vanguard of the fertility transition in Verviers, and their experience suggests three major lessons about the early stages of fertility decline. First, it emphasizes that voluntary fertility control within marriage was not the only or even the most important factor affecting family size. The Malthusian checks, high mortality and late marriage, were still very much in evidence in Verviers in the 1870s. On one hand, the average married woman in Verviers experienced one or more child deaths before her family was complete. On the other hand, completed family size was reduced by about one child for every two years that marriage was delayed. With an average age at marriage of 26 years, the women of Verviers were well below their biological reproductive potential.

Second, we have discovered that the fertility transition in Verviers took place at a time of rising fertility. In fact, fertility control in the transitional generation simply offset the increase in fertility between generations, leaving completed family size about the same. The examination of factors affecting birth intervals in each cohort suggests that the increase in fertility was somehow linked to the effects of breastfeeding. There is strong evidence that the transitional cohort was breastfeeding, but the effect of breastfeeding on ovulation had apparently decreased between cohorts. This change may have been due to improved nutrition, to a decrease in the intensity of breastfeeding, or to other behavioral changes between generations.

The evidence of a "replacement effect" in the hazard model of birth intervals casts a new light on this apparent change in the balance between fertility and mortality. It reveals that couples in the transitional cohort were not passive in the face of mortality. The high infant and child mortality in Verviers in the 1870s did not prevent the onset of fertility control, because couples actively responded to the threat posed by child mortality. In the hazard analysis we see that couples increased their fertility in the wake of a child's death. This behavior has important implications for our understanding of the fertility transition. It suggests that the onset of fertility control may have been delayed or even hidden by the Malthusian factors reducing family sizes. In the terminology used by Richard Easterlin (1978), pretransition cohorts may have lacked motivation to control fertility, because their "supply" of children was still below their "demand." If couples did have target family sizes in mind, changes in fecundity, in age at marriage, or in child survival could have triggered increased fertility control. Furthermore, the extent of fertility control in the earliest stage of the transition will be hidden, because some couples returned to childbearing to "replace" children who had died.

Finally, an examination of explanatory variables usually linked to lower fertility points to a cultural explanation of the decline in the birth rate. When we look at fertility differentials by occupation, literacy, and migrant status, only migrant status is clearly related to fertility control in the transitional cohort. Women who had entered Verviers after age 15 were much less likely to show signs of family limitation than women born or raised in the city. The difference between migrants and nonmigrants points to the importance of the city as a cultural influence. Migrants faced the same economic conditions as nonmigrants in Verviers, and their husbands had similar occupations. The most plausible interpretation is that they brought different expectations and values with them from their rural backgrounds.

These results fit the general trend in historical demography away from explanations resting on economic factors toward those emphasizing changes in attitudes (Knodel and van de Walle, 1979). Occupation, clearly the most economic variable examined here, had no association with fertility differences. Whether we interpret occupation as an indicator of economic, social, or demographic differences, its lack of association with fertility is surprising. Even though the relative economic benefits of child labor must have been much greater among industrial workers, especially those in the textile industry, they were not less likely to restrict their fertility.

While the Verviers data do not point to a "trickle-down" or class diffusion model of the fertility transition, there is some evidence of an important class difference. The elite in Verviers did have substantially lower fertility, and they may have begun fertility control earlier. This elite was in some ways more a part of an international European culture than of the local culture of Verviers. The industrialists and merchants in Verviers had business contacts all over the globe, and many had traveled widely. Furthermore, the social distance between the elite and the rest of the community was much wider than any other social distinction. Outside of the elite, fertility decline seems to have reached all social strata at about the same time.

In an impressive study of demographic change in protoindustrial villages surrounding Liège, René Leboutte (1984–85, 1985) has documented a change in attitude toward children in the late nineteenth century. Leboutte uses an extraordinary journal written by a worker in the cottage manufacture of firearms to describe the rising aspirations for children in both material and career terms. The village school teacher, Leboutte argues, had become the symbol of social mobility that was now within reach of even poor families. Parents saw not only the benefits that this new path would hold for their children but also began to base their own social status on the success of their children (Leboutte, 1984–85). The diarist ridiculed the pretentions of workers whose children were being introduced to the outward signs of prosperity at younger and younger ages. The death of a young woman prompted him to remark upon the vanity and false grandeur of her parents. On Sundays and holidays these poor people had dressed their daughter in expensive clothes and had even given her a parasol, while the rest of the week she had worked at the heaviest and dirtiest work and become quite red from exposure to the sun (Leboutte, 1985, p. 20).

The changes in attitudes described by Leboutte may explain the evidence of greater fertility control among women raised in Verviers. It is reasonable to believe that new attitudes spread somewhat earlier in a city like Verviers than in the smaller towns and villages. Visiting socialist leaders from Ghent were astounded at the prosperity of the skilled workers of Verviers, one of whom even owned a piano (Bertrand, 1927, p. 133). Higher wages were prerequisites for this new life style, but a change in attitude toward children and the family economy is also implied. As long as parents emphasized the economic contribution that children could make to the family, there was no reason for them to limit their fertility. As we saw in Chapter 6, parents seem to have been successful in

194

directing the labor of their unmarried children toward the benefit of the family as they defined it. The vigorous, if ambivalent, defense of child labor by both workers and employers in the 1870s suggests that economic development by itself had not yet changed the economics of the family. Only when the economic bargain within the family changed—in Caldwell's terms, when the intergenerational flow of wealth was reversed to flow from parents to children—would a small family become the goal.

8

Conclusion

This study has offered a new perspective on the tension between individualism and family values, which is the central theme in the history of the European family. Did industrial society free the individual from constraints and obligations inherent in the patriarchal organization of peasant agriculture? The life histories of women in Verviers demonstrate the continued importance of family in the nineteenth century by showing the influence of parents and siblings on the lives and actions of women.

To reveal these patterns I have proposed an individual-centered rather than a household-centered approach to family history. Unlike family-cycle typologies, which are based upon stages in the history of a married couple, the life course approach follows individuals within families. Most studies of the household tend to emphasize characteristics of the household head and largely ignore the experiences of those who do not marry or head their own households. The life course approach views the family "from the inside out" rather than "from the top down" and considers the diversity of roles within families.

Previous writers have not been uninterested in family dynamics, but sources and methods suitable to this task have not been available. The life course approach calls for longitudinal sources and dynamic analysis rather than the static cross-sectional analysis most often used in family history. This study taps a new source of data, the Belgian population registers, and develops a methodology for examining transitions in the life course. Samples drawn from the Verviers registers follow the cohort of women who experienced the industrial expansion of the 1850s and 1860s and participated in the first stage of the fertility transition of the 1870s. The time and movement recorded in the population registers complicates their analysis, and the categories and methods used here have not been widely used by historians. For example, I have classified households to show when women moved away from their household of origin or to a household of procreation, rather than classifying them along a scale from nuclear to extended. Life tables and hazard analysis have been used to calculate time

196

spent in different statuses and the likelihood that a woman will migrate, marry, or give birth.

Chapter 2 provides an introduction to the methods of event-history analysis used in the rest of the monograph. I have suggested ways of conceptualizing the longitudinal aspects of data contained in the population registers and problems such as censoring and the changing composition of samples over time. Each life history must be placed in a social context reflecting the interactions among family members and elements of the individual's own history. The sequence of events matters, and each decision is contingent upon the actions of others. Event history analysis recasts the study of life course transitions from a description of average ages of transition (migration, marriage, childbirth, widowhood, etc.) to a discussion of the conditional probabilities of each type of transition. These conditional probabilities reflect the influences of other family members and the consequences of earlier actions. Each of the subsequent chapters applies these tools to a major transition in the life course: household formation, migration, entry and exit from the labor force, courtship, and the initiation of sexual activity, marriage, and childbirth.

The importance of the family is not diminished by organizing our analysis around individuals rather than family groups. Instead, we find new ways of posing questions about the influence of family in individual lives. The discussion of residence patterns in Chapter 3 recasts the historical debate about household structure by stressing that unmarried women remained in their families of origin. Even though mortality rapidly reduced the numbers of two-parent households as women aged, lengthy coresidence with widowed parents and unmarried siblings shows the persistence of family ties. This indicates a continuity in the experience of women who did not marry that the family cycle approach does not address. The marriage model in Chapter 6 also emphasizes the interactions among siblings within a household. Marriages were affected by the family's need for labor as well as by such noneconomic factors as birth order.

Thus, the life course approach enriches our understanding of the importance of the nuclear family in European society. The lives of women in nineteenth-century Verviers emphasize both the exclusiveness and cohesiveness of the European family system. Despite evidence of solidarity among unmarried siblings, married couples rarely accepted unmarried sisters into their households. The exclusion of nonnuclear kin is another aspect of the pattern of small nuclear families which we have come to expect in historical studies of western Europe.

Chapter 3 also shows that the marriage prospects of women in Verviers were strongly affected by the in-migration associated with the city's expanding textile industry. Migrants from surrounding rural areas moved into the city to work in both the textile industry and in the jobs in domestic service, which natives avoided. Most young adult migrants were unmarried women who stayed a short time before moving on. Although only a minority of this type of migrant was likely to remain in Verviers, such a large number of these women moved through the city that they had an important impact on the marriage market for native women. As a result, high proportions of women born in Verviers remained unmarried and attached to their families of origin.

Most authors have stressed the opposition between wage employment and family values; a more complex interaction is presented in Chapter 4. The structure of industrial opportunities in Verviers had effects on both employment careers and marriage, some of which reinforced the importance of family in women's lives. The economic and social impact of family background appears in the evidence that occupational inheritance strongly affected the employment careers of young women. Female occupational choices were very limited, but there were important differences in prestige if not in earning potential. Skilled workers directed their daughters to the more respectable needle trades, whereas daughters of textile workers followed their fathers into the factories. The avoidance of wage employment was itself a sign of high social status. Only women from better-off families could avoid entering the labor force, and the privilege of having "no occupation," not even ménagère, was limited to the elite who could hire domestic servants. This intergenerational transfer of occupations and the social position that it conveyed may have been as important in the lives of women as it was for men.

Family considerations determined a woman's exit from the labor force as well as her choice of occupation. Wage labor in factories was incompatible with the domestic responsibilities that followed soon after marriage. However, opportunities for part-time work and petty commerce allowed married women to continue to make important contributions to the family economy. Large numbers of women did out-work for textile factories or took in sewing and laundry. Those with a little capital ran small shops and cabarets or simply peddled in the streets. These small sources of income could mean the difference between hunger and comfort in the working-class families of the mid-nineteenth century.

The rising rate of illegitimacy in nineteenth-century cities has always been considered the strongest evidence that industrial society undermined the family. Even here, a close look at conceptions outside of marriage in nineteenth-century Verviers reveals a more complicated picture in which family and parents played important roles. Sexual activity outside of marriage took place in a social and cultural framework fundamentally disadvantageous to women. Under the "double standard" young men could demand sexual favors during courtship, while the legal system put full responsibility for any offspring on the mother. The high proportion of bridal pregnancies shows that parents did not prevent coresident daughters from engaging in sexual activity before marriage, and it suggests that sexual intimacy was a normal part of courtship in Verviers.

I have argued in Chapter 5 that illegitimacy and bridal pregnancy resulted from a three-sided bargaining process. On one side were young men who demanded sexual intimacy as a part of courtship. Whether they promised marriage or not, most men recognized that courtships reaching the stage of sexual activity were expected to lead to marriage, even if many did not. On another side were parents who discouraged early marriages that robbed them of the labor of their unmarried daughters. Finally, the young women themselves had to weigh family pressures against their prospects in the marriage market. Most women did wait until their mid-20s to engage in sexual activity, and pregnancies that precipitated marriages were common and probably not unwelcome events. Unwed mothers tended to be older than the average bride and less likely to be residing with their families. These women may have been motivated to take greater risks in the marriage market, and they were less able to bring social pressure to bear on their partners.

The marriage-choice model in Chapter 6 suggests that control of economic resources was not the source of parental power. Working-class parents had few assets to transfer to their children, and contemporary observers frequently remarked that they lived "day to day" without any savings. The women of nineteenth-century Verviers dowered themselves, and parental control was normative rather than economic. The tradition of parental authority had survived the transition from rural to urban life; indeed it had always been an urban tradition as well. Parents could still expect the urban community to support their authority, and rebellious daughters ran the risk of being labeled unruly women and unsuitable prospective wives.

It is surprising to find that women living with both parents were less likely to marry than those living with a widowed father or with no parents at all. A mother's death had a small effect on the economic assets of the household and even increased the widowed father's need for his daughter's domestic labor, but a woman was more likely to marry after her mother died. Such marriages were disproportionately characterized by prenuptial pregnancies, perhaps as a result of conflict with widowed fathers. The marriage-choice model suggests that even the low marriage rates of daughters of widowed mothers were due to the labor needs of households bereft of a male wage-earner, not to the expectation that widows would receive extra emotional support from offspring. I have suggested that the nuclear family had a special hold on children, and that parents were successful in prolonging the contributions of their children to the family as an ongoing enterprise. The death of either parent disrupted the continuity of this social unit and weakened its hold on children.

An instructive comparison can be drawn between the women of nineteenth-century Europe and the young working women in Hong Kong interviewed by Janet Salaff (1981). Salaff has found that the incomes these women bring to their families increase their autonomy and influence on decision-making within the family. But this evidence of change should not mislead us; the dominant aspect of their family lives is the continued authority of parents. These young women have relatively little influence over major decisions, and the patriarchal orientation of their families is hardly threatened. Daughters contribute much of their earnings and postpone their own marriages to enhance the marriage prospects of their brothers. Wage employment and exposure to new influences have had noticeable effects in Hong Kong, but we can still wonder why young women continue to defer to parents within a family system that apparently offers them few rewards.

The nineteenth-century European family was not as strongly patriarchal as the Chinese family; nevertheless, women did make significant contributions to a family system that overtly ignored their interests. Misogynist echoes of Proudhon are evident in *Le Mirabeau* (28 June 1874, BV), the local organ of the International Workingmen's Association, and female employment was usually mentioned as an unfortunate necessity that undermined male wages. Most workers in Verviers would probably have agreed with the French delegation to the international meeting of 1866 in Geneva, who declared unmarried women a violation of the "laws of nature" (Freymond, 1962, p. 93). Under the assumption of patriarchal authority evident in the speeches and writings of working-class leaders, the needs of the family always prevail over the individuals within it, especially its younger female members.

I have not attempted to construct a comprehensive theory of the late marriages in nineteenth-century cities, but several elements of such a theory can be identified. First, most cities encouraged more female than male migration, and this demographic imbalance made later and less universal female marriage more likely. Second, the logic of the independent nuclear family system required the accumulation of savings before marriage, the urban equivalent of access to a farm in Hajnal's description of the "European marriage pattern." Under the low wages found in early industry both males and females tended to marry later. Third, there was probably some active discouragement of marriages by parents who sought to prolong the economic contributions of their children.

Future research should consider whether nineteenth-century cities offered an alternative lifestyle to women who preferred not to marry. The culture of the times was unfavorable to unmarried women, and there are few signs in Verviers of a movement asserting the desirability of unmarried life. Nevertheless, Susan C. Watkins (1984) has emphasized that no other major culture has allowed as high a proportion of unmarried women as European society. She also points out that the Catholic religion always actively promoted the virtues of celibacy. The large numbers of unmarried and widowed women in cities were a potential source of social support for a woman without husband or family. A woman need not have abandoned the ideal of marriage to conclude that spinsterhood in the company of other women was better than an indifferent or brutal husband.

After their marriages the demands of childbearing dominated the lives of nineteenth-century women, as they had for all previous generations, but signs of change are evident in the 1870s. Intervals between births became shorter, probably because of changes in nutrition and infant-feeding practices. However, completed family sizes were little different from those of the older women examined in the 1850s, because the increase in fecundity was offset by the introduction of birth control. Age-specific birth rates began to show a "stopping" pattern associated with family limitation, and birth-interval analysis reveals a "replacement effect" in which fertility was higher after a child's death. These changes in fertility behavior herald a new demographic regime under voluntary control, which advanced in spite of the continued influence of high infant and child mortality.

The economic and social elite was in the vanguard of the fertility transition in Verviers, as earlier studies have found elsewhere in Europe. Women from the wealthiest families show much stronger and more complete control of their fertility. Family limitation does not, however, appear to have spread slowly through the social structure from top to bottom. There is evidence of family limitation in all occupational groups in the cohort of women born during 1826–35. Even education, measured here by literacy, does not identify the couples most likely to have practiced fertility control. The clearest dividing line is between women who were born or reared in the city and those who arrived as adults. The industrial and urban experience was at least partly responsible for the transition to smaller families, but European history cautions us not to expect a simple relationship between economic change and lower fertility (Coale and Watkins, 1986; Knodel and van de Walle, 1979).

Caldwell (1982) has argued that high fertility is maintained by a family system in which the "intergenerational flow of wealth" moves from children to parents. As long as parents believe that large families offer them economic and social advantages, family limitation is not desirable. Children in nineteenth-century Verviers were not a bargain in simple economic terms, but the long coresidence of unmarried adult children made them an important economic asset in the long run. As older children entered the labor force, their earnings brought prosperity to the family and more than offset the costs of additional children. These later-born siblings could then sustain the family into the parents' old age. Thus, the expectation of income from children encouraged large families.

The working-class family in nineteenth-century Verviers depended upon the income of children, and the debate over regulation of child labor reveals an ambivalence regarding the balance of obligations between parents and children. Neither workers nor employers were willing to endorse legislation that would have limited the employment of children. Working-class leaders both attacked the industrial system that paid them too little to support their families, and defended the decision to send children into the factories when their earnings were needed.

Economic development in the late nineteenth century undoubtedly affected attitudes about child labor and the family in general. René Leboutte (1984–85) has found that parents' desire to see the social advancement of their children in a protoindustrial Walloon village was increasing at the time that fertility began to decline. It is likely that the experience of rising incomes changed the bargain between generations within the family in Verviers as well. As it became possible for the family to survive and even prosper on the income of a male wage-earner, parents began to desire a better life for their children. They could not expect sons and daughters to satisfy their ambitions and support a host of younger siblings, so families needed to be limited in size. The lower fertility of women reared in the city probably reflects their longer exposure to urban opportunities and aspirations for their children that were incompatible with large families.

The picture of nineteenth-century women painted here is at odds with the themes of individualism, economic emancipation, and female independence found in historians like Michael Anderson and Edward Shorter and dating back to contemporary observers like Frédéric Le Play. Anderson (1971, 1978) correctly encourages us to view the family in terms of exchange, but he creates the impression that the bargaining power of children was directly proportional to their economic contribution. Like Louise Tilly and Joan Scott, I have emphasized the continued importance of the family in the urban environment. My conclusion is that parents maintained a moral authority rooted in culture and supported by the urban community throughout the transition to modern industrial society. The question is whether changes in the family occurred because parental authority was weakened or because parents changed their attitudes and expectations about children. Contemporary commentators certainly saw conflict between parents and children in working-class families. However, it may be that contemporaries judged evidence of individualistic attitudes on the part of children by standards that we would not use today. Conflicts within the family can also arise because parents demand a great deal of their children. The lives of women in nineteenth-century Verviers are best understood in terms of the competition between demands of parents and siblings and the desire to establish families of their own. Changes in the family since the nineteenth century have not simply involved the intrusion of individualism. European families have also developed a new conception of the responsibilities of parents to children and a new balance for the obligations between generations.

Appendix   References   Index

Appendix

Explanatory Variables in the Coale-Trussell Model

The Coale-Trussell model describes fertility rates by the equation

$$\frac{b_x}{t_x} = M n_x e^{m v_x}$$

in which

b_x is the number of births at age x,
t_x is the birth of person years exposed to the risk of a birth,
M is the parameter indicating the level of fertility compared with the natural fertility model,
n_x is the age-specific marital fertility rate in the natural fertility model,
e is the base of the natural logarithms,
m is the parameter indicating the level of fertility control,
v_x is the schedule of deviations from the natural fertility model.

This model is modified by taking logarithms on both sides, which yields a linear equation

$$\log b_x - \log t_x = \log M + \log n_x + m v_x$$

and

$$\log b_x = \log M + m v_x + \log n_x + \log t_x.$$

Next, the estimated parameters, M and m, are replaced by linear equations of explanatory variables

$$\log b_x = a_0 + a_1 y_1 + \cdots + a_j y_j + v_x(b_0 + b_1 z_1 + \cdots + b_k z_k) + \log n_x + \log t_x,$$

in which

$a_1 \ldots a_j$ and $b_1 \ldots b_k$ are estimated coefficients, and
$y_1 \ldots y_j$ and $z_1 \ldots z_k$ are explanatory variables.

This model can be analyzed by one of several computer packages for estimating log linear models. The estimates reported here were produced by the GLIM program.

The estimated values of the Coale-Trussell parameters are

$$M = e^{a_0 + a_1 y_1 + \cdots + a_j y_j}$$

and

$$m = b_0 + b_1 z_1 + \cdots + b_k z_k.$$

References

Archival Sources

ADL: Archives Diocésaines de Liège
"Réponse de S. G. Mgr l'Evêque de Liége à une consultations de la Société de St. François Régis," Liège, 28 February 1883. Fonds Doutreloux, No. 64.

AEL: Archives de l'état à Liège
Enterprises Peltzer. 18 January 1854, No. 87. 29 November 1856, No. 116.
Fonds David. 1842, No. 5157. 1844, No. 5144.
Fonds Flagontier et de Thier. 1861–65, Nos. 6–9.

AV: Archives communales de Verviers
Conseil communal. 1836. "Procès-verbaux de la séance du conseil communal du 6 septembre 1836." 19D4.2, No. 12.
"Echoppes, mannes, et autres objets étalés dans les rues, sur les trottoir et autres lieux, les jours autres que ceux de marché." 2 and 3 December 1847, XIXe siècle F. 5/8.
Exposé de la situation de la ville de Verviers sous le rapport de son administration. n.p. 1.F1.1. 1844–80.
L'Industriel de Verviers. 1842–50. 47 F1.3.
"Livre aux déclarations sur la fortune présumée." 1848 and 1856, Vols. 2 and 47, 41 F1.1.
Nouvelliste de Verviers. 1835–1904. 47 D1.2.
H.B., "Une histoire très véritable." *Nouvelliste*, 14 August 1844.
Frédéric Thomas, "Un couplet en action." *Nouvelliste*, 16 November 1844.
"Pièces diverses." 16 January 1852, XIXe siècle, F. 6/32.
"Pièces diverses—fortune présumée." 1849. 29 F3.4 farde 31.
Registres de population. 1846, 1849, 1856, 1866.
Registres de l'état civil. 1844–80.
Relevés des habitants. 1843–45.
Registre des patentables. 1871. 40 D2.5, No. 115.

BV: Bibliothèque de Verviers
"L'Etude cercle d'émancipation intellectuelle. Procès-verbaux, première et seconde années, 1865–66–67." Fonds de la Ville, 24 February–2 March 1867, No. 75-4, pp. 150–57.

Le Mirabeau. 1867–80.
   H. R., "Section des femmes. Appel aux femmes." 24 October 1873, 6 année, No. 214. [Théo Pirard (1971, p. 200) identifies "H. R." as Hubertine Ruwette.]
   "L'Emancipation de la femme." 17 April 1870, 3me année, No. 39.
   C. G., "L'Instruction et l'émancipation (L'Union conjugale)." 28 June 1874, 7 année, No. 258.
   "Procès verbaux des séances entre patrons et ouvriers 1870–1877." Photocopy of handwritten manuscript. n.d. BR IV.0129
MVW: Musée de la vie Wallonne
   Nouveau trésor des amants. n.d. Liège: Bertrand-Forck.
   Le Catéchisme des amants ou l'art de faire l'amour. [1896]. Paris: S. Bornemann.

OTHER SOURCES

Allison, Paul D. 1982. "Discrete-Time Methods for the Analysis of Event Histories." In *Sociological Methods,* ed. S. Leinhardt, 61–98. San Francisco: Jossey-Bass.

Alter, George. 1978. "The Influence of Social Stratification on Marriage in Nineteenth Century Europe." Ph.D. dissertation, University of Pennsylvania.

Alter, George. 1984a. "Work and Income in the Family Economy: Belgium, 1853 and 1891." *Journal of Interdisciplinary History* 15: 255–76.

Alter, George. 1984b. "Fertility Limitation in Historical Population Registers: Methods and Results from Nineteenth Century Belgium." Unpublished working paper, Indiana University, 12 June.

Anderson, Michael. 1971. *Family Structure in Nineteenth Century Lancashire.* Cambridge: Cambridge University Press.

Anderson, Michael. 1978. *The Family and Industrialization in Western Europe.* St. Louis: Forum Press.

Anderson, Michael. 1980. *Approaches to the History of the Western Family 1500–1914.* London: The Economic History Society.

Anderson, Michael. 1984. "The Social Position of Spinsters in Mid-Victorian Britain." *Journal of Family History* 9: 377–93.

Anderson, Michael. 1985. "Continuity and Turmoil in Industrial Cities." *Journal of Family History* 10: 196–205.

André, Anne-Marie. 1976–77. "Le Mariage chez les fabricants de drap verviétois XVIIIe-début XIXe siècle. Essai de démographie historique et structure de l'alliance." Mémoire de licence, Université de Liège.

Appert, B. 1848. *Voyage en Belgique.* Brussels: A. Garcin et Aug. Beelaerts.

Arminger, Gerhard. 1984a. "Analysis of Event Histories with Generalized Linear Models." In *Stochastic Modelling of Social Processes,* ed. Andreas Diekman and Peter Mitten, 245–82. New York: Academic Press.

Arminger, Gerhard. 1984b. "Compound Linear Models." Paper presented at the annual meeting of the American Sociological Association, San Antonio, 27–31 August.

Banks, J. A. 1981. *Victorian Values, Secularism and the Size of Families*. London: Routledge and Kegan Paul.

Baugniet, Jean. 1956. "Le Statut juridique de la femme." In *La Condition sociale de la femme*, xxve Semaine sociale universitaire du 17 au 22 octobre 1955, pp. 103–15. Brussels: Université libre de Bruxelles, Institut de sociologie Solvay.

Becker, Gary S. 1973. "A Theory of Marriage: Part I." *Journal of Political Economy* 81: 813–46.

Becker, Gary S. 1974. "A Theory of Marriage: Part II." *Journal of Political Economy* 82: S11–16.

Becker, Gary S. 1981. *A Treatise on the Family*. Cambridge, Mass.: Harvard University Press.

Belgium, Commission du travail. 1887. *Réponses au questionnaire concernante le travail industriel*, Vol. 1; and *Procès-verbaux des séances d'enquête concernante le travail industriel*, Vol. 2. Brussels: A. Lesigne.

Belgium, Ministère de l'intérieur. 1846. *Enquête sur la condition des classes ouvrières et sur le travail des enfants*, Vol. 2. Brussels: Th. Lesigne.

Belgium, Ministère de l'intérieur. 1849. *Statistique de la Belgique. Population. Recensement général, 15 octobre 1846*. Brussels: Th. Lesigne.

Belgium, Ministère de l'intérieur. 1851. *Statistique de la Belgique. Industrie. Recensement général, 15 octobre 1846*. Brussels: Th. Lesigne.

Belgium, Ministère de l'intérieur. 1852. *Statistique générale de la Belgique. Exposé de la situation du royaume*. (Période décennale de 1841–1850). Brussels: Th. Lesigne.

Belgium, Ministère de l'intérieur. 1872. *Statistique de la Belgique. Population. Recensement général, 31 decembre 1866*. Brussels: Th. Lesigne.

Berkner, Lutz K. 1972. "The Stem Family and the Developmental Cycle of the Peasant Household: An 18th Century Austrian Example." *American Historical Review* 77: 398–418.

Bertrand, Louis. 1927. *Souvenirs d'un meneur socialiste*, Vol. 1. Brussels: Maison nationale d'édition "L'Eglantine."

Blake-Davis, Judith. 1967. "Parental Control, Delayed Marriage, and Population Policy." In *World Population Conference*, United Nations Department of Economic and Social Affairs, Vol. 2, 132–36. New York: United Nations.

Borscheid, Peter. 1986. "Romantic Love or Material Interest: Choosing Partners in Nineteenth Century Germany." *Journal of Family History* 11: 157–68.

Boserup, Ester. 1970. *Women's Role in Economic Development*. London: George Allen and Unwin.

Brostrom, Goran. 1985. "Practical Aspects of the Estimation of the Parameters in Coale's Model of Marital Fertility." *Demography* 22: 625–31.

Bruno, M. A. 1842. *Code administratif de Belgique*. Brussels: M. Hayez.

Caldwell, John C. 1982. *Theory of Fertility Decline*. New York: Academic Press.

Caspard, Pierre. 1974. "Conceptions prénuptiales et développement du capitalisme dans la principauté de Neuchâtel (1678–1820)." *Annales: Economies, sociétés, civilisations* 29: 989–1008.

Christensen, Harold T. 1960. "Cultural Relativism and Premarital Sex Norms." *American Sociological Review* 25: 31–39.

Coale, Ansley J., and T. James Trussell. 1974. "Model Fertility Schedules: Variations in the Age Structure of Childbearing in Human Populations." *Population Index* 40: 185–258.

Coale, Ansley J., and T. James Trussell. 1978. "Technical Note: Finding the Two Parameters That Specify a Model Schedule of Marital Fertility." *Population Index* 44: 203–7.

Coale, Ansley J., and Susan Cotts Watkins. 1986. *The Decline of Fertility in Europe.* Princeton: Princeton University Press.

Collier, Frances. 1965. *The Family Economy of the Working Classes in the Cotton Industry 1784–1833.* Manchester: Manchester University Press.

Commission médicale de la province de Liège. 1847. C. Wasseige, rapporteur. *Mémoire sur la condition des ouvriers et le travail des enfants dans les mines, manufactures et usines de la province de Liège*, 86. Brussels: Th. Lesigne.

Coomans, J.-B. [1849]. *Pauperisme. Causes et remèdes. Discours prononcé par M. Coomans sur le budget de l'intérieur dans la séance de la Chambre des représentants du 30 janvier 1849.* N.p.

Courtois, Richard. 1828. *Recherches sur la statistiques physique, agricole et médicale de la province de Liège*, 2 vols. Verviers: M.-R. Beaufays.

Dauby, J. 1873. *De l'élévation des classes ouvrières en Belgique au point de vue moral et intellectuel.* Brussels: Librairie de A.-N. Lebegue.

Daumard, Adeline. 1970. *Les Bourgeois de Paris au XIXe siècle.* Paris: Flammarion.

Davis, Natalie Z. 1971. "The Reasons of Misrule: Youth Groups and Charivaris in 16th-Century France." *Past and Present* 50: 41–45.

De Camps. 1890. *L'évolution sociale en Belgique: ses pèripèties au point de vue de classes ouvrières. L'Enquête ouvrière de 1886.* Brussels: Bruylant-Christophe.

Dechesne, Laurent. 1908. *L'Avènement du régime syndical à Verviers.* Paris: Libraire de la Société du recueil général des lois et des arrêts.

Dechesne, Laurent. 1932. *Histoire économique et sociale de la Belgique.* Liège: Libraire Joseph Wykmans.

Dejardin, Joseph. 1891–92. "Dictionnaire des spots ou proverbes wallons." *Bulletin de la Société liégeoise de litérature wallonne.* 2d ser., 17 and 18.

de Montpellier, Theodore-Alexis Joseph. 1867. "Mandement de carême." *Lettres et mandements de l'évêque de Liège*, Vol. 4. Liège: Evêché de Liège.

Demos, John. 1970. *A Little Commonwealth, Family Life in Plymouth Colony.* New York: Oxford University Press.

De Paepe, P. 1887. *Pasinomie, collection complète des lois, décrets, arrêtés et règlements généraux qui peuvent être invoqués en Belgique.* Brussels: Bruylant-Christophe.

Desama, Claude. 1985. *Population et revolution: Evolution des structure démographiques à Verviers dans la première moitié du 19e siècle.* Bibliothèque de la faculté de philosophie et lettres de l'Université de Liège. Paris: Société d'édition "Les Belles Lettres."

Ducpetiaux, Edouard. 1855. *Budgets economiques des classes ouvriers en Belgique*, 1–11. Brussels: M. Hayez.

Duncan, O. D. 1965. "Farm Background and Differential Fertility." *Demography* 2: 240–49.

Easterlin, Richard A. 1978. "The Economics and Sociology of Fertility: A Synthesis." In *Historical Studies of Changing Fertility*, ed. Charles Tilly, 57–133. Princeton: Princeton University Press.

Elder, Glen H. 1974. *Children of the Great Depression.* Chicago: University of Chicago Press.

Elder, Glen H. 1978. "Family History and the Life Course." In *Transitions: The Family and the Life Course in Historical Perspective*, ed. Tamara K. Hareven, 17–64. New York: Academic Press.

El Kefi-Clokers, Christiane. 1975–76. "La population féminine active de l'industrie textile verviétoise: Essai d'interpretation du recensement de 1856." Mémoire de licence, Université de Liège.

Entwisle, Barbara, and William M. Mason. 1985. "Multilevel Effects of Socioeconomic Development and Family Planning Programs on Children Ever Born." *American Journal of Sociology* 3: 616–49.

Evans, David-Owen. 1930. *Le Roman social sous la Monarchie de juillet.* Paris: Presses universitaires de France.

Fairchilds, Cissie. 1978. "Female Sexual Attitudes and the Rise of Illegitimacy: A Case Study." *Journal of Interdisciplinary History* 8: 627–67.

Fairchilds, Cissie. 1984. *Domestic Enemies: Servants & Their Masters in Old Regime France.* Baltimore: Johns Hopkins University Press.

Featherman, David L. 1983. "Life Perspectives in Social Science Research." In *Life-Span Development and Behavior*, ed. Paul B. Baltes and Orville G. Brim, Jr., Vol. 5, 1–57. New York: Academic Press.

Fleury, M., and L. Henry. 1956. *Nouveau manuel de dépouillement et d'esploitation de l'état civil ancien.* Paris: Editions de l'Institut national d'études démographiques.

Fohal, Jean. 1927–28. "La Disette à Verviers en 1845." *Bulletin de la Société verviétoise d'archéologie et d'histoire* 21: 30–31.

Fohal, Jean. 1928. *Verviers et son industrie il y a quatre-vingt-cinq ans 1843.* Verviers: G. Leens.

Fossion, N. G. 1845. *Rapport sur la condition des ouvriers et le travail des enfants dans les manufactures, mines et usines de la province.* Liège: Félix Oudart.

Frey, Michel. 1978. "Du mariage et du concubinage dans les classes populaires à Paris (1846–1847)." *Annales: Economies, sociétés, civilisations* 33: 803–29.

Freymond, Jacques, Ed. 1962. *La première Internationale, Recueil de documents*, Vol. 1. Genève: Librairie E. Droz.

Furstenberg, Frank. 1976. *Unplanned Parenthood.* New York: Free Press.

Goldberg, David. 1959. "The Fertility of Two Generation Urbanities." *Population Studies* 12: 214–22.

Goldberg, David. 1960. "Another Look at the Indianapolis Fertility Data." *Millbank Memorial Fund Quarterly* 38: 23–36.

Goldin, Claudia. 1979. "Household and Market Production of Families in a Late Nineteenth Century American City." *Explorations in Economic History* 16: 111–31.

Goldstein, Sidney, and Alice Goldstein. 1981. "The Impact of Migration on Fertility: An 'Own Children' Analysis for Thailand." *Population Studies* 35: 265–84.

Green, Arnold W. 1941. "The 'Cult of Personality' and Sexual Relations." *Psychiatry* 4: 343–48.

Guillaume, James. 1910. *L'Internationale. Documents et souvenirs (1864–1878).* Paris: P.-V. Stock.

Guillaume, Pierre. 1972. *La Population de Bordeaux au XIXe siècle.* Paris: Armand Colin.

Gutmann, Myron P., and Etienne van de Walle. 1978. "New Sources for Social and Demographic History: The Belgian Population Registers." *Social Science History* 2: 121–43.

Haines, Michael. 1979a. *Fertility and Occupation: Population Patterns in Industrialization.* New York: Academic Press.

Haines, Michael. 1979b. "Industrial Work and the Family Life Cycle, 1889/90." In *Research in Economic History*, ed. Paul Uselding, Vol. 4, 289–356. Greenwich, Conn.: JAI Press.

Hajnal, John. 1965. "European Marriage Patterns in Perspective." In *Population and History*, ed. D. V. Glass and D. E. C. Eversley, 101–43. London: Edward Arnold.

Hajnal, John. 1983. "Two Kinds of Pre-industrial Household Formation." In *Family Forms in Historic Europe*, ed. Richard Wall, 65–104. Cambridge: Cambridge University Press.

Hareven, Tamara K. 1977. "Family Time and Historical Time." *Daedalus* 106: 57–70.

Hareven, Tamara K. 1978a. "Cycles, Courses and Cohorts: Reflections on Theoretical and Methodological Approaches to the Historical Study of Family Development." *Journal of Social History* 12: 97–109.

Hareven, Tamara K., Ed. 1978b. *Transitions: The Family and the Life Course in Historical Perspective.* New York: Academic Press.

Hareven, Tamara K. 1982. *Family Time and Industrial Time: The Relationship between the Family and Work in a New England Industrial Community.* Cambridge: Cambridge University Press.

Hareven, Tamara, and Louise A. Tilly. 1981. "Solitary Women and Family Mediations in Two Textile Cities: Manchester and Roubaix." *Annales de démographie historique*: 253–71.

Harrison, Brian. 1967. "Underneath the Victorians." *Victorian Studies* 10: 239–62.

Henau, M. 1847. "Recherches sur les causes de la criminalité dans la province de Liège." *Bulletin de la Commission centrale de statistique* 3: 184–207.

Henry, Louis. 1961. "Some Data on Natural Fertility." *Eugenics Quarterly* 6: 81–91.

Henry, Louis. 1977. "Current Concepts and Empirical Results concerning Natural Fertility." In *Natural Fertility*, ed. Henri Leridon and Jane Menken, 15–28. Liège: Ordina editions.

Henry, Louis. 1980. *Techniques d'analyse en démographie historique.* Paris: Editions de l'Institut national d'études démographiques.

Hervitz, Hugo M. 1984. "Origin-Destination Comparisons of Migrant and Stayer

Fertility Differentials: The Case of Brazil." Project paper prepared for the Fertility Determinants Group, Indiana University, Bloomington, Indiana.

Hillman, Arthur. 1960. "Eilert Sundt: Pioneer Student of Family and Culture in Norway." In *Norway's Families*, ed. Thomas D. Eliot and Arthur Hillman, 36–46. Philadelphia: University of Pennsylvania Press.

Hogan, Dennis P., and David I. Kertzer. 1985a. "Longitudinal Approaches to Migration in Social History." *Historical Methods* 18: 20–30.

Hogan, Dennis P., and David I. Kertzer. 1985b. "Migration Patterns during Italian Urbanization, 1865–1921." *Demography* 22: 309–26.

Hoggart, Richard. 1971. *The Uses of Literacy*, 84–85. London: Chatto and Windus.

Houget, Adrein. 1875. *La Réforme du travail des enfants, encore pourquoi une loi?* Verviers: A. Remacle.

Kälvemark, Anne-Sofie. 1980. "Illegitimacy and Marriage in Three Swedish Parishes in the Nineteenth Century." In *Bastardy*, ed. P. Laslett, K. Oosterveen, and R. M. Smith, 327–35. Cambridge, Mass.: Harvard University Press.

Katz, Michael B. 1975. *The People of Hamilton, Canada West: Family and Class in a Mid-Nineteenth Century City*. Cambridge, Mass.: Harvard University Press.

Kertzer, David I. 1985. "Future Directions in Historical Household Studies." *Journal of Family History* 10: 98–107.

Kertzer, David I., and Dennis P. Hogan. 1985. "On the Move: Migration in an Italian Community, 1865–1921." *Social Science History* 9: 1–24.

Kertzer, David I., and Andrea Schiaffino. 1983. "Industrialization and Coresidence: A Life Course Approach." In *Life-Span Development and Behavior*, ed. Paul B. Baltes and Orville G. Brim, Jr., Vol. 5, 360–91. New York: Academic Press.

Knodel, John. 1975. "The Influence of Child Mortality on Fertility in European Populations in the Past: Results from Individual Data." In *Seminar on Infant Mortality in Relation to the Level of Fertility*, 103–118. Paris: Committee for International Coordination of National Research in Demography.

Knodel, John. 1981. "Child Mortality and Reproductive Behavior in German Village Populations in the Past: A Micro-Level Analysis of the Replacement Effect." Research Report No. 81-1. Population Studies Center, University of Michigan, Ann Arbor, Michigan.

Knodel, John. 1986. "The Demographic Transition in German Villages." In *The Decline of Fertility in Europe*, ed. Ansley J. Coale and Susan Cotts Watkins, 337–89. Princeton: Princeton University Press.

Knodel, John, and Steven Hochstadt. 1980. "Urban and Rural Illegitimacy in Imperial Germany." In *Bastardy*, ed. P. Laslett, K. Oosterveen, and R. M. Smith, 284–312. Cambridge, Mass.: Harvard University Press.

Knodel, John, and Mary Jo Maynes. 1976. "Urban and Rural Marriage Patterns in Imperial Germany." *Journal of Family History* 1: 129–68.

Knodel, John, and Etienne van de Walle. 1979. "Lessons from the Past: Policy Implications of Historical Fertility Studies." *Population and Development Review* 5: 217–45.

Kooy, Gerrit A., and Iteke Cramwinckel-Weeda. 1975. "Forced Marriages in the Netherlands: A Macrosociological Approach to Marriages Contracted as a Consequence of Unintended Pregnancy." *Journal of Marriage and the Family* 37: 954–65.

Landais, Napoleon. 1847. *Lettres à Amélie sur le mariage*. Brussels: Ad. Wahlen.

Laslett, Peter. 1972. [with the assistance of Richard Wall]. *Household and Family in Past Time*. Cambridge: Cambridge University Press.

Laslett, Peter. 1977. *Family Life and Illicit Love in Earlier Generations*. Cambridge: Cambridge University Press.

Laslett, Peter. 1980a. "Introduction." In *Bastardy*, ed. P. Laslett, K. Oosterveen, and R. M. Smith, 1–65. Cambridge, Mass.: Harvard University Press.

Laslett, Peter. 1980b. "The Bastardy Prone Sub-society." In *Bastardy*, ed. P. Laslett, K. Oosterveen, and R. M. Smith, 217–40. Cambridge, Mass.: Harvard University Press.

Laslett, Peter, Karla Oosterveen, and Richard M. Smith. 1980. *Bastardy and Its Comparative History*. Cambridge, Mass.: Harvard University Press.

Leboutte, René. 1983. "L'Apport des registres de population à la connaissance de la dynamique des ménages en Belgique au XIXe siècle." Paper presented at the international conference "Strutture rapporti familiari in epoca moderna: esperienze italiane e riferimenti europei," Trieste, Italy, 5–7 September.

Leboutte, René. 1984. "Les Registres de population en Belgique: Point d'ancrage d'une future banque de données." Paper presented at the conference "On Methods for Using Population Registers in Historical Research," Umea, Sweden, 13–17 August.

Leboutte, René. 1984–85. "Reconversions industrielles et transition demographique dans la Basse-Meuse liégeoise 1750–1976." Thèse de doctorat, Université de Liège.

Leboutte, René. 1985. "The Socio-Psychological Basis for the Demographic Transition in Belgium." Paper presented at the Social Science History Association, Chicago, 21–24 November.

Leboutte, René, and Rashidi Obotela. 1982. "Les registres de population en Belgique, XIXe–XXe siècles." Unpublished paper, Université de Liège, Liège, Belgium, November.

Lebrun, François. 1979. "Naissances illegitimes et abandons d'enfants en Anjou au XVIIIe siècle." *Annales: Economies, sociétés, civilisations* 27: 1183–89.

Lebrun, Pierre. 1948. *L'Industrie de la laine à Verviers pendant le XVIIIe et le début du XIXe siècle*. Liège: Bibliothèque de la faculté de philosophie et lettres de l'Université de Liège, Fascicule 114.

Lebrun, Pierre, Marinette Bruwier, Jan Dhondt, and Georges Hansotte. 1979. *Essai sur la révolution industrielle en Belgique 1770–1847*. Brussels: Académie royale de Belgique.

Lee, W. R. 1977. "Bastardy and the Socioeconomic Structure of South Germany." *Journal of Interdisciplinary History* 7: 403–25.

Lejear, J. 1906. "Histoire de la ville de Verviers. Période hollandaise et revolution belge de 1830. 1814–1830." *Bulletin de la Société verviétoise d'archéologie et d'histoire* 7: 1–264.

Lepas, André Jos. 1844. "Coup d'oeil sur la situation de la classe ouvrière de Verviers." *Nouvelle revue de Bruxelles*: 199–214.

Le Play, Frédéric. 1878. "Epilogue de 1878." In *Les Ouvriers Européens*, Vol. 6, 538–60. Tours: Alfred Mame.

Lesthaeghe, Ron J. 1977. *The Decline of Belgian Fertility, 1800–1970.* Princeton: Princeton University Press.

Levine, David. 1983. "Proto-Industrialization and Demographic Upheaval." In *Essays on the Family and Historical Change*, ed. Leslie Page Moch and Gary D. Stark, 9–34. College Station: Texas A & M University Press.

Levine, David, and Keith Wrightson. 1980. "The Social Context of Illegitimacy in Early Modern England." In *Bastardy*, ed. P. Laslett, K. Oosterveen, and R. M. Smith, 158–75. Cambridge, Mass.: Harvard University Press.

Lockridge, Kenneth A. 1983. "The Fertility Transition in Sweden." Report No. 3 from the Demographic Data Base, University of Umea, Sweden.

Lottin, Alain. 1970. "Naissances illegitimes et filles-mères à Lille au XVIIIe siècle." *Revue d'histoire moderne et contemporaine* 17: 278–322.

Mareska, J., and J. Heyman. 1845. *Enquête sur le travail et la condition physique et morale des ouvriers employés dans les manufactures de coton, à Gand.* Gand: F. et E. Gyselynck.

Martine, G. 1979. "Migrant Fertility Adjustment and Urban Growth in Latin America." *International Migration Review* 9: 179–91.

Mathieu, Joseph. 1946. *Histoire sociale de l'industrie textile de Verviers.* Dison, Belgium: J.-J. Jespers-Gregoire.

Mathieux, A.-J. 1954. *L'Industrie drapière du pays de Verviers et au duché de Limbourg.* Verviers: S. A. G. Nautet-Hans.

Mayhew, Henry. 1861–62. *London Labour and the London Poor.* 4 vols. London: Griffin, Bohn.

Menken, Jane, James Trussell, and Susan Watkins, 1981. "The Nutrition Fertility Link: An Evaluation of the Evidence." *Journal of Interdisciplinary History* 11: 425–42.

Menken, Jane, James Trussell, Debra Stempel, and Ozer Babakol. 1981. "Proportional Hazards Life Table Models: An Illustrative Analysis of Socio-Demographic Influences on Marriage Dissolution in the United States." *Demography* 18: 181–200.

Mitterauer, Michael, and Reinhard Sieder. 1983. *The European Family.* Chicago: University of Chicago Press.

Moch, Leslie Page. 1983. *Paths to the City: Regional Migration in Nineteenth Century France.* Beverly Hills, Calif.: Sage Publications.

Moch, Leslie Page, and Louise A. Tilly. 1985. "Joining the Urban World: Occupation, Family, and Migration in Three French Cities." *Comparative Studies of Society and History* 27: 33–56.

Modell, John. 1978. "Patterns of Consumption, Acculturation, and Family Income Strategies in Late Nineteenth-Century America." In *Family and Population in Nineteenth-Century America*, ed. Tamara K. Hareven and Maris A. Vinovskis, 206–40. Princeton: Princeton University Press.

Modell, John, Frank Furstenberg, and Theodore Hershberg. 1976. "Social Change and the Transition to Adulthood in Historical Perspective." *Journal of Family History* 1: 7–32.

Monseur, Eugène. [1892]. *Le Folklore wallon*. Bibliothèque belge des connaissances modernes, No. 6. Brussels: Charles Rozez.

Morgan, Edmund S. 1966. *The Puritan Family*. New York: Harper and Row.

Moses, Claire Goldberg. 1984. *French Feminism in the Nineteenth Century*. Albany: State University of New York Press.

Mueller, Eva. 1976. "The Economic Value of Children in Peasant Agriculture." In *Population and Development: A Search for Selective Interventions*, ed. Ronald Ridker, 98–153. Baltimore: The Johns Hopkins University Press.

Myrdal, Alva. 1968. *Nation and Family*. Cambridge, Mass.: MIT Press.

Neuman, R. P. 1972. "Industrialization and Sexual Behavior: Some Aspects of Working Class Life in Imperial Germany." In *Modern European Social History*, ed. Robert Bezucha, 270–98. Lexington, Mass.: D. C. Heath.

Ogle, William. 1890. "On Marriage Rates and Marriage Ages with Special Reference to the Growth of Population." *Journal of the Royal Statistical Society* (London) 53: 253–80.

Oukhow, C. 1967. *Documents relatifs à l'histoire de la première Internationale en Wallonie*. Centre interuniversitaire d'histoire contemporaine, Cahiers 47. Leuven-Louvain: Editions Nauwelaerts.

Phayer, Michael. 1974. "Lower Class Morality: The Case of Bavaria." *Journal of Social History* 8: 79–95.

Pickens, Gary. 1978. "A Stochastic Model of Natural Marital Fertility: Theory and Analysis of Some Historical Population Data." *Mathematical Biosciences* 48: 129–51.

Piette, Emile. 1876. [Pol Ether, pseud.]. *Pétitionnement pour l'abolition du travail des enfants jugé au point de vue révolutionnaire*. Verviers: E. Piette.

Pirard, Théo. 1971. "Le Mouvement ouvrier verviétois et 'Le Mirabeau' au temps de la 1ère Internationale (1867–1874)." Mémoire de licence, Université catholique de Louvain, juin.

Poetgens, Henri. 1895. [Joseph Krahli, pseud.]. *Coutumes et silhouettes du Verviers ancien*. Verviers: Aug. Nicolet.

Pope, Hallowell, and Dean D. Knudsen. 1965. "Premarital Sexual Norms, the Family, and Social Change." *Journal of Marriage and the Family* 27: 314–23.

Preston, Samuel H., and Alan Thomas Richards. 1975. "The Influence of Women's Work Opportunities on Marriage Rates." *Demography* 12: 209–22.

Rainwater, Lee. 1966. "Some Aspects of Lower Class Sexual Behavior." *Journal of Social Issues* 22: 96–108.

Reiss, Ira L. 1960. *Premarital Sexual Standards in America*. Glencoe, Ill.: Free Press.

Renier, J. S. 1881. *Histoire de l'industrie drapière au pays de Liège et particulièrement dans l'arrondissement de Verviers*. Liège: Leon de Thier.

Richards, Toni, Michael J. White, and Amy Ong Tsui. 1985. "Changing Living Arrangements: A Hazard Model of Transitions among Household Types." Paper presented at the Population Association of America, Boston, 28–30 March.

Roberts, Robert. 1973. *The Classic Slum: Salford Life in the First Quarter of the Century.* Harmondsworth, Middlesex: Penguin Books.

Rodriguez, German, John Hobcraft, John McDonald, Jane Menken, and James Trussell. 1984. "A Comparative Analysis of Determinants of Birth Intervals." *World Fertility Survey Comparative Studies,* No. 30.

Rossiaud, Jacques. 1976. "Prostitution, jeunesse et société au xve siècle." *Annales: Economies, sociétés, civilisations* 31: 289–325.

Rowntree, B. Seebohm. 1903. *Poverty: A Study of Town Life.* London: Macmillan.

Rowntree, B. Seebohm. 1910. *Land and Labour: Lessons from Belgium.* London: Macmillan.

Ryder, Norman B. 1975. "Fertility Measurement through Cross-Sectional Surveys." *Social Forces* 54: 7–35.

St. Lewinski, Jan. 1911. *L'Evolution industrielle de la Belgique.* Brussels: Misch et Thron.

Salaff, Janet. 1981. *Working Daughters of Hong Kong: Filial Piety or Power in the Family?* Cambridge: Cambridge University Press.

Scott, Joan, and Louise Tilly. 1975. "Women's Work and the Family in Nineteenth-Century Europe." *Comparative Studies in Society and History* 17: 36–64.

Segalen, Martine. 1978. "Amour et liberté entre les jeunes en milieu rural: l'exemple opposé de la Cornouaille et de la Maurienne." In *Actes du colloque international: "Amour et Mariage en Europe,"* 13–23. Liège: Musée de la vie walonne.

Segalen, Martine. 1980. *Marie et femme dans la société paysanne.* Paris: Flammarion.

Servais, Jean. 1911. "Les femmes wallonnes: ce qu'on en dit." *Wallonia* 19: 195–97.

Shaffer, John W. 1980. "Family, Class, and Young Women: Occupational Expectations in Nineteenth Century Paris." In *Family and Sexuality in French History,* ed. Robert Wheaton and Tamara K. Hareven, 179–200. Philadelphia: University of Pennsylvania Press.

Shorter, Edward. 1972. "Capitalism, Culture and Sexuality: Some Competing Models." *Social Science Quarterly* 53: 338–56.

Shorter, Edward. 1973. "Illegitimacy, Sexual Revolution, and Social Change in Modern Europe." In *Family in History,* ed. Theodore K. Rabb and Robert I. Rotberg, 48–84. New York: Harper Torchbooks.

Shorter, Edward. 1977. *The Making of the Modern Family.* New York: Basic Books.

Shorter, Edward, John Knodel, and Etienne van de Walle. 1971. "The Decline of Non-Marital Fertility in Europe, 1880–1940." *Population Studies* 25: 375–93.

Smelser, Neil J. 1959. *Social Change in the Industrial Revolution: An Application of Theory to the British Cotton Industry.* Chicago: University of Chicago Press.

Smith, Bonnie G. 1981. *Ladies of the Leisure Class: The Bourgeoises of Northern France in the Nineteenth Century.* Princeton: Princeton University Press.

Smith, Daniel Scott. 1973. "Parental Power and Marriage Patterns: An Analysis of Historical Trends in Hingham, Massachusetts." *Journal of Marriage and the Family* 35: 419–28.

Smout, Christopher. 1980. "Aspects of Sexual Behavior in Nineteenth Century

Scotland." In *Bastardy*, ed. P. Laslett, K. Oosterveen, and R. M. Smith, 192–216. Cambridge, Mass.: Harvard University Press.

Spagnoli, Paul G. 1983. "Industrialization, Proletarianization, and Marriage: A Reconsideration." *Journal of Family History* 8: 230–47.

Stolnitz, George J. 1984. "Urbanization and Rural-to-Urban Migration in Relation to LDC Fertility." Project paper prepared for the Fertility Determinants Group, Indiana University, Bloomington, Indiana.

Sundt, Eilert. 1980. *On Marriage in Norway*. Trans. Michael Drake. Cambridge: Cambridge University Press.

Tennent, Emerson. 1844. *Excursion industrielle en Belgique*. Trans. P. Justin. Brussels: Société belge de librairie.

Thomas, Keith. 1959. "The Double Standard." *Journal of the History of Ideas* 20: 195–216.

Thomassin, Louis François. 1879. *Mémoire statistique du Departement de l'ourte (commencé dans le courant de l'année 1806)*. Liège: L. Grandmont-Donders.

Thonnar, Albert. 1904. "L'Industrie du tissage de la laine dans le pays de Verviers et dans le Brabant wallon." In *Les industries à domicile en Belgique*, Vol. 6, Belgium, Ministère de l'industrie et du travail, Office du travail. Brussels: J. Gomaere.

Tilly, Louise A. 1978. "Structure de l'emploi travail des femmes et changement démographique dans deux villes industrielles, Anzin et Roubaix, 1872–1906." *Le Mouvement Social* 105: 33–58.

Tilly, Louise A. 1979. "Individual Lives and Family Strategies in the French Proletariat." *Journal of Family History* 4: 137–52.

Tilly, Louise A., and Joan W. Scott. 1978. *Women, Work, and Family*. New York: Holt, Rinehart and Winston.

Tilly, Louise A., Joan W. Scott, and Miriam Cohen. 1976. "Women's Work and European Fertility Patterns." *Journal of Interdisciplinary History* 6: 447–76.

Trussell, James. n.d. "Program Mm." Available from the Office of Population Research, Princeton University, 21 Prospect Avenue, Princeton, New Jersey 08544.

Trussell, James. 1984. "Estimating the Determinants of Birth Interval Length." Paper prepared for the International Union for the Scientific Study of Population Conference on "Integrating Proximate Determinants into Analyses of Fertility Levels and Trends," London, April.

Trussell, James, Linda G. Martin, Robert Feldman, James A. Palmore, Mercedes Concepcion, and Datin Noor Laily Bt. Abu Bakar. 1985. "Determinants of Birth-Interval Length in the Philippines, Malaysia and Indonesia: A Hazard Model." *Demography* 22: 145–68.

Tuma, Nancy B., Michael T. Hannan, and Lyle P. Groeneveld. 1979. "Dynamic Analysis of Event Histories." *American Journal of Sociology* 84: 820–54.

Uhlenberg, Peter. 1978. "Changing Configurations of the Life Course." In *Transitions: The Family and the Life Course in Historical Perspective*, ed. Tamara K. Hareven, 65–97. New York: Academic Press.

Vanden Broeck, V. P. 1843. *Aperçu sur l'état physique et moral de certaines classes ouvrières*. Brussells: J. Voglet.

Vandereuse, Jules. 1940–48. "Le Mariage du cadet ou de la cadette." *Le Folklore brabançon* 20: 101–21.

van der Linden, Renat, and Roger Pinon. 1978. "Abortus provocatus, le faiseur et la faiseuse d'anges." In *Actes du colloque international: "Amour et mariage en Europe,"* 34–56. Liège: Musée de la vie walonne.

van de Walle, Etienne. 1976. "Household Dynamics in a Belgian Village, 1847–1866." *Journal of Family History* 1: 80–94.

van de Walle, Etienne, and Olivier Blanc. 1975. "Registre de population et démographie: La Hulpe." *Population et Famille* 36: 113–28.

Van Houtte, François-Xavier. 1949. *L'Evolution de l'industrie textile en Belgique et dans le monde de 1800 à 1939.* Louvain: Institut de recherches economiques et sociale.

Van Houtte, J. A. 1943. *Esquisse d'une histoire économique de Belgique.* Louvain: Editions universitas.

Vincent, Clark E. 1960. "Unmarried Fathers and the Mores: 'Sexual Exploiter' as an Ex Post Facto Label." *American Sociological Review* 25: 40–46.

Vinovskis, Maris A. 1977. "From Household Size to the Life Course: Some Observations on Recent Trends in Family History." *American Behavioral Scientist* 21: 263–87.

Wall, Richard, Ed. 1983a. *Family Forms in Historic Europe.* Cambridge: Cambridge University Press.

Wall, Richard. 1983b. "The Household: Demographic and Economic Change in England, 1650–1970." In *Family Forms in Historic Europe,* ed. Richard Wall, 493–512. Cambridge: Cambridge University Press.

Watkins, Susan C. 1980. "On Measuring Transitions and Turning Points." *Historical Methods* 12: 181–86.

Watkins, Susan C. 1984. "Spinsters." *Journal of Family History* 9: 310–325.

Watkins, Susan C., and Myron P. Gutmann. 1983. "Methodological Issues in the Use of Population Registers for Fertility Analysis." *Historical Methods* 16: 109–20.

Watkins, Susan C., and James McCarthy. 1980. "The Female Life Cycle in a Belgian Commune: La Hulpe, 1847–1866." *Journal of Family History* 4: 167–79.

Weir, David. 1982. "Fertility Transition in Rural France, 1740–1829." Ph.D. dissertation, Stanford University.

Wrightson, K. 1980. "The Nadir of English Illegitimacy in the 17th Century." In *Bastardy,* ed. P. Laslett, K. Oosterveen, and R. M. Smith, 176–91. Cambridge, Mass.: Harvard University Press.

Xhoffer, J.-F. 1866. *Verviers ancien. Conférence sur les anciennes coutumes de Verviers donnée au Cercle littéraire verviétois.* decembre 1865. Verviers: Ch. Vinche.

Yernaux, E., and F. Fievet. 1956. *Folklore wallon.* Charleroi: Imprimerie de Charleroi.

Zarate, A., and A. U. Zarate. 1975. "On the Reconciliation of Research Findings of Migrant-Nonmigrant Fertility Differentials in Urban Areas." *International Migration Review* 9: 115–56.

Zylberberg-Hocquard, Marie-Hélène. 1981. "L'ouvrière dans les romans populaires du XIXe siècle." *Revue du nord* 62, 250 (juillet-septembre): 603–35.

Index

Anderson, Michael, 4, 5, 7, 9, 64, 144, 160

Banks, Joseph A., 187
Berkner, Lutz K., 9, 65n
Birth control. *See* Fertility control
Birth interval: first birth, 131–32; analysis of, 131–32, 164, 177–85
Birth rate. *See* Fertility; Verviers, demographic history
Birth registers, 59
Blake, Judith, 148
Breastfeeding. *See* Fertility
Bridal pregnancy: in Verviers, 21; as marriage strategy, 22, 115; attitude of Catholic Church, 123; ages of brides, 127; and social class, 130–31, 134; and household composition, 134–36. *See also* Premarital pregnancy
Brostrom, Goran, 187
Brothels, 54. *See also* Prostitution
Business. *See* Commerce

Caldwell, John, 6, 161, 169, 201
Celibacy, 76, 203
Censoring: in life histories, 14, 36–38; in Verviers samples, 47
Censuses: compared to population registers, 32
Charivari, 124
Child labor: and weakening of family, 3; legislation, 7, 173, 202; attitudes toward, 23, 172, 195, 202; in textile industry, 167; and fertility, 170–72
Children: attitudes toward, 6, 202; economic contribution to family of, 115, 121, 140, 164, 200; labor force entry, 158; costs and benefits of, 167–73

Christensen, Harold J., 132–33
Civil Code, Belgian, 110, 111, 123, 145, 147, 149
Coale, Ansley J., 174, 185, 186–87
Coale-Trussel model of fertility control, 174–75, 182, 185–87
Cockerill, John, 16
Cohen, Miriam, 21–22, 114, 137
Collier, Frances, 105
Commerce: petty, 9, 105–11; retailing, 92; kinds of, 105–8; legal restrictions on women in, 110, 111
Concubinage. *See* Consensual unions
Conditional probabilities in life histories, 61–62
Consensual unions, 136, 136n
Contraception. *See* Fertility control
Courtship: urban, 22, 113, 115–16, 118, 120–21, 139, 140; rural, 22, 113, 116, 137; and bridal pregnancy, 138

Death rate. *See* Verviers, demographic history
Demographic transition, 163
Domesticity, 3, 7, 21, 92
Domestic servants, 84, 92, 96
Dowries, 149
Duncan, Otis Dudley, 191

Education. *See* Literacy
Elder, Glenn, 10, 12
El Kefi-Clokers, Christiane, 102, 105
Employment: in textile industry, 66; and decision to marry, 150–52; part-time, 198
Engels, Friedrich, 7
European Fertility Project, 163
European marriage pattern, 4, 20, 63, 141, 142, 153

223